RIGHT OF THE DIAL

RIGHT
OF THE DIAL

THE RISE OF CLEAR CHANNEL AND THE FALL OF COMMERCIAL RADIO

ALEC FOEGE

FABER AND FABER, INC.

AN AFFILIATE OF FARRAR, STRAUS AND GIROUX / NEW YORK

Faber and Faber, Inc.
An affiliate of Farrar, Straus and Giroux
18 West 18th Street, New York 10011

Distributed in Canada by Douglas & McIntyre Ltd.
Printed in the United States of America
First edition, 2008

Library of Congress Cataloging-in-Publication Data
Foege, Alec.
    Right of the dial / by Alec Foege. — 1st ed.
        p.   cm.
    ISBN-13: 978-0-571-21106-7 (hardcover : alk. paper)
    ISBN-10: 0-571-21106-2 (hardcover : alk. paper)
    1. Clear Channel (Firm)—History.   2. Radio broadcasting—United
States—History.   I. Title.

HE8698.F64 2008
384.5406'573—dc22

                                                      2007045426

Designed by Gretchen Achilles

www.fsgbooks.com

1   3   5   7   9   10   8   6   4   2

FOR ERICA, ALWAYS

They say you better listen to the voice of reason
But they don't give you any choice 'cause they think that it's
  treason.

—ELVIS COSTELLO, "Radio Radio," 1978

CONTENTS

PREFACE

Here it comes again. The repetitive, droning notes. The slowly yawning crescendo. Then a sharp, keening voice pipes in with that familiar refrain:

Oh let the sun beat down upon my face, stars to fill my dream
I am a traveler of both time and space, to be where I have been

I'm on a road trip from Connecticut to Maine with my wife and two-year-old daughter. They're both in the backseat of our Honda SUV, snoozing. I'm at the wheel trying to find something fun to listen to on the radio. Not surprisingly, I've lost track of exactly where we are.

For the fourth time in four states, I've unwittingly tuned in to "Kashmir," the eight-and-a-half-minute-long, Middle Eastern–influenced epic song released by the legendary British rock band Led Zeppelin on their 1975 album, *Physical Graffiti*. For me, like millions of other radio listeners, it is instantly recognizable from its throbbing opening bars, which seductively wend their way to lead singer Robert Plant's vocals—powerful, affecting, inimitable . . . and phenomenally annoying, once you've heard them a thousand times.

This is how it's been for as long as I can remember. Classic-rock radio, the stations that keep "Kashmir" and other rock "classics" in heavy rotation, is practically a public utility in the United States.

Simply turn on the faucet (in this case, the radio knob) and familiar hits from the 1960s and '70s by Zeppelin, the Beatles, the Rolling Stones, Aerosmith, and the Doors—peppered with maybe a few similar-sounding tracks from the 1980s and '90s—come flowing out. For most Americans of my generation and younger (I was born in the late 1960s), this, or some other genre variation of this, is what radio is.

Clear Channel Communications, the world's largest radio conglomerate for nearly a decade, didn't invent classic-rock radio. But one could easily argue that the company perfected it, whittling a familiar playlist of thirty- to forty-year-old rock songs into what sometimes feels like the same hour-and-a-half mix played over and over ad infinitum. Then they saturated the nation's airwaves with the formula, as well as a handful of other equally rigid radio formats. They also turned talk radio into a nationwide monolith, making (mostly conservative) big names like Rush Limbaugh, Glenn Beck, Dr. Laura Schlessinger, and Howard Stern even bigger and more ever present than before. Simultaneously, the company reduced resources devoted to local news coverage and hired matchless personalities such as "Bubba the Love Sponge," the Florida-based Clear Channel DJ who famously castrated and killed an actual boar as part of a comedy routine during a live radio broadcast.

Anyone who complains that there's nothing to listen to on the radio anymore could certainly lay most of the blame on Clear Channel. Since the late 1990s, Clear Channel has been the biggest radio company in the country, in terms of both revenue and the number of stations it owns. Clear Channel dramatically increased its advertising revenues, even as it alienated scores of radio listeners who had grown weary of what they perceived as unimaginative programming and who eventually would abandon commercial radio for good.

Then there's the concert industry. Since Clear Channel became the nation's dominant popular-music promoter in 2000, ticket prices for shows have gone through the roof. Add to that price the inflated costs of parking, food and drink, T-shirts, and other incidentals, and many fans have found themselves priced out of attending shows by their favorite musical artists.

But the real trouble started when Clear Channel tried to create synergies between its radio and its concert divisions in the few years that followed. In the course of trying to maximize profits, it alienated a whole generation of concertgoers by turning arenas and amphitheaters into cross-promotional billboards for captive audiences. Furthermore, artists complained that they were being bullied into playing Clear Channel–controlled venues or else risk being banned from the company's radio stations. If the average person heard the name "Clear Channel" in the early years of the twenty-first century, it was usually followed by the word "sucks," as in "Clear Channel sucks."

In time, Clear Channel became a Rorschach test for whatever observers liked or disliked about major media companies. Opponents saw a company that was tearing away at the very fabric of American media, not just because it was turning pop music into a pure commodity and news radio into an inane shout-fest, but because it was making loads of money while producing the dullest radio programming in the history of the medium, and doing so in quantities hard to ignore. The concerts it produced were overpriced and poorly managed. Its billboards littered the landscape. And the company made it known, in no uncertain terms, that it did not care, since it regarded advertisers—not consumers—as its customers. And its supporters? Well, its supporters tended to be employees of the big-league radio business.

Financially speaking, however, the story was very different. When I first bumped into the idea of writing a book on Clear Channel, the company was coming off a banner year: in 2003, Clear Channel reported a net income of $1.15 billion on revenue of $8.9 billion. An investment of $1,000 in Clear Channel stock in 1994 would be worth upwards of $10,000 now. This was an old media company seemingly making it in the new media universe, perhaps the one merger-manufactured monolith that seemed to have crunched the numbers right. In an era in which fortunes were bet and lost on all manner of new technology, Clear Channel squeezed double-digit gains from unfashionable, old-world media outlets like radio and billboards and live entertainment. In recent times, success continued apace, landing Clear Channel among *Fortune*'s 100 Most Admired Businesses in America and one of the top five stocks on Wall Street.

And yet that's not what most people knew about Clear Channel.

Since 2002, Clear Channel had been involved in no fewer than five major, headline-making scuffles regarding its business practices. Major media sources had published stories on how Clear Channel was suffocating the radio business and killing the concert business. Dark tales circulated about the company's rough-and-tumble negotiating tactics and its coarse internal corporate culture. Its harshest critics claimed the company was actually stomping on the First Amendment by systematically trying to wrest the radio airwaves from their rightful owner, the American public.

"We must preserve radio as a medium for democracy," said Senator Russ Feingold of Wisconsin on January 30, 2003, before the Senate Commerce Committee Hearing on Media Concentration and Ownership in Radio, invoking Clear Channel, if not by name, then certainly by inference.

The shock jock Howard Stern vilified the company on his syndicated radio show. And when Clear Channel dropped Stern from six of its stations after a run-in on obscenity charges with the FCC, Stern sued his former employer and fled commercial radio for good, taking up in the greener pastures of subscription-based satellite radio. In early 2005, the indie singer-songwriter Conor Oberst, better known by his stage name, Bright Eyes, proudly declared that he would not play any Clear Channel–controlled venues on his upcoming concert tour and kept to his promise.

No doubt about it: Clear Channel had developed one heck of a public-relations problem.

Sure, one could chalk up some of the controversy to the conservative bent of the company's leadership, somewhat unusual in the media world. Clear Channel's founder and chairman, Lowry Mays, is a longtime friend and supporter of fellow Texan George W. Bush. And rallies supporting the war in Iraq staged by local Clear Channel affiliates at the war's outset did little to quell the worst fears of the liberal-leaning mainstream media. But fellow media-world conservative Rupert Murdoch has courted far less controversy with his relatively diversified News Corp. Somehow Clear Channel had turned the very act of doing business into a political gesture. Its business-worthy strategies practically oozed a complete set of cultural values with every deal it made.

Then everything started to unwind for Clear Channel. Advertising revenues from radio began to dwindle, and competing technologies began challenging its relevance; Wall Street began punishing the company's stock price. With the concert industry in a slump, Clear Channel decided to spin off its entertainment division and part of its billboard division. By the time the public company decided to sell itself to a group of private investors at the end of 2006, it no longer seemed like much of a threat, either as a monopolistic venture or as a cultural force.

Still, perhaps against reason, I felt there was something to admire about Clear Channel. From his early days as an investment banker, Lowry Mays had taught himself a certain discipline about numbers. As a budding radio entrepreneur in the early 1970s, he developed a keen eye for a good deal. Ultimately, his philosophy about pooling resources and the economy of scale was as ingenious as Henry Ford's, and every bit as American in its attention to the details that constitute mass taste.

Gathering media properties that complemented each other and created financial efficiencies came as second nature to Mays. How could he have known that the practice would become a global trend? Clear Channel established itself by catering to its clients, advertisers, not by worrying about what others thought of Mays's plan. As for the bad press and the lawsuits and the terrible mess with Congress, who is to say in another time, perhaps a few years from now, all of Clear Channel's actions won't seem so nefarious? After all, as I write, the Internet has blown a hole in the information

pipeline. Wireless technology is wreaking havoc on the telecommunications industry. File sharing is injuring the music industry and
possibly the television and movie industries. And blogs are eviscer-
ating the newspaper and magazine businesses. In today's media environment, it's all about delivering consistency and reliability at a
reasonable cost.

Lowry Mays built his career on such principles. These days,
however, his legacy is being handled by his two sons, Mark, Clear
Channel's chief executive and president, and Randall, its chief financial officer. The jury is still out on their long-term effectiveness,
though, generally speaking, their track record doesn't fare very well
when compared with their dad's.

Finally, I wanted to write a book about Clear Channel because I
thought the company's story was a fascinating one that somehow
seemed to encapsulate many of the major media dilemmas of our
time.

I also had a couple big questions to answer: How did a $9 bil-
lion media conglomerate, named one of America's most admired
companies by *Fortune* magazine in 2003, simultaneously become
one of the most hated corporate entities in the history of our country? And how did the company once proclaimed the radio industry's
white knight come to be held responsible for radio's decline? And
what was the effect of all of this on American popular culture and
the contemporary music scene? In my mind, it had all the makings
of an epic business fable, and a suspenseful one at that.

When I first told friends, particularly those in the music business, that I was writing a book on Clear Channel, however, many
warned me to proceed with caution, mumbling asides about the
"Evil Empire," as the company had become known during its most
powerful days in the early twenty-first century. Some even went so
far as to suggest that I might face some professional, or even physical, harm in the course of reporting my story. Of course, these
warnings only served to pique my interest further. I assured the

naysayers that I was not out to do a hatchet job, but rather to get to the bottom of a company that I suspected had gotten a raw deal as its bad publicity had snowballed.

I was only half right about the raw-deal part. During the course of my research, I was impressed by the humanity and openness of a number of the company's founding executives, who gave generously of their time and remembrances to a "Yankee" they hardly knew. The honesty and integrity of these men (yes, they are all men) shone through in many of their colorful anecdotes—as did their unabashed rapaciousness.

On the other hand, the powers that be at Clear Channel did little to counter the general impression that they had a lot to hide. When I received the go-ahead for this book, I wrote multiple letters to Lowry Mays, Mark Mays, and Randall Mays, informing them of my plans and encouraging their participation. In return, I received complete and utter silence—not even a "no thank you." Then I contacted Clear Channel's head of communications. Before responding to any of my inquiries for interviews with Clear Channel's top executives, this executive fired off a letter to my publisher, threatening a lawsuit if I got any of my facts wrong. The company also had the maddening habit of denying all accusations lobbed against it when I inquired about responses—through a New York public-relations firm it now employs to spin its image in the press—while insisting many of its obvious blunders in the name of boosting revenues were actually noble gestures to improve the reach of quality radio. Clearly the company had learned little since its most embattled days, at least from a publicity perspective. Despite Clear Channel's role as the key architect of the radio, concert, and billboard advertising industries over the past two decades, the company was convinced I was only interested in tearing it to shreds.

Having spent a lot of time talking to some of the company's most prominent critics, as well as some of its most devout supporters, I have concluded that Clear Channel is indeed to blame for much of what it has been accused of. Perhaps I would have come to a different conclusion had the company itself done a better job of responding to questions about its actions. Whether the company behaved in an uncouth manner out of maliciousness or simply due to its genetic disposition is a matter that I hope the facts held within this book will clarify.

But the soul of this story emanates from countless road trips like the one described above, taken over a period of two decades. Trips filled with hours upon hours of what seemed like the same two dozen or so songs. Why had commercial rock radio hardly changed since I was a teenager in the 1980s? And it wasn't just rock radio: Top 40, talk, urban contemporary, country, classical—nearly every other radio category had turned to stone as well. Ask radio listeners of any age—except those in the radio business—and they'll likely tell you something similar, how terrible it is listening to *anything* on commercial radio these days.

And as I waded deeper into the subject of Clear Channel, I began wondering what effect it was having on the legacy of commercial radio and on American culture as a whole. With 1,250 radio stations coast-to-coast—nearly 1,000 more than its closest competitor—as well as much of the North American concert-touring business (it owns 130 venues and all the major promoters), 770,000 billboards, 41 television stations, and the largest sports management business in the country, Clear Channel at its height truly dominated the pop-cultural landscape. Was it altering our cultural DNA? That is, did it matter in any quantifiable way that radio, well, sucked—and did the benefits outweigh the downside? After all, modern popular music was invented (and perfected) in this sprawling country of ours, a freewheeling soundtrack that mimicked our pioneering spirit, the land's wide-open spaces, and a promise of future creativity, innovation, rule breaking. Today's mainstream pop culture is none of those things. Blockbuster movies, choreographed arena pop-music shows, advertising-saturated TV programming—big and bland is all around us. It's what we know and have come to expect. Indeed, all of these mega-sized media phenomena represent another strong trend in American history: capitalism.

In the course of my research, I learned that Clear Channel was started by a group of genuine radio people, many of whom at some point in their younger years had a genuine passion for the medium. Over time, they channeled that passion into a creative, even brilliant vision for a modern radio company. Unfortunately for today's radio listeners, though, that creativity was expressed far more in a business context than in a programming one. And quality radio indisputably suffered the consequences.

In my mind, and apparently many others, Clear Channel Communications is an exemplar of a trend in the media business. It may not be the world's most surprising one: big companies get bigger to gain more power and make more money. But what if there was more to this predictable money trail than met the eye? Aside from a brief respite in the post–September 11 economy, the media business has been busily consolidating for about two decades. Right now, less than 20 percent of our newspapers are independent and locally owned. In the past decade, the ten largest owners of local television stations have tripled the number of stations they own. And, thanks to Clear Channel, more than one-third of the American population listens to radio stations owned by the same company.

General Electric and RCA; Viacom and CBS; America Online and Time Warner; Bertelsmann and everybody. In recent times in the American economy, mega-sized media mergers have become as regular as bizarre weather. But over the past few years, a handful of deals dramatically upped the stakes. Suddenly it was no longer enough to have more content than the other guy. Now you needed distribution to win.

As far back as 2000, America Online swallowed Time Warner in an attempt to create the perfect content-plus-distribution cocktail. In late 2003, Rupert Murdoch, owner and operator of News Corp., acquired the satellite service DirecTV. In early 2004, the cable operator Comcast attempted (and failed) to take over Disney. Of course, Clear Channel was there first: its acquisition in 2000 of the concert-booking powerhouse SFX ensured that many big musical acts would have no choice but to do business with Clear Channel in many major cities.

And with the pro-business Michael Powell at the helm of the FCC (he stepped down in March 2005), such deals were explicitly encouraged as a response to the diffusing effect of the Internet and other new media technologies.

In this heated climate, media regulation of any sort almost seemed like a relic. Why, then, were so many people upset by the actions of Clear Channel? The first reason seems obvious: jealousy. The company has made buckets of money for its investors. Media properties traditionally operate on thin margins, yet Clear Channel's annual rate of return to investors from 1993 to 2002 was around 26 percent. By comparison, Viacom, Clear Channel's next-biggest competitor, coughed up a mere 7.1 percent return rate during the same period. Everyone other than its investors and the Wall Street analysts who advised them began to wonder what Clear Channel was doing differently—what did it know, and was it legit?

Most all-encompassing media operations, after all, start with a big splash only to make a mockery of the term "synergy" over time. AOL Time Warner was a perfect example: The world's best-known Internet company swallowing a top movie and media corporation made perfect sense at the height of the dot-com era. But when the house of cards finally fell, AOL Time Warner understood its big plan didn't make sense. It discreetly dropped the "AOL" from its corporate name and went back to the sensible business of creating content people actually wanted.

The second reason was harder to pin down, and I must admit at first I was skeptical, despite my own personal biases. But I'm here to report it's true: Americans really do care about culture, however they define it. They like choice and variety and a sense that the media they enjoy are vibrant and alive, no matter what their particular preferences are. Americans also have an innate sense of entitlement about radio and the public airwaves. They seem to understand that a commercial radio universe that is a true reflection of the populace at large is crucial to democracy. Clear Channel, in building its position of dominance, ignored that fact, and hurt itself and the radio business as a whole in the process. The gifted executives who built

Clear Channel were creative in their pursuit of capitalism but not in their approach to culture.

I have nothing against big media companies. Quality content is an expensive and risky proposition, and often a large corporation is one of the few entities with deep enough pockets to absorb major missteps. But whereas in the late 1990s and early twenty-first century major media conglomerates were the norm, the winds have recently shifted, partly due to the increase in entertainment options afforded by the Internet. Clear Channel has often argued that as it has grown, it has created more variety and more choices for consumers. I found little evidence of this in the course of my research. Instead, I found a company whose undeniable innovations have been overshadowed by the cultural damage wrought by its lack of regard for the content that has made its prodigious advertising revenues possible. I believe there is a lesson in Clear Channel's story about the one-size-fits-all approach to producing and marketing entertainment that has become so popular in this country. The company's recent merger with a group of private equity investors—along with its plan to sell off at least 450 of its smaller radio stations and all of its TV stations—suggests its executives ultimately came to a similar conclusion.

And last, this book is an attempt to explain how two undeniably American traditions—capitalism and creativity—battled to coexist within the confines of one uniquely American media conglomerate. It also, I believe, shows how capitalism nearly snuffed out creativity, but then ultimately lost the war.

Led Zeppelin's lead singer, Robert Plant, is once again delivering his signature high-pitched wail, eminently predictable and as solid as bedrock, as "Kashmir" continues to wend its way out of my car speakers. The drums pound with a tribal intensity. Twin guitar lines intertwine and spiral up in a nearly Zen-like koan. It seems as if the song has been playing forever. I don't even think about it as music anymore, but rather as a mild condition of being. Like a toothache or a strained knee. Something now causing discomfort that's likely to dissipate over time. I'd change the station, but I have little faith that I'd find anything much more appealing.

This lack of faith is at the heart of the Clear Channel story. At its center is a man who had a revolutionary way of running a radio company and who became very successful at it. He made plenty of enemies in the process, but he also made some unlikely friends. In early 2005, for example, Clear Channel Entertainment partnered with the Public Broadcasting Service (PBS) in a deal that gave the concert promoter the option to mount tours stemming from performance-driven programs featured during pledge-drive broadcasts on PBS affiliates. In other words, Clear Channel convinced the not-for-profit PBS, a media outlet committed more than most to upholding the public's trust, to hand over the reins of its fund-raising arm to a for-profit entity that has a reputation for violating the public's trust in the name of profits. No matter how one feels about this unusual business arrangement, one can't deny it is a pure and, in many ways, truly American moment. Whether you feel good about it or not depends on where your sympathies lie.

We finally arrived in Maine. My wife and daughter awoke. My daughter at once declared the radio was "too loud" and demanded that I turn it down. I simply decided to turn it off. We rode the final two hours of our journey in silence.

Clear Channel wasn't to blame for the predictable programming I experienced during my teen years, but, as I try to show in the following pages, it certainly has a lot to do with what has—and hasn't—changed since. How could one man's vision of a new way of doing business mutate into a trend in culture that many would come to view as a plague? There was no doubt that Clear Channel had forever altered the way we listen to music. The lingering question was, were we better or worse off for it?

RIGHT OF THE DIAL

1.

THE CONTROVERSY

Howard Stern shuffled onto the stage of the *Late Show with David Letterman* on the eve of November 18, 2004, much in the way he had on plenty of other occasions over the previous fifteen years. Clad in jeans, a black T-shirt, black sport coat, and dark sunglasses, the tall, shaggy-haired radio host looked a lot like an aging rock star but with none of the attitude or bitterness. Instead, he flashed a warm smile, waved to the studio audience, amiably rubbed the bald head of Letterman's bandleader, Paul Shaffer, and greeted Letterman with a hearty handshake. The self-proclaimed King of All Media—and the man for whom the term "shock jock" was practically minted—in a word, *ruled*.

And why not? With more than twelve million daily listeners and an annual salary of more than $30 million, Stern was one of the biggest stars the radio business had ever known. For more than two decades, he had thrived on the controversial humor that filled his meandering five-hour daily morning broadcast, where guests over the years had included porn stars, dwarfs, strippers, and his personal favorite, lesbians. A magnet for criticism and censure, Stern was responsible for more than half of the $4.5 million in fines for obscenity meted out by the Federal Communications Commission since 1990.[1] But for years his employer, Infinity Broadcasting (now CBS Radio), didn't seem to mind, since he also brought in multimillions per year in revenue. At the time of his 2004 *Late Night* appearance, Infinity was a division of Viacom, the same corporation that owned CBS Television, Letterman's employer.

But on this particular night, Stern was neither outrageous nor particularly funny. He had a serious announcement to make. "Always a lot of controversy when I come here," he told Letterman, as he slouched into the guest chair. "My career is never normal, there's always a lot of pressure."

The biggest personality in radio was leaving radio. And he was blaming it on the nation's biggest radio company, Clear Channel.

Indeed, the occasion for Stern's appearance was the official announcement of his newest job. Just six weeks earlier, Stern had revealed his plan to abandon free broadcast radio for good and to begin appearing on Sirius Satellite Radio, a relatively new company that sold a subscription-based medium whose business model was akin to cable television: "In recent years because of the government interference and what's been going on with the FCC [and] Clear Channel Broadcasting, doing my job every day has become increasingly difficult." Sirius had agreed to pay Stern $100 million per year for the next five years, which included the costs of producing his show. In return, Stern was expected to draw untold millions of new listeners to a kind of radio they had to pay for.

In February of that same year, in the wake of a highly contentious incident during the broadcast of the Super Bowl halftime show in which the singer Janet Jackson bared a single breast while performing a musical dance number choreographed by MTV, the FCC decided to flex its muscles by fining Clear Channel Communications $495,000 for broadcasting a twenty-minute segment of Stern's show featuring sexually suggestive humor on some of its stations. On April 9, 2003, Stern discussed the discomforts of anal sex and a potion the FCC characterized as "a purported personal hygiene product designed for use prior to sexual activity." The sophomoric bit was accompanied, according to the FCC report, "by sound effects of flatulence and evacuation." In response, Clear Channel dropped Howard Stern's network program from six of its radio stations in mostly conservative markets. It later paid $1.75 million in fines to the FCC for obscenity on Stern's show and others, including that of an outrageous Florida disc jockey known as "Bubba the Love Sponge," who had been fired a few months earlier after racking up $755,000 in fines from the FCC for his lewd on-air patter.[2]

Had the incident involved anyone else, it likely would have faded away. But Stern was different. For one, he was so huge for radio. Second, he seemed genuinely radicalized by the event.

In a presidential election year, Stern, not usually regarded for his political banter, started delivering on-air political tirades against President George W. Bush, blaming Republicans and the religious right for creating a culture of censorship. Then, on *Letterman* that night, he introduced the nation to another, far more tangible target: Clear Channel Communications, the world's largest radio company.

As for Letterman, he seemed peculiarly impassioned by Stern's diatribe that night, his trademark wire-rimmed glasses adding an air of erudition. "Here's what I know about Clear Channel," Letterman said, interrupting Stern. "And, you know, I'm not paying attention to anything, I'm just doing my little dog-and-pony show here," he said, pausing for a breath. "I read an article in *Rolling Stone* this summer: Clear Channel owns 1,200 radio stations, many stations in the same markets. They've essentially wiped out individuality of the radio stations and played havoc with the record industry and the music industry and live concerts. I was stunned." Letterman went on to note that three corporations controlled more than 60 percent of the nation's radio audience.

Then Stern added, "When I was working for Clear Channel, they fired me I think from nine stations on a whim. And one of the reasons they fired me is I didn't support President Bush. Clear Channel is busy throwing parties in markets for the Iraq war. And I hardly think that's something you should be throwing a party for. They're throwing rallies. So I didn't support that and the next day I was fired. My fellow broadcasters are not standing up for me. I am turning my back on regular terrestrial radio. I believe in five years . . . satellite radio will be the dominant medium in radio broadcasting."

Within a mere five minutes of late-night network television programming, Clear Channel Communications had been introduced to an unsuspecting general public, a large portion of which had probably never even heard its name before that night. On the other hand, they were probably familiar with some of the company's products. At the time of the broadcast, Clear Channel stations reached nearly 60 percent of the nation's radio audience and represented around 20 percent of the radio industry's total revenue. Its concert division had a virtual headlock on America's live-entertainment market. And its outdoor billboard displays lined ribbon after ribbon of highways from New York to California.

Just as MTV dominated the 1980s, and Microsoft defined the 1990s, Clear Channel became the defining media and technology story of the early years of the twenty-first century.

In 1995, when Congress was reconsidering media ownership rules, Clear Channel ran just forty-three radio stations and sixteen TV stations across the country. The next year, when Congress deregulated radio, allowing radio groups to own as many stations as they wanted (with some regional restrictions), Clear Channel began to gobble up stations at an incomparably breathtaking rate. In that very same year, it acquired forty-nine more radio stations, more than doubling its holdings. And in an industry built on leveraged capital, Clear Channel liked to pay cash. By 2001, the company had acquired several rivals and laid claim to more than twelve hundred stations. It also got into the billboard business in a very big way, purchasing Eller Media, a large Arizona-based billboard company, in 2000, adding 700,000 billboards nationally to its advertising-friendly roster. Clear Channel's idea was to buy broadly, working its way into a wide variety of local markets. The basic plan was to sell ads nationally and regionally, as well as locally. The word for this plan was "synergy."

Around 2000, the music business got its first wake-up call about Clear Channel when the company extended its synergistic plan by buying SFX Entertainment for $4.4 billion. Suddenly the world's largest radio company was also the world's largest concert promoter. For Clear Channel, the logic was crystal clear: It could promote its concerts on Clear Channel radio stations. In addition, local Clear Channel stations could advertise at the concert venues. Clear Channel's local ad sales teams could drum up business on all platforms—radio, billboards, and concerts. It was a music-biz slam dunk. Or as one music manager and producer put it to *Fortune*, "They are the devil."

Clear Channel had ruined radio, according to its critics. It was a leader in employing some of radio's most controversial practices, including "voice tracking"—in which DJs dial in their "local" broadcasts from centralized locations and simply customize them with a few local references, some syndicated programming, and a high-tech national network that seamlessly enables the implementation of the first two. Since purchasing the largest concert tour promoter, SFX, in 2000, it was now ruining the concert business. And, unlike most other concert promoters, Clear Channel also ran the venues. In the New York City area, traditionally known for its diverse ownership, the company controlled major venues such as Irving Plaza, Roseland Ballroom, the Beacon Theatre, and the Jones Beach amphitheater.

Regulators and watchdog groups regularly excoriated the company for its insensitive, overtly political, and monopolistic tendencies. New York State's attorney general, Eliot Spitzer, had roped Clear Channel into his investigation of the music biz's anticompetitive practices. In a typical deal, Clear Channel reached an agreement in December 2004 with Fox News in which Fox would become the primary news provider for Clear Channel stations. Though the deal only ran in the millions, it greatly benefited the conservative-leaning Fox by providing a strong radio presence for the fledgling news operation to do battle against larger competitors like ABC Radio and CBS Radio.

Yet Clear Channel, at the time, was hardly a household name. Even in corporate media circles, Clear Channel was something of a cipher. But thanks to the censure of a high-profile talk-show host, Clear Channel hit the national consciousness as a brand literally overnight.

The only problem was that this was a brand established almost wholly on negative connotations. Stern and Letterman didn't create it; they merely reflected an opinion that had been simmering for months, in a host of places, from the halls of major recording labels to the minds of legions of concertgoers. Prior to Stern's appearance on *Letterman*, "Clear Channel sucks" had already become something of a mantra in popular-music circles; and online, ClearChannelSucks.net was a popular destination.

Some sly marketers might have argued that brand awareness was valuable regardless of the connotations. But this was different. Very different. Never before had the American citizenry seemingly come to loathe a public corporation so quickly. It seemed almost unfathomable. Not even the animus that had built up against Microsoft over the decades could match the out-and-out hostility that Clear Channel engendered in a matter of months. The controversy had stirred a latent American passion for radio that had lain buried in the nation's collective psyche.

Despite all the newfangled tech-comm innovations, the airwaves were still owned by the public, presciently established by the federal government as a cornerstone of democracy during the post-industrial era of the early twentieth century. An electrified forum to amplify the views and desires of "the people."

Sure, radio had taken its hits. Smeared even in its earliest days as being overly commercial, it lost serious economic ground in the first years of television. By the end of the 1950s, it was all but a footnote in the histories of ABC, NBC, and CBS, once its largest producers. Then, with the birth of rock and roll, radio got a much-needed jolt. The rise of Top 40 and later FM radio revived its prospects, but in the early 1960s the payola scandals, whereby record labels proffered illegal payments or gifts in return for highly coveted airplay, established radio forever after as a slightly shady, morally dubious corner of the American economy.

But at the end of the day, radio still mattered. For the millions of commuters who drove to and from work for more than a hundred hours a month per year on average, it was a reassuring companion, a relatively pleasant and undemanding way to pass the time. For music fans, it remained a way to hear the most popular music in the nation. For musicians, it was still the best route to jump-starting a career.

How did Clear Channel, once a sleepy little company from Texas, arrive at the center of an American institution that traces its roots back to Thomas Edison? Did it deserve such pointed attacks? Who were the people behind this corporate monolith? And what were they actually doing that pissed so many people off?

Just a few years earlier, Clear Channel was the darling of Wall Street. Between 1986 and 2000, the company's revenues grew at an annual rate of 46 percent. Shareholder return averaged 36 percent annually during that same period, at a rate 21 percent higher than shareholder cost of equity. Clear Channel was the fourth-largest media conglomerate in the United States—rivaling NBC and Gannett in revenues—and the subject of case studies pored over at prominent business schools.[3] It was the shining example of media consolidation done right. It had rescued radio, a national treasure, from history's dustbin and built itself into an Internet-age corporate beacon. Even its detractors, who dubbed it the Evil Empire, grudgingly had to concede the reach of its power and influence. Certainly Stern didn't provide any real clues that fateful night on *Letterman*. Indeed, it was entirely possible that the radio giant was just looking for some free publicity. (Clear Channel would later settle a pair of competing lawsuits involving Stern, his relating to his termination and Clear Channel's to Stern's refusal to adhere to the FCC's indecency rules.)

How did it come to this?

Radio is the oldest of the electronic mass media, tracing its roots back to the late nineteenth century, as well as the most ubiquitous. Most households in America still have more radio receivers than occupants. It's also the most underappreciated, long ago relegated to third-tier status as a kind of bush league for the entertainment world, where flashier media such as movies, television, and the Internet easily overshadow it.

It also is the most profitable of the traditional media, due to its relatively low overhead, and thus regarded as a bellwether of the media industry.

But in the last few years, radio hit a snag. In 2005, broadcast radio advertising expenditures grew at a paltry rate of 0.3 percent while total listenership dropped 0.8 percent to 27.4 million, its worst year since 2002.[4] And that was before new competing technologies, such as subscription-based satellite radio, portable iPods, Internet radio, and podcasting, had really begun to take root.

Suddenly the idea of Clear Channel's owning 1,200 radio stations (the actual number had dropped slightly to 1,182 by the end of 2005) didn't seem like such a great thing, at least in purely financial terms.

How would radio compete, particularly in its current content-hobbled state (homogenized programming plus indecency monitoring equals subpar ratings)? And more important, was it all Clear Channel's fault?

To be fair, media consolidation became something of a disease beginning in the late 1990s. In the 1970s, the media business was still regarded as a noble calling tied to rationality and intelligence, run by serious people with a sense of the power involved and all of the social responsibility that came with that power. In the two decades following, the landscape changed dramatically as others realized how much cash some media businesses generated. The margins, particularly in advertising-based media businesses with relatively low ownership barriers like radio, were nothing short of spectacular. So by the mid-1990s, the media business was filled with "assholes run amok," in the words of the trenchant media critic Michael Wolff.[5]

By the first half of 1998, the media business was all about mergers, nothing but mergers. An unprecedented $99 billion of media mergers and acquisitions took place in that six-month period as compared with $77 billion for all of 1997.[6] Then came the onslaught of mega-big, mega-unimaginable, mega-moneyed mega-deals. Vivendi and Universal, then Viacom and CBS, and finally AOL and Time Warner. It was as if a collective idea bulb had lit up over the heads of the world's media moguls: *This is the way.*

Audience fragmentation had begun taking its toll. And media consolidation was just about the best method in theory with which to hedge one's bets. The thought process went like this: an economy of scale created certain cost efficiencies that would result in historically high profits for segments of the American economy that traditionally did not worry themselves so much about profits.

And if a media corporation could boil down popular taste to sell more units of fewer choices, greater revenues would surely follow. The paradigm in the music industry was Michael Jackson's 1982 album, *Thriller*, which sold more than sixty million copies worldwide. In movies, James Cameron's *Titanic*, released in 1997—which ultimately grossed over $1.8 billion in worldwide box-office sales alone—became the standard by which all others were judged.

Blockbuster hits became the real currency of the media industry. Outrageously expensive to make (*Titanic* cost a reported $285 million), but even more outrageously profitable once they were released, blockbusters, so the theory went, financed everything else put out by a big media conglomerate, relieving countless niche products of their various worldly burdens, namely profitability.

In radio, the equivalent was, as always, the hit single. But in an increasingly consolidated media world, hits suddenly had a lot more riding on them. Record labels no longer permitted artists to develop over a series of albums but rather expected big debut sales built upon the number of radio plays of one or more hit singles.

The reality was that media companies started getting so large that no one really controlled them, or even understood them. By the earliest years of the twenty-first century, it had become clear that the media moguls who had engineered these feats of magic were at the top of the list when it came to lack of comprehension.

Michael Wolff writes eloquently of that period in his 2003 book, *Autumn of the Moguls*: "You couldn't say what seemed pretty obvious: that nobody knew how to run the superaggregated and radically transformed companies that came into being during the past decade. That these companies defied control, were too vast and far-flung and composed of too many recalcitrant people and inimical functions. This, together with the fact that the guys who ran these companies often clearly had no idea what they were doing."[7]

It was within this cultural-industrial petri dish that Clear Channel began getting huge. Until 1998, it had made money the old-fashioned way. It bought stations it found to be financially attractive and ran them better than most other radio companies. But in the late 1990s, it changed tack and initiated a series of megadeals that transformed at least two industries and cornered another.

In recent years, Clear Channel has had some second thoughts. No wonder. From September 18, 1984, the date of Clear Channel's first recorded stock price, through October 19, 2004, the day Lowry Mays officially stepped down as chief executive, the company's total annual return was 25 percent. That figure was nearly double the Standard & Poor's 500's 13 percent rate of return for the same period.[8]

From that same day—the day Mark Mays became CEO—going forward to March 24, 2006, Clear Channel's total return was 2.4 percent per year, compared with 15 percent total annual return for the S&P 500. Put another way: some 79 percent of companies in the S&P 500 index outperformed Clear Channel during that period.

The ascents of Mark and Randall Mays dovetailed with a period in which Clear Channel's corporate DNA was irrevocably altered. And by all accounts, the new species was not faring well. By the time a majority of Clear Channel's shareholders voted in favor of management's plan to go private again in September 2007, the company was a pale shadow of its former self.

In the 1950s, radio had reinvented itself as a purely local

medium. Then Clear Channel came along in the late 1990s and eradicated radio's localism, making it more formatted and formulaic, less personalized and more national. The world's biggest radio company deconstructed a medium that prided itself on its intimate connection with its listeners and made it as uniformly bland and anonymous as anyone could bear.

This was what was necessary, Clear Channel argued, to save radio from almost certain and painful death. To give the people what they wanted. What they *really* wanted, which, as it turned out, wasn't all that unique—at least according to Clear Channel's extensive research.

So listeners got fewer musical formats and insanely repetitive playlists. And advertisers were happy. And investors were happy.

Radio would survive. It always had before. And Clear Channel would find new ways to preserve its famously rich margins.

Or would it? Clear Channel, by dint of its size in comparison to its closest competitors, had the power to shape radio's future. But for the first time in its nearly thirty-five-year history, Clear Channel was facing a future it couldn't control. New technologies were gushing out of the pipeline, and Clear Channel was still holding more conduits for the old technology than anyone else on the planet.

Radio had commenced a whole new phase, one of reinvention and revision. Was Clear Channel up for the challenge? Was the company really the media monster Howard Stern and nearly everyone else claimed it was? Or was Clear Channel an innovator that simply saw radio's future before anyone else could own up to it?

Of course, nobody knew the answers to these questions yet. But at least there was the history. To understand Clear Channel's current ability to compete required a parsing of the past, an analysis of these San Antonio firebrands from the very beginning.

If radio was dying, could Clear Channel save it? Or had Clear Channel pumped the offending bullet into its heart?

I was determined to find out.

2.

THE BIRTH OF MODERN
RADIO, TEXAS-STYLE

Growing up in the small West Texas town of Cisco in the late 1950s, Stan Webb caught the rock-and-roll bug like so many other teenagers of his generation. A tall, gawky teen, Webb fell hard for performers like Elvis Presley and Buddy Holly, a native of Lubbock, Texas, and began playing guitar in rock bands soon after that. "I had a real interest in music and ended up playing in a variety of bands for quite a while," Webb recalls, "until I got drafted into the army."[1]

By the time he got out of the military in the mid-1960s, Webb had decided that, as much as he loved music, his chances of becoming a rock idol were slim. He felt his chances of becoming a disc jockey were marginally better, so when a friend told him about a DJ school in Dallas, Stan decided almost immediately to enroll. After just six months at the school, he got offered his first job as DJ at a small station called WGLB, in, of all places, Port Washington, Wisconsin, a suburb north of Milwaukee on the shore of Lake Michigan. "It was a small station," says Webb matter-of-factly, "and I was cheap."

For the young Texan, the move to Wisconsin was something of a culture shock. For one, it was the winter of 1966–67, one of the coldest in Wisconsin history. Also, Webb had a heavy Texas drawl, not the obvious choice for a Milwaukee-area station that played everything from big band to Top 40 to polka. Webb had never traveled out of Texas other than to Fort Polk, Louisiana, and Washington, D.C., with the army. "I knew nothing about polka music," he recalls. "That just wasn't a music genre that was popular in Texas. I absolutely knew nothing about it. But this little community was filled with German and Polish families, and so that music was very popular. And they would call in and request these songs, so anyway I would dig it out and play these tunes."

The polka hour, which ran in the middle of the day, was the most popular show on the station.

That Christmas, Webb returned home and married his girl-friend. After the holidays, he brought her back with him to Wisconsin. They both quickly decided it was time for a change. During the miserably cold winter of 1967, Webb got the lucky break he was hoping for. The twenty-three-year-old DJ spotted an ad in *Broadcasting* magazine looking for young creative types to join a radio company owned by Gordon McLendon. Webb couldn't believe it. Back in Texas music circles, McLendon was an idol. "Gordon was really the father of modern radio," says Webb, "particularly Top 40."

"McLendon was like the Ted Turner of his era," says the radio industry veteran Gary Stevens, who today works as a station broker. "He came from a big family with money, but did things that probably the rest of the family wouldn't do and was very good at it because he was so incredibly creative."[2]

Needless to say, Stan answered the ad. "Gordon was looking for what he was calling the Magnificent Seven," he says, "which would be seven bright young guys that could be real promotion-oriented and get what his company philosophy was. So I was, I'm told, one of five thousand or so applicants. And somehow I cut through all of that. I'm not really sure how he picked me up from that lineup. But I got hired."

Webb could hardly have suspected that the then-marginal industry in which he had chosen to make a living would ultimately lead to a high-flying career at the largest radio corporation in the world.

Until the 1920s, radio was thought of primarily as a wireless telegraph.[3] Yet concerns about anticompetitive practices, due to the powerful nature of the first electronic broadcasting medium, were a part of radio's history from its earliest days in the late nineteenth century. The technology behind the medium is usually traced back to two physicists—the Scottish James Clerk Maxwell, who studied electromagnetic waves in the 1860s, and the German Heinrich Hertz, who generated radio waves with an electric spark and detected them with a receiver made of iron filings he called a "coherer."[4] Others in the late 1880s and early '90s also developed various devices that produced and received radio waves. But a young British transplant from Italy named Guglielmo Marconi was the first to put together a device that could be marketed to the masses.

Marconi's work was funded by his Scottish-Irish mother, an heir to the Jameson whiskey fortune; after pitching an early radio prototype to the Italian postal service, where it received a lukewarm reception, the two relocated to London in 1896. There, at the age of twenty-two, Marconi won the first patent for what was then called radiotelegraphy, a wireless technology that at first only transmitted Morse code.[5] The next year he and his financial backers started the Wireless Telegraph and Signal Company. But the British Post Office refused to purchase Marconi's technology; his first major customer was in fact the British War Office, which gave his technology a test run during the Boer War and later made it the Royal Navy's exclusive wireless technology.[6]

Almost immediately, the navy's endorsement allowed Marconi to build a viable commercial business out of ship-to-shore communication, including a key contract with Lloyd's, which fitted ships it insured with wireless stations. As Marconi's business grew, though, he thwarted potential competitors by banning his operators from communicating with stations using another firm's equipment. Marconi's company constructed its own shore stations, leased communications units to ships, and trained its own telegraph operators. Critics of the company complained that Marconi's policy was monopolistic and, furthermore, endangered lives at sea. But the inventor argued that since he paid to maintain his own equipment, others should not be able to use it.[7]

In the United States, the reception to Marconi was decidedly mixed. He was praised by the press for his technological accomplishments, but the federal government, and in particular the U.S. Navy, was unwelcoming due to his no-intercommunication policy. Though the navy had been slow to adopt any radio technology in the first years of the twentieth century, it outright refused to work with Marconi. Instead, it experimented with various devices while committing to none; naval officers opposed wireless for fear that it eroded their independence, presumably by enabling their superiors to keep closer tabs. Instead, marine wireless grew as a private operation—ultimately, to Marconi's benefit. In 1911, the industry nearly became dominated by American Marconi after the company won a patent infringement suit against a rival, United Wireless, and took over its assets.[8]

The sinking of the *Titanic* in 1912 helped galvanize the fledgling business after Marconi operators were praised for the part they played in rescuing survivors. The tragedy led to the passage of the Radio Act of 1912 by Congress, which required all radio operators to have licenses and all ships to have wireless equipment. It also for the first time allocated bands of spectrum for different uses, relegating amateurs to the less desirable shortwave frequencies. Ironically, the legislation practically handed Marconi a monopoly by restricting the activity of smaller players. But the advent of continuous-wave radio, a technology developed in the United States by Reginald Fessenden and others that allowed the transmission of voices and music in addition to dots and dashes, quickly blew open the market.[9]

The commercial radio industry as we know it began after World

War I; during the war, radio was still understood primarily as a way to send wireless communication. As late as the early 1920s, radio enthusiasts were known as hobbyists, since most listeners built their own radio sets from mail-order kits.[10]

David Sarnoff, a former wireless operator who became president of the Radio Corporation of America (RCA), is often credited with turning radio into a mainstream phenomenon. But Herbert Hoover, who served as secretary of commerce in both the Harding and the Coolidge administrations prior to being elected president in 1928, deserves nearly as much credit. Radio was a perfect vehicle for Hoover's approach to encouraging economic growth, known as "associationalism," in which the government assisted industry in organizing and resolving disputes outside the realm of federal control. Starting in 1922, Hoover put together a series of four national radio conferences intended to organize the industry. The big issue at the time was signal interference.[11]

The first commercial radio station, KDKA, was launched in 1920 by Westinghouse Electric and Manufacturing Company, based in Pittsburgh, Pennsylvania, after a Westinghouse engineer drew a local following by playing phonograph records on the air. WWJ in Detroit and KCBS in San Francisco are also often cited as some of the earliest commercial radio outlets.[12]

In 1922, AT&T linked stations via long-distance telephone lines and two years later created the National Broadcasting System, which reached 65 percent of American homes with radios, mostly in the Northeast and Midwest. By the early 1920s, radio plays had become a form of popular entertainment. In late 1924, AT&T aired a speech by President Calvin Coolidge coast-to-coast over a network of twenty-six stations.

The commercial radio industry met up with its first monopolistic skirmish in 1925 when RCA, General Electric, and Westinghouse, known together as the Radio Group, cut a deal with AT&T, which supplied telephone lines for their stations. The compromise created a separate radio network called the National Broadcasting

Company (NBC), owned by RCA, GE, and Westinghouse, that guaranteed AT&T a minimum of $1 million a year in revenue under a ten-year contract.[13]

Then, in 1926, chaos broke out after the federal government lost a lawsuit against a radio station run by Zenith, a radio manufacturer. Zenith had purposely defied a governmental order restricting radio licenses by broadcasting on a vacant frequency allotted for Canada. The Justice Department then announced that the government had no right to regulate broadcasting, and soon more than two hundred unregulated stations flooded the airwaves—stations jumping from frequency to frequency, changing hours, and increasing power were not uncommon, creating confusion and chaos for listeners and programmers alike.

In response, Congress passed the Radio Act of 1927, which gave authority over radio to an independent commission rather than to the Department of Commerce. From this point on, broadcasting in the United States would be privately owned but under federal licenses. The independent Federal Radio Commission, established the same year, was meant to exist on a temporary basis, but the Department of Commerce never regained control of radio.

From the first time NBC went on the air—on November 15, 1926, live from the Grand Ballroom of the Waldorf-Astoria hotel in Manhattan—radio ceased to be a hobby and a local phenomenon.[14] The broadcast featured the singer Mary Garden warbling from Chicago and the legendary humorist Will Rogers delivering his monologue from Independence, Kansas. A few years later, the Columbia Broadcasting System (CBS) debuted. In 1934, four high-powered stations—WOR in New York, WGN in Chicago, WLW in Cincinnati, and WXYZ in Detroit—organized the Quality Group, later known as the Mutual Broadcasting System.

The period that followed, from the mid-1930s to the early 1950s, is generally known as the golden age of radio. Live orchestras, *Amos 'n' Andy*, *Burns and Allen*, Orson Welles's *War of the Worlds*, *The Lone Ranger*, *The Jack Benny Show*, *Dragnet*, *The*

Green Hornet. Families gathered around the living-room console as vivid sound dramas brought heartwarming narratives and humor into the home.

The story of Clear Channel begins in the period that followed radio's golden age, the era in which television seemed to threaten radio's very existence. The period in which radio stations were forced to slash budgets with their very survival at stake.

NBC won the first commercial television license from the FCC in 1941; by the end of 1954, there were 354 television stations in operation. Network radio advertising revenue plummeted from $134 million in 1948 to $103 million in 1952. On the other hand, television ad revenue went from $2.5 million in 1948 to $172 million in 1952.[15]

Most radio stations in those days, though, were independent operators. And independent stations relied mostly on local advertising revenue, which they pursued more fervently once the threat of television began to emerge. Local and regional ad revenues amounted to $417 million in 1948. By 1952, they had reached $473 million.

Network radio suffered as all the big-name talent was drawn to television, and it began cutting budgets by eliminating live bands and orchestras and sometimes airing the audio tracks from popular television shows. Independent stations had to make do with whatever they could manage; the frugal approach was to determine as accurately as possible the listening preferences of their local audiences.

The most cost-effective solution? Disc jockeys, of course, since playing records eliminated the high cost of live musicians. Ever since the 1930s, radio announcers like Martin Block at WNEW in New York and Al Jarvis at KELW in Los Angeles had played musical recordings on the air, both under the name *Make Believe Ballroom*. They were first known as record jockeys, an apparent reference to the fact that they often needed to control the volume of their records, otherwise known as "riding the gain." Unlike his predecessor, the disc jockey—the term was reportedly coined by the gossip columnist Walter Winchell—did not read from a script, as did most radio announcers, but improvised his on-air patter in a natural, conversational tone.[16]

In the early 1950s, music began to change, too. Disc jockeys began noticing that rhythm-and-blues records, created mostly by black Americans, held appeal among young white mainstream audiences as well. Elvis Presley was the galvanizing figure in the cultural revolution known as rock and roll. In one corner of the country, however, the effects of this musical sea change seemed to spark a creativity of another sort, a giddy but profit-minded business environment that would help shape the modern era of radio over the next fifty years.

The oversize influence of Texas radio on the modern history of the medium is virtually unknown outside a small circle of radio lifers and some exceptionally knowledgeable Texans. From its earliest days, the Texas broadcasting community operated, like so many other Texas institutions, as its own self-sufficient country-community, virtually independent—and oblivious—of the world around it. Broadcasting existed in Texas as early as 1911, when J. B. Dickinson, manager of the Texas Fiscal Agency in San Antonio, erected wireless facilities on the campuses of the University of Texas and the Agricultural and Mechanical College (later Texas A&M) in College Station to teach engineering students about radio technology. In 1915, a UT professor, S. Leroy Brown, started broadcasting weather and crop reports from a physics laboratory; on November 24, 1921, a station known as 5XB, on the campus of Texas A&M, aired what was likely the first football game broadcast in American history. The play-by-play commentary for the University of Texas–Texas A&M game was sent in Morse code via ham radio equipment and then decoded and announced on public-address systems from stations that received the broadcast.[17]

The first Texas radio station was WRR in Dallas, which was owned by the city and officially went on the air in 1920. By the end of 1922, the year commercial broadcasting started in Texas, the state had twenty-five commercial stations, including WOAI in San Antonio, which went on the air on September 25, 1922. In February 1928, WOAI joined the world's first radio network, the National Broadcasting Company, and later became a "clear channel," a 50,000-watt station that could be heard for thousands of miles.

A Fort Worth station, WBAP, laid claim to launching the first country-music variety show, broadcast in 1923, a precursor to Nashville's Grand Ole Opry. KFJZ, also in Fort Worth, debuted the Light Crust Doughboys, a pioneering group that played the popular Western swing sound. But it wasn't until the 1950s rock-and-roll era that Texas, and specifically Gordon McLendon, would make a lasting mark on the national radio business.

Gordon Barton McLendon was born on June 8, 1921, in Paris, Texas, near the Oklahoma border. A precocious youth and the son of a well-to-do attorney, McLendon got hooked on radio as a teenage sports fan listening to local football announcers such as Ted Husing, Bill Stern, and Graham McNamee. Soon enough, the teen was practicing his radio delivery by reading newspaper columns aloud.[18]

After graduating from Yale and dropping out of Harvard Law School, McLendon joined the U.S. Navy and studied Japanese at the navy's Japanese-language school in Boulder, Colorado, later spending five months in Pearl Harbor interrogating Japanese prisoners and translating seized documents. After World War II ended, he moved his young family to Palestine, Texas, in 1946 and purchased half of a local station, KNET, with his father's financial backing. (Gordon's father, B. R. McLendon, was something of an accidental entrepreneur who had spun one movie theater, purchased from a struggling law client in Idabel, Oklahoma, into the profitable Tri-State Theater Circuit.) Within months, the railroad moved out of Palestine, greatly diminishing the town's financial prospects; Gordon McLendon sold the station. Soon, the younger McLendon set his sights on Dallas, where he was granted an FCC license in 1947. He founded his new station in the Dallas suburb of Oak Cliff and, his first sign of showmanship, picked its call letters, KLIF, to remind listeners where the station was located.

Aware that his new station—which initially featured music programs, a homemakers' advice program, and an on-air finishing school called *How to Be Charming*—would need to distinguish itself in the competitive Dallas market, McLendon came up with an innovative programming idea: daily broadcasts of professional sports games. On November 9, 1947, its first day on the air, KLIF featured its owner re-creating a pro football game between the Chicago Cardinals and the Detroit Lions. Game highlights were telegraphed to KLIF, and McLendon fleshed out his commentary over recorded crowd sounds. Many listeners of the broadcast reportedly thought they were listening to coverage direct from the game.[19] Soon after, he paid major-league baseball, then still largely an East Coast phenomenon, a mere $1,000 for the rights to broadcast play-by-play accounts received by Teletype from back East and deliver them to fans in the boondocks.[20] McLendon himself would often reprise his sportscaster role, using a sketchy script and ad-libbing the details complete with the sounds of the bat hitting the ball and cheering crowds dubbed in by technicians at the station.

McLendon quickly realized he had a knack for the creative side of radio rather than the sales and managing chores. One of his first promotional gimmicks was to train a parrot to say the call letters K-L-I-F on the air. Klif the parrot, as the bird became known, even had his own American Federation of Radio Artists union card.[21]

McLendon, then in his late twenties, also dubbed himself "the Old Scotchman," often claiming on air to be eighty-three years old, figuring that having an easy-to-remember moniker had some marketing value. He claimed he chose the nickname in part because nobody disliked the Scots.

"Gordon was a very eccentric character," says Stan Webb. "He was almost like a mad scientist."[22] John Barger, who would go on to be the chief architect of Clear Channel in its earliest years and also worked for McLendon as a young man, puts it this way: "He was the first guy [in radio] with what they now call out-of-the-box thinking."[23]

Finding it difficult to attract local advertisers based on ratings, which were determined in those days through audience surveys, McLendon surmised that the way to get higher ratings was to imprint the station's call letters on the minds of its listeners. In that spirit, KLIF pioneered the use of jingle songs, commonly used in radio commercials since the late 1930s, for station identification.

Within a year, KLIF was an unabashed hit, as were McLendon's baseball broadcasts. During that time, the manager of a small station in Denison, Texas, approached McLendon and asked if he could pay him a fee to air his baseball broadcasts. Soon stations in nearby towns such as Tyler, Mount Pleasant, and Mineral Wells had made similar arrangements with McLendon. By the end of 1948, McLendon's "network" included 50 stations. Three years later, Liberty Broadcasting System, as Gordon's father dubbed the operation, had 458 affiliates, making it the second-largest radio network in the country.[24]

With the baseball rebroadcasts at the center of its programming strategy, Liberty gained an audience of sixty to ninety million. Yet despite its size, Liberty earned only $20,000 before taxes in 1949 and $50,000 in 1950; McLendon's outlay to service the stations apparently outweighed his revenue from affiliation fees. The next year he sold half the company to Hugh Roy Cullen, a Houston oilman known as the "king of the wildcatters." Liberty was further decimated when the big-league ball clubs raised their fees from $1,000 to more than $225,000 a year.[25] It seems the majors were concerned that Liberty's broadcasts were affecting attendance at minor-league ballparks; during the 1952 season, many National and American League teams refused to renegotiate with Liberty.

McLendon filed a $12 million antitrust lawsuit against the thirteen major-league teams that opposed him, but the damage had already been done. Liberty shut its doors on May 15, 1952. Still in his early thirties, McLendon, with his father's help, decided to focus on owning stations, including KLIF, of which he was still proprietor.

Other than Liberty's network sportscasts, KLIF aired a mix of "block programming"—distinct shows or blocks scheduled at regular times, most of them popular-music-oriented—similar to that of other radio stations at the time. After Liberty's demise, the only distinguishing factor of KLIF's programming roster was its incessant station-identification jingles. McLendon realized he had to come up with more compelling programming that would appeal to local audiences. He also recognized that particular audiences, such as teenagers, were underrepresented on the air.

Soon a solution presented itself: In the early 1950s, the owner of an Omaha radio station, KOWH, a former disc jockey named Todd Storz, and his assistant, Bill Stewart, noticed how bar patrons liked to play their favorite songs over and over on the jukebox. Storz—who like McLendon had gotten into the radio business with the help of his father's checkbook—decided to try a similar concept on the air at KOWH, allowing repeated plays of a limited selection of songs based on local tastes. By 1953, the station was the highest rated of six stations in Omaha. That same year Storz took the concept to New Orleans, a much larger market, where he had just acquired WTIX. In a year's time, the station was number one in New Orleans.

McLendon took note and applied a similar formula to KLIF that same year. Reluctant to repeat songs, he ordered KLIF disc jockeys not to repeat any tracks during their four-hour shifts. They were to play ten different local hit tunes every hour for a total of forty songs per shift. McLendon also insisted that two oldies and a Glenn Miller song be added to every hour. Later, DJs were allowed to pick the oldies hits themselves.[26]

The term "Top 40" evolved over time, as did the elements of what constituted hits. Initially, the hits were derived from local record store sales, but in smaller markets that often meant that the lower-ranking selections were anything but hits. Increasingly, other factors became as important as the music, namely the disc jockey's patter, the timing and pace of the programming, and the emotional attachment of the listener.

By the mid-1950s, KLIF had a programming schedule unlike most radio stations in the country: rather than the block programs such as *Coffee Capers, Mellow's the Mood,* and *Candlelight and Gold* that KLIF itself had run just months earlier, a day's schedule simply included names of DJs and their time slots. By the middle of 1954, KLIF had gone from 2 percent share of the marketplace to 45 percent. The station was later credited with developing more programming innovations than any other station in the country.

While McLendon often preached a philosophy of programming over sales in interviews, he was open about his utter lack of interest in rock and roll, the hot new musical style that would catapult his new format to commercial success.[27] His son, Bart, told McLendon's biographer, Gordon "knew nothing at all about music and cared nothing at all about music."

Still, he stuck with what worked. Soon radio executives from around the country were traveling to Dallas, taping KLIF broadcasts, and leaving with a recorded blueprint for their own stations. Young would-be Top 40 disc jockeys soon dreamed of working at KLIF.

McLendon was one of the first leaders in the radio business who voiced what was to become its virtual credo: Give the people what they want. That meant a fairly pat version of the Top 40 records and news breaks, a formula McLendon acknowledged accounted for about 90 percent of the time on the air.

McLendon, however, was energized by that other 10 percent. First, he expected his DJs to be funny and informative, to have a real personality. More important, though, was his rapt enthusiasm for station promotions, a catchall category that included any tactic he could think of to draw listeners in.

The classic McLendon promotion was the Money Drop. In 1954, KLIF aired an announcement five times a day for a week telling Dallas listeners "to gather at Elm and Akard streets at five o'clock on Good Friday and 'watch the skies.' " Two hours before the designated time, a crowd of nearly ten thousand people had gathered on the appointed street corner. Then KLIF employees dropped balloons from a window of a Dallas hotel; 250 of the balloons had dollar bills attached to them. The ensuing traffic nightmare prompted the arrival of Dallas police and a ban on anything but armchair contests.

Another early promotional giveaway concocted by McLendon was the KLIF Treasure Hunt. The goal was to find a soda bottle buried in the dirt somewhere—with only the bottle cap showing—that contained a $50,000 check signed by McLendon. He even paid Lloyd's of London $1,250 for insurance that guaranteed 90 percent of the check's value if it was unearthed. Beginning in December 1956, KLIF broadcast clues twice daily, though they were intentionally deceiving, making the discovery of the bottle unlikely. Eventually someone found it, the station (or rather Lloyd's of London) paid up, and in return McLendon received a priceless amount of publicity.

Other on-air contests featured a wide range of awards concocted by McLendon, including "radio's biggest prize" (a one-acre "mountain" in the Texas hill country), free pizza, concert tickets, and even a "live baby" (in actuality, a live baby pig).

McLendon wasn't above manufacturing a scandal as a promotional gimmick. In January 1954, a KLIF news team that had been monitoring the police radio showed up at the scene of an armed robbery in time to score an on-site interview with the victim. The agitated interviewee apparently used a few off-color words in describing what had happened. KLIF's program director, reportedly dismayed by the small number of listeners who called in to complain, decided to place ads in all the local newspapers apologizing for the slipup. He later claimed nearly six thousand people called in to find out what had happened. McLendon immediately saw the "Oops, Sorry" ads as an opportunity and in the following years ran similar ads in local papers in Louisville, San Antonio, Shreveport, and Houston, where he owned stations. The advertisements would always allude to "unfortunate language" that had allegedly been used on the air. Despite that in most cases no incident had occurred, people would call in to the radio station referred to in the ad and ask exactly what had transpired. Many, McLendon surmised, would later tune in to try to catch another slipup.

In mid-April 1967, the so-called Magnificent Seven reported to Dallas and began McLendon's training program while living at Gordon's ranch and film studio, Cielo, just north of Dallas. The group included Stan Webb, Don Barrett, Rick Johnson, Dennis Rodriguez, Jack Hogan, and Luis Carrillo (the seventh guy fell out in the very beginning). "I have always believed that much of my radio success was founded in the education I received during those three months of training," says Webb.

In 1967, KLIF was still going strong, though primarily as an adult contemporary station, playing a mellower, less teen-oriented version of the Top 40 formula. "I was really kind of pinching myself to make sure this is really, really happening to me," recalls Webb of being hired by McLendon. "It was a very exciting time."

As both a Texan and a radio geek, the twenty-three-year-old Webb idolized McLendon. Despite the older man's eccentricities, Webb was not disappointed. "Here I am at Mecca for radio," says Webb. "Seven of us began this training course that was put on by Gordon and many of his leaders at the company, a real intensive three-month program. The idea was going to be that once we were so-called finished with our training we were going to be sent out to one of the seven McLendon markets."

In 1959, McLendon produced the first of three Z-grade horror movies, *The Killer Shrews*, in which he played the part of the mad scientist who gets chewed to death by one of the titular shrews, in actuality a dog wearing a costume. An elfin-looking man with dark, stringy hair, McLendon acts stiffly (hardly a distinguishing factor in this drive-in disaster) but nonetheless communicates a simmering, distracted energy, as if he has world-changing secrets he can't bother to explain to his cast mates. "The mad scientist in the movie was a little bit of his character," says Webb. "He was a bit of a carny who also had a penchant for enlarging the truth of the story."

The training program, however, was everything Webb had dreamed of. "Gordon had saved every memo that had ever really been written, and they were saved in what were known as the policy books." Webb was thus given the opportunity to read McLendon's notes back and forth with his programming executives about how they had come up with various programming and promotional gimmicks. One thing he learned very quickly was that McLendon had an innate distrust of his sales managers. "I think he had a couple bad experiences with guys who hadn't been on the up-and-up with him business-wise," says Webb.

Though McLendon himself always preached the importance of programming over all other concerns, Webb was left with a slightly different impression of his priorities. "Gordon believed the most important thing was to get a competitive signal, and by that I mean you don't want to get a small 1,000-watt daytimer," a station that only broadcast during the day, he says. McLendon had built up KLIF to eventually become a 50,000-watt powerhouse. His number-two priority was programming. "So you build an engineering piece and a product and go hire these sales guys and somehow all this magic will occur."

John Barger, who worked for McLendon twice, first on the programming end in 1966 for WISL in Buffalo and then as his general counsel in the early 1970s, recalls Gordon's inspiring if unorthodox way of brainstorming. "He used to sit us around a table and say, okay, let's come up with a hundred things that are in the newspaper, and he'd throw around copies of the *San Francisco Chronicle*, which he thought was the best newspaper in the country at that time."

Once the group—which often also included the company's chief financial officer and the head of public relations—had compiled a list of topics, they discussed whether any of them had any relevance or application to radio. "Gordon would just grab people whose intellect and outlook he respected and bring them in," says Barger, chuckling. "Of course, we would all have to stop what we were doing. But they were fabulous brainstorming sessions, and for a young man twenty-four, twenty-five, or twenty-six, however old I was, this was just unbelievable."

For Stan Webb, the McLendon whirlwind soon carried him to the far corners of the country. After "graduating" from the McLendon training program, Webb was dispatched to Boston to monitor the local market by listening to every station and taking notes on a legal pad. "Sometime in early July we were all given our market assignments and sent on our way," he says. "I was sent to Boston for a quick two-week assignment, then to New York, where I would be assigned to McLendon 25, a new sales and promotions representation firm for FM stations that Gordon was starting." The concept was pretty revolutionary for its time (representing just FM stations). The New York assignment was interrupted with a brief two-month jump out to the McLendon station KABL in San Francisco.

When Webb hadn't received a paycheck for a couple of weeks, he called in to Gordon's secretary, Bonnie Owens, who promptly asked him where he was. "I told her I was in Boston," Webb recalls. "And she said, 'Gordon doesn't know where you are.' Sometimes during the cocktail hour he would do certain things he would not remember the next day."

In the coming months, Webb, now twenty-four, would often traverse the nation, seemingly at McLendon's whim, to pursue some new project or notion to the utmost of his relatively undeveloped abilities.

One night, McLendon pulled Webb aside at a company event and told him he had just bought a station in Detroit that he wanted the young exec to program just like KABL. By this time, even the ever-enthusiastic Webb was getting weary. "I said, 'I still have an apartment in New York,'" Webb recalls. "He said, 'Send me the lease.'"

So Webb and his wife packed their belongings into their Volkswagen and headed for Detroit, where McLendon had purchased an ailing classical-music station and redubbed it WWWW. "He wanted to call it W4," says Webb. The idea was to automate the station as much as possible. It was housed in an old brownstone on Jefferson Street that included a twenty-foot-long room filled with broadcast machinery.

Alas, the conversion to easy listening was a bust. Webb offers his own theory of why McLendon's formula didn't work in Detroit: "San Francisco is a very romantic city, and all the programming nuances of KABL were very romantic. Detroit was not romantic. It was the summer of 1967, right after the Detroit riots; the streets were still smoking when I got there."[28]

Sensing it was time to move in another direction, Webb started looking for a new job, this time in radio advertising sales. "I began noticing that the sales guys in the radio stations drove the newer cars and had better-looking sport coats," he says. He also learned that his McLendon credential had some value: despite no sales experience, he quickly got his first sales job at KTSA in San Antonio, a former McLendon station owned by Bernie Waterman, an independent owner.

Finally, Webb found something he was good at. "I really cut my teeth in sales," he says. Working at KTSA and a small R&B station in San Antonio, he honed his skills until "I could sell just about anything." Then, still in his mid-twenties, Webb got the call from the number-one Top 40 station in San Antonio, KONO-AM, owned by Jack Roth, who had competed with McLendon in San Antonio for years and had eventually won the battle.

For the next five and a half years, Webb worked his way up through the ranks in San Antonio, eventually becoming general manager for both KONO and KITY, its FM counterpart, an adult pop station. Before he knew it, it was 1975. "By that time, my wife and I had bought a starter home," he recalls, and had begun a family. Success knew his name: Webb had developed something of a reputation as a competent sales guy in San Antonio.

One day that same year he got a call from John Barger, who had just arrived in San Antonio from a stint at KRLD in Dallas. Barger informed Webb that he was representing L. Lowry Mays and his business partner, a local car dealer named Billy Joe "Red" Mc-Combs. Together, they were planning to purchase a local underperforming Top 40 station, WOAI. The idea was to transform it with an all-talk format, a concept Barger had cribbed from his old boss, Gordon McLendon.

Before he knew it, Webb was sitting at a table in a local restaurant with Barger, who mapped out the terms of a possible deal on a napkin. "Johnny really put the pitch on me," Webb says. By the end of their meeting, Webb had agreed to become WOAI's sales manager with Barger in place as the station's general manager. Mays and McCombs took over the station on June 13, 1975. A month later, Stan Webb began work as Clear Channel's very first sales manager.

3.

CLEAR CHANNEL'S BEGINNINGS

I f the story of Clear Channel bears the flavor of a father-and-sons epic, then the early life of the father offers some tantalizing clues about the current state of the family legacy. Though Mark Mays and his younger brother, Randall, were brought up in the privileged surroundings of East Coast prep schools and Ivy League universities, their dad, L. Lowry Mays, survived some pointedly difficult periods as a child and young man.

Lester Lowry Mays was born on July 24, 1935, into a middle-class family in Houston, Texas. His father, Lester T. Mays, was a steel-industry executive who, with his wife, Virginia Lowry Mays, raised Lowry and his younger sister, Joanne, in the upscale University Park neighborhood of Dallas. But according to Mays, he was raised in a culture of frugality. He once recalled how during World War II, the family grew a "victory garden" of vegetables in the backyard to augment reduced food supplies. He also remembered visiting the farm his father grew up on to collect eggs to sell to add to the family's income. "Having to do those types of things made you appreciate the value of a dollar," said Mays.[1]

Life would get even tougher for Lowry at the age of twelve, when his father was killed in a car accident. To make ends meet, his mother took up a career as a real estate agent and built up her own business to support the family. At Highland Park High School in

Dallas, Lowry was a good student but seemingly took more pride in his work ethic than in his exemplary studies. A friend from that time once called him a "straight arrow": he was a member of the student council, was in the Air Force ROTC, and earned a varsity letter as a member of the high school football team. The six-foot-two teenager was well liked, according to classmates, but "I wasn't born to be the most successful," Mays said. "I was just a normal kid in high school that did well academically. I was not the brain of the class."

Lowry held various after-school jobs, including one as a surveyor; shortly after graduating, he put in time on a Louisiana oil rig as a roughneck, the workers who take on most of the heavy-lifting and dangerous tasks in the oil fields. His pay was $3.50 an hour, money he saved for college. The oil business seemed a good fit, and, soon after, when he attended Texas A&M University, he majored in petroleum engineering. "That's what I thought I would do the rest of my life."[2]

After graduating from Texas A&M in 1957, he was called into service by the U.S. Air Force, stationed at Brooks Air Force Base in San Antonio, also the site of a blind date with his wife to be, Peggy Pitman. A young teacher who had attended Wellesley College in Massachusetts and the University of Texas at Austin, Peggy was Mays's entrée into San Antonio society. She had grown up in San Antonio and attended a prestigious local all-girls school, St. Mary's Hall. She had also been 1958's Queen of the Order of the Alamo, a debutante-like honor awarded each year during San Antonio's springtime Fiesta, a bizarre, Texas-style version of Mardi Gras, mixing Anglo old-money aspiration with flamboyant Mexican-influenced pageantry.

Mays was assigned to the Republic of China, Taiwan, during the skirmish between the two Chinas over the islands of Quemoy and Matsu, where he worked as a pipeline engineer adviser.[3] His position was a vital one: Taiwan needed a pipeline to link all its air-bases.[4] While in Taiwan, Mays worked with the Chinese nationalist air force general Tiger Wong; and when the project was completed, he celebrated with his hosts at a "monkey feast," which entailed a live monkey prepared at the table.[5]

His future career path seemed clearer than ever. Lowry and Peggy wed in San Antonio on July 25, 1959. But Mays's time in the military also hammered home the fact that reservoir engineering was a rapidly changing field and his skills were already getting rusty. To keep up to speed, he knew he would need a master's degree in engineering. Instead, in 1960 he left the air force to attend Harvard Business School, where he earned a master's in business administration in 1962. After that he returned to San Antonio with Peggy to begin work at Russ & Company, a regional investment-banking firm where he eventually became vice president of corporate finance.

Mays's knack for creative salesmanship displayed itself from the start. In his early days at Russ, he once identified potential investors for the stock of a budding photo processing company by paying a local teen $10 to write down the license plate numbers of cars that were parked outside the company's San Antonio store. Then he paid another youth to visit the Department of Motor Vehicles and retrieve the address for each plate. He sent a letter to each one with a recommendation to invest in the company.[6]

In 1970, he formed his own investment firm, Mays & Company.

San Antonio in the 1970s was about as unlikely a site for a nascent media company as anywhere on the planet. The home of the Alamo, the miniature fortress that serves as the symbol of Texas's independence and rebelliousness, it was a sleepy, regional city—the most multiethnic in the state—until the boom of the 1980s. It now sports a population of about 1.2 million, making it the ninth-largest city in the United States; but back in 1970, it ranked as the fifteenth-largest city, with a population just over 650,000.[7] Nearly doubling its number of inhabitants had major effects.

San Antonio's historic downtown area remains compact, centering on the River Walk, a winding canal twenty feet below sea level designed as a tourist attraction in the 1930s and now lined with cheesy Tex-Mex joints and cowboy bars, as well as a Hard Rock Cafe. But the story of today's San Antonio glows in the gleaming modern office towers that dot the landscape north of the downtown area, along I-287 and I-10, the city's two main thoroughfares.

Tom Frost, the seventy-eight-year-old chairman emeritus of Frost National Bank—the largest Texas-based bank, founded by his great-great-grandfather in 1868—recalled the 1970s era one February morning in his modern downtown San Antonio office. Surrounded by wood paneling and oil paintings of Western nature scenes, Frost, a tall, lanky white-haired gentleman who is now a philanthropist and something of a town elder, said he knew Mays's wife, Peggy, before Mays did, as the younger sister of his best friend and the daughter of some of his parents' best friends. Both families attended Christ Episcopal Church and belonged to the same social clubs; Frost's wife taught Mark and Randall as little boys in Sunday school. Frost still passes Mark Mays's Alamo Heights residence every day on his morning walk.

Until the 1970s, the biggest employers in San Antonio were two beer companies, Lone Star and Pearl, that catered almost exclusively to Texans. One hundred and fifty miles from Mexico with a high poverty rate and a strong manufacturing base, San Antonio lacked the flash and good-ole-boy moxie of larger Texas towns like Dallas and Houston. But slowly, drawn in by the city's low cost of living and nearly California-like climate, a handful of Fortune 500 companies began to take root and grow. USAA, the insurance company founded by military for military; Valero and Tesoro, two locally run oil-refinery conglomerates; and SBC, the Southwestern telecommunications giant, all found San Antonio to be fertile territory for big business. It should be no surprise that the recently merged AT&T chose the San Antonio home of SBC, over AT&T's New York City base, for its new corporate headquarters. In 2006, Toyota opened a new plant in San Antonio, scheduled to spit out more than 150,000 Tundra pickup trucks a year and employ more than four thousand local residents.[8]

Texans, according to Frost, are known for their character; and San Antonians in particular are well regarded for their humility and lack of ostentation. "The thing about Lowry is, what you see is what you get," says Frost. "He doesn't live any high-binding life—he doesn't fly his friends on a jet to Paris for an anniversary dinner with his wife or anything like that. When you see Lowry up and down the street and going anywhere, he's just like anybody else. That's why he was accepted in this community. This community at that time was a pretty small place and everybody could tell that what you saw is what you did get. There was no fooling around here with anybody."[9]

Even longtime employees recall Mays's folksiness. "I don't know that Lowry came from a tremendous amount of money," says Jim Smith, later a top Clear Channel executive. "So even though he enjoys being very wealthy, there's an aura about Lowry that allows him to sit down with the common man and appreciate everything they do, too."[10]

With the retrial of the Enron executives Kenneth Lay and Jeffrey Skilling just igniting in Houston at the time of our talk (both were later convicted), Frost was quick to point out that Mays was made of different stuff. First and foremost, says Frost, Lowry Mays is a Texan. "He's very up-front," he says. "I don't think you'll ever catch Lowry Mays working behind the scenes at something else, and saying one thing and doing another. That's just not his style. If you're at a dinner party or in a boardroom, when you hear it from him, that's what he thinks and you can bet on that and depend on that."

And while media wasn't a core San Antonio industry, WOAI had long played a dominant role in the city. "When I grew up, you couldn't go to bed without listening to Ken McClure or Henry Guerra on the WOAI ten o'clock news," recalls Frost.

After putting together some real estate deals with B. J. Mc-Combs, the successful local car dealer who liked to boast he had sold more Edsels than any other Ford dealer in the country, Mays happened into the financial transaction that would forever change his life's path.

The details of Mays's purchase of his first radio station have taken on almost mythic proportions in the industry. Due, to some extent, to a bit of apparent embellishment by Mays himself, most would later get the impression that he was so inept he bought it purely by accident.

The basic facts are clear: In 1972, a couple of local investors asked Mays to go in on the purchase of a local country-music station, KEEZ-FM, that was teetering on the brink of failure. As the story goes, Mays politely declined to participate in the investment opportunity but agreed to co-sign the note.[11]

Almost immediately, the investors ran into financial problems, and there was only one solution to repaying the debt. As Mays told it, he bumbled his way into ownership. "Ninety days later, I found myself owning the station," recalls Mays, who convinced Red Mc-Combs to take the plunge with him (with some help from John Schaefer, a local real estate developer who later cashed out). "He bought radio advertising [as a car dealer]," Mays said, "so he knew more about it than I did." Mays was thirty-six years old.

In another version of the story, McCombs convinced Mays of the financial merits of the radio business. But when Mays approached McCombs to invest in KEEZ, McCombs balked—he wanted to buy WOAI.[12] McCombs, a strong San Antonio booster, apparently was displeased by the idea of an out-of-town company owning a local institution. WOAI may have been a better investment, but KEEZ was a lot cheaper, and buying it kept it in the hands of San Antonians.

Together the pair took out a loan of $125,000 to purchase the station for $185,000. "It was not that I had any great, great fever about the radio business," said McCombs, but he described Mays as someone he wanted to do business with, "whether or not it was radio or plowing up turnips in Uvalde."[13]

Mays soon regretted his decision to partner with McCombs. "I said, 'Do you know anything about radio?' And he said, 'Yes' [and Mays believed him], which was the second mistake I made," said Mays. "The first mistake I made was co-signing the note."[14] Even as late as 1992, Mays told *Forbes* magazine, in no uncertain terms, "I had no intention of getting into the broadcast business."[15]

"He and Red McCombs, as I understand the story," says Stan Webb, "had made a loan to a fella who wanted to buy this FM station there in San Antonio. Well, they get in there and they try to operate it and they can't pay their bills. So Lowry and Red literally take back the station because their name is on the note. So suddenly they have a radio station and neither one of them had any experience in running a radio station."[16]

But other accounts suggest that Mays became attuned to the upside of the radio business rather early in his exposure to it. For instance, he took careful note that the radio industry had not seen a decline in revenues year after year since 1950. He also is credited by some with understanding early the value of amassing a large group of radio stations. But Jim Smith, who would go on to be one of Mays's most trusted deputies, disputes such accounts. "There are stories floating around out there that Lowry was some kind of broadcasting genius that started this company with that in mind and built it up," says Smith. "And that's just complete bullshit. He didn't know anything about the business."

Lowry named his fledgling concern San Antonio Broadcasting Company. Tom Frost says he didn't believe Mays even had a significant game plan for his business back then: "I think he was more of an incremental-step guy rather than a big-picture guy."

Still, there were many factors working in his disfavor. For one, in 1972, 90 percent of the radio audience still listened to AM. Not only that, the Federal Communications Commission prohibited any one company from owning more than seven radio stations.[17]

Mays's venture did not thrive. FM radio was not really making its mark yet. "The changeover in San Antonio came very, very late," says John Barger. "It wasn't until 1978 that an FM station became number one in the market." Besides, Mays was trying to run KEEZ as an easy-listening station, but there was already a successful easy-listening station in the area, Stan Webb recalls.

In those first years, Mays burned through a host of concepts and programmers trying to make the station work. After a while, the goal was simply to minimize their expenses.

John Barger recalls the problems somewhat differently: "It was a single FM station. It struggled because it was up against a big twenty- to twenty-five-share radio station named KTSA that just dominated. KTSA-AM at 550. And they were trying to do Top 40 up against it. To make things worse, 80 percent of your potential listeners didn't have a receiver that could get you."[18]

Eventually, though, the station began to turn a profit, and somewhere along the way Mays developed a taste for the radio business. Years later he would make clear exactly what had whet his appetite. "During every other recession except for the one in 1991, radio revenues grew through the downturn," he observed. "Traditionally, people have advertised more on radio when there's a downturn."[19]

He also had a sense that with FM he had gotten in on a new trend early. And lucky for him, FM stations didn't cost a whole lot in those days. In 1973, Mays acquired two more failing FM stations in Tulsa, Oklahoma, from TracyLocke Advertising. By 1974, all three of his stations were losing money.

Pretty soon Mays was paying his employees with his own cash instead of company earnings. That same year, despite his stations' losses, Lowry decided to leave investment banking and focus all of his time and energy on his radio stations.

As luck would have it, an opportunity soon presented itself that Mays found irresistible. That opportunity was the availability of WOAI-AM in San Antonio. Owned by Avco Broadcasting, WOAI held a particular appeal to Mays, and not only because it was one of only twelve stations at that time with a clear channel, or a Class 1 AM radio license, which allowed it to be heard nationwide in the evening.

Founded in 1922, with an initial power of 500 watts, WOAI was one of South Texas's earliest stations. Ironically, it was also one of the first stations in the country licensed as a clear channel by the FCC, the government agency that Clear Channel would later lock horns with over ownership rules. In 1928, WOAI had joined the

National Broadcasting Company and later became known as one of
the first radio stations in the country to employ a local news staff. It
was one of the four largest stations in Texas. It also happened to be
an AM station, of crucial significance for Mays's foundering FM operation.

In the seven years Avco had owned WOAI, the company had
changed it to a Top 40 format and run it into the ground, despite a
fifty-year history with NBC News and a locally popular agricultural
news show, or ag report, that ran every weekday at noon. Avco, a
diversified conglomerate that manufactured farm equipment and
many of the helicopters used by the United States in the Vietnam
War, had gone on a wild acquisition binge in the late 1960s and
early '70s as the war began to unwind, buying its way into many
businesses it didn't understand, including broadcasting.[20]

The team of investors with whom Mays arranged to purchase
WOAI was slightly different from the one that purchased the FM
stations, in part because the cost would be so much higher. Indeed,
it would take nearly a year for the $1.5 million deal to close.[21] The
investors included the former Dallas mayor Erik Jonsson, the owner
of KRLD-FM in Dallas, who as a bonus offered the services of
KRLD's program director as part of the deal, to help position
WOAI for a new era. Apparently, it took a while for Mays to raise
all the capital needed for the purchase, though some close to the
deal joked that he was simply waiting, in those difficult days of the
mid-1970s recession and gas crisis, for interest rates to drop.

One day in the weeks before the deal finally went down in
June 1975, Mays dropped in to the offices of KRLD and for the first
time met the station's young programmer, John Barger. The tall,
slightly plump, but otherwise unassuming Barger had brought the
all-news format to KRLD with great success.

But Barger was hungry for more. When he first worked for
Gordon McLendon, he spent his days brokering leases for drive-ins
and helping to build McLendon's sports radio network. "He was
kind of a frustrated non-player in the business because he was doing networks," says one former colleague.

Prior to that, after his second stint working for McLendon, Barger had left the radio business for Washington, where he worked for President Lyndon Johnson, a fellow Texan, on his much-vaunted War on Poverty project. In 1968, Barger returned to Dallas, to spearhead Gordon McLendon's ambitious if short-lived gubernatorial campaign. (McLendon, a conservative Democrat, withdrew early, it is commonly believed, due to the large number of conservative candidates.)

Barger suggested to Mays in their brief chat that perhaps a similar all-news talk format would work for WOAI in San Antonio. Mays immediately liked the idea. "It wasn't brain surgery," says Barger, who credits the bright idea to his McLendon background and his friendship with a Westinghouse executive named Herb Humphries, who had programmed news-talk powerhouse 1010 WINS in New York ("You give us 22 minutes, we'll give you the world") and, later, KFWB and KABC in Los Angeles.

Barger had worked under Humphries in Austin, Texas, a decade earlier. During that time, Humphries showed Barger the ins and outs of the "news wheel" he had helped develop at Westinghouse, an outline for how to pace an engaging hour of news-talk radio.

Barger reasoned that any idiot off the street could have figured out that sandwiching the new Rolling Stones single between the hog report and an update on cotton futures was not a productive programming concept deep in the conservative, mid-1970s heart of South Texas.

He also believed, rightly or wrongly, that news-talk radio was a lower-risk solution. "I knew from experience you could do a lot more with a news-talk radio station regardless of ratings," says Barger, "because in Dallas we were like number two or number three in the market always, but we were just knocking the hell out of everybody in terms of billing."

After the fact, though, Barger wondered whether a better idea for San Antonio might have been a Spanish-language station since 85 percent of the population south of San Antonio is Spanish-speaking, with 75 percent preferring to speak Spanish.[22] Mays also had an interest in the Spanish-language market, having noted that a local Spanish-language-formatted station owned by the Dallas-based Tichenor family controlled a 30 percent market share. Unfortunately, Barger didn't have a clue about Spanish-language radio.

But San Antonio, with its Mexican-American population that goes back nine generations, was different from other Spanish-language markets: Barger later learned that even Spanish-speaking stations in San Antonio peppered their on-air banter with English phrases—and all phone numbers in advertisements were given in English.

Nonetheless, after his meeting with Mays, Barger quickly contacted his friend Herb Humphries. "Herb had given me a quick, short course in Dallas when I put the news talk on at KRLD," says Barger. "So now I called him back and I said, 'I think we committed to the same thing in San Antonio.' " Despite San Antonio's differences, Barger says he became convinced the same formula could work in Dallas.

By most accounts, WOAI had been through some tough times, and through many formats. In the seven years that Avco had owned the station, it had become the number-three-rated Top 40 station in its market.

On June 13, 1975, Mays and his partners took over at WOAI. The name of his new company, which consisted of only the one AM station, was Clear Channel Communications, named after WOAI's powerful clear channel signal. Mays's other three stations included different partners and continued to operate as San Antonio Broadcasting Company.

On June 16, Mays hired Barger as WOAI's general manager. In one of their first meetings, Mays enthusiastically described his plan for structuring the new business, using the management-by-objective method he learned at Harvard Business. The idea was to define the problem, set firm goals, develop a strategy for achieving them, and then, finally, solve the problem. Barger shook his head and chuckled after hearing this from his new boss, and then informed him as politely as possible what the plan was: "We're just gonna reward the guys who sell the most ads."[23]

Days after arriving in San Antonio to start work, Barger knew things weren't going to be as easy as they looked. After his first meeting with the station's sales manager, the sales manager decided to quit. Within two or three weeks, most of the rest of the sales staff had walked out, too. Almost immediately, the new boss had set a new tone. "I was kind of nutsy about accountability," explains Barger. "You know, I just said, I need to know what you're going to be doing this next week, and I want to know what your goals and objectives are insofar as the accounts that we've assigned to you."

The good news was that change was on the horizon. The bad news? With the station's relaunch only weeks away, Barger was desperate to hire a new sales staff and, being new to San Antonio, had no choice but to inquire around town for available talent. The same name kept coming up no matter where he went: Stan Webb. You've got to talk to Stan Webb.

Barger had never met the guy, but he certainly knew his name. After all, Webb was one of McLendon's Magnificent Seven. But in mid-June 1975, Barger couldn't find him. It seems Stan Webb had walked out of his job as sales manager at KONO over a dispute with the owner and had plans to take his family for a two-week vacation to Montana to visit his sister. Desperate and determined, Barger hunted him down before he left and met with him at a local restaurant.

The man he finally met was not exactly what Barger expected. Stan Webb stood an imposing six feet three with a big, neatly groomed Afro, not an unusual style for would-be white hipsters in Texas in that era, but far from the buttoned-down "suit" Barger was prepared to encounter. Webb also had a taste for wild-looking sport jackets. But his manner was cool and collected. "He was a plain and very amiable but yet no-nonsense Central Texan," recalls Barger. "And he was an extremely unassuming pitchman."

The two men got along swimmingly. They bonded about their

McLendon experiences and connected on the business lessons they had learned at the knee of the master. But both agreed there was plenty about the model to improve upon. "[At McLendon], there was very little emphasis on concept selling [selling the product to advertisers] and a lot of emphasis on creativity and programming [developing ideas for listeners]," says Barger with a chuckle. "And it was my idea that you could have your cake and eat it, too."

The new duo ended up hashing out Webb's employment deal on a napkin in the aforementioned restaurant. On July 4, WOAI switched to the news-talk format mapped out by Barger. Clear Channel Communications was officially in business.

Webb had already bought his vacation plane tickets, so he insisted on not starting at WOAI until mid-July. Meanwhile, Barger set out to re-create the classic WOAI lineup from scratch. Once again, he asked around town about talent, this time the news personalities who had made the station great before Avco botched it up. The first name that came up was that of Henry Guerra, a local legend who had appeared on San Antonio radio in the 1930s and '40s and was a regional television news anchor in the 1940s. Barger asked Mays what had happened to Guerra; Mays told him that Guerra was running the Angelus Funeral Home in San Antonio, founded by his grandfather. So Barger tracked him down and rehired him for the afternoon shift as a business reporter.

Then he approached Bob Guthrie, WOAI's morning news anchor, who normally got two and a half minutes an hour in the Top 40 format, and offered him a three-hour morning slot.

Guthrie was thrilled.

Barger also decided to keep Bill McReynolds, the station's beloved agricultural report commentator and another local legend. The way he saw it, farmers were loyal listeners and a strong selling point for the station to advertisers.

By the time Stan Webb returned from Montana, Barger had transformed the station from a middling Top 40 embarrassment to a news-talk contender. Now all Webb had to do was sell the thing to advertisers.

Yet even in those early days, according to both men, Lowry Mays had little to do with the day-to-day business of running the station. Mays often stopped by the station's offices, but rarely did he offer his opinion on programming and sales decisions. "Lowry really never got involved in operations," says Webb. "He just wasn't interested in that." Mays quickly established a reputation as a trusting, hands-off manager. "He really let us run the business, and Lowry knew what to do with the money once he got it."

As a result, these two young radio diehards got a solid chance to test their wildest ideas about how to build a better station.

Webb quickly realized that the road to the future was a rocky one. For one thing, he had only worked for music stations in the past, never a news station. For another, he didn't have a sales staff.

To make matters worse, the new format was a tough sell to advertisers. While the all-news-and-talk format was thriving in New York City, it was an entirely new concept in San Antonio. To the local media buyers, radio was all about music. At least 60 percent of WOAI's listeners in its previous incarnation spoke only Spanish. The rest were young white teenagers tuning in to hear the latest hits. Neither of those constituencies seemed likely to tune in to a station filled with a bunch of guys talking and ads. So, wondered the local ad buyers, who the heck would? Never mind that WOAI's ratings were abominable, placing it not even in the top ten in a relatively small market.

The consummate sales professional, Webb saw the situation called for drastic measures. "The ratings were very poor," he says, "so the advertising agencies who tried to put together this formula of how they buy stations based on cost per rating point, or in those days it was a cost per thousand, they couldn't do that, because the audience was so small." Webb's only option was to go to the clients directly, some of whom he already knew from his previous stint in San Antonio.

"So rather than calling on the advertising agency for Lone Star beer," Webb recalls, "I would just go and see Barry Sullivan, who was the advertising manager for Lone Star, which was based right there in San Antonio, and I would take him to lunch. And you know, after he had drunk about ten Lone Star beers, I'd sell him the schedule. And WOAI was really not in their target, but I knew that the chairman of Lone Star beer, who was a guy named Harry Jersig, loved the new WOAI. Here's a guy in his sixties, not in the target for beer advertising, but Barry had to buy it because his boss listened to the station. And so I figured out very early that they liked to hear themselves on the radio. It's like if you're selling outdoor advertising, you always want to make sure you find out where the client's work is, so you can put one of the billboards up on his way to work. Because you're selling him on his own advertising."

In another sales coup, Webb sold a plan to Handy Andy, the largest supermarket chain in town. Handy Andy was represented by one of San Antonio's top advertising agencies, the Pitluck Group. Pitluck had no interest in WOAI, claiming their spots were too expensive when considering their lackluster ratings. But Webb found out that Charlie Becker, president of Handy Andy (and San Antonio's mayor from 1973 to 1975), also liked WOAI's news-talk format. Again, he made a visit to the company's advertising manager and sold him a schedule. The manager then had the unwelcome task of calling the ad agency and telling it what Handy Andy had just bought. Webb had set a new precedent, "that those clients are our clients, not just the advertising agencies'," he says. "So we had a little bit of a low-heat relationship with the advertising agencies."

Webb also credits Barger's hiring of Henry Guerra as an early stroke of genius from a sales perspective. Armed with Guerra's local name recognition and credibility, Webb began pitching the idea of the well-respected Guerra delivering advertisements during his business reports. Such was Guerra's reputation that, Webb surmised, his participation in commercials would come off as endorsements, not shilling.

The strategy worked and almost immediately translated into new revenue. Webb sold business news spots to Frost National

Bank. Then he tried selling time during the sports report to Lone Star and Pearl, two local breweries.

With Webb and Barger playing off each other, WOAI quickly made an impression with the business community as a fast-growing newcomer in the local media market. Emphasis on the word "impression." In fact, Clear Channel's corporate office in July 1975 consisted only of Mays, his secretary, the accountant Tom Klein, and one other administrative employee. The head count in operations was two: John Barger and Stan Webb. And already Clear Channel was having money troubles. WOAI was bringing in $25,000 to $30,000 per month and operating at a loss.

"It was a very intense time," says Webb. "Johnny would say, 'We've gotta speed up our collection process because we've gotta make payroll.' " So Webb would implore the sales department the next morning to turn up the heat on collections. "I wouldn't say, 'Hey, we're trying to make payroll,' but it was literally that."

Still, impressions counted for a lot in a small American city that was still reeling, like so many others, from a national recession. That August the *San Antonio Light* ran a full-page feature on Lowry Mays under the headline "Exec Tunes in on S.A."[24]

Accompanied by a photo of the handsome, smiling young executive, the article portrayed Mays as an "extremely confident" booster of the business community and downtown revitalization of his adopted hometown. Mays was interviewed in his office, which included an antique partner desk, as well as bookshelves filled with titles such as Peter Drucker's *Effective Executive, The Success System That Never Fails,* and *Reality in Advertising,* along with a copy of the *Texas Almanac.*

"Sure, San Antonio has its share of problems," he told the reporter, "but this city is going to continue to grow and industry will eventually come to San Antonio because this is such an outstanding place to live. With the proper leadership, it's just a matter of time."

Mays's prescription for economic growth in San Antonio at the time included more corporate headquarters and a plan to make the city the industrial and business hub for South Texas, as well as a gateway to the north for Mexican businesses. "I just hope the private sector will continue to support all these things," he added ominously, "because it's a long-term proposition."

Credited in the story for acting more like a native son of San Antonio than a transplant, Mays also earned points for being a member of the Greater San Antonio Chamber of Commerce and for being active with the YMCA, where he liked to get in some jogging, golf, and tennis when he had time. In many ways, much of what he proposed later came to pass: in the coming decades, corporate headquarters such as Clear Channel's helped put San Antonio on the national business map. And in the 1990s, ground was broken on a new state-of-the-art gym facility in San Antonio, the Mays Family branch of the YMCA.

What was not reported was how poorly WOAI was doing in the local ratings battle. The ratings started out very low, and then they stayed pretty low. Although in the category of men thirty-five years and older, it didn't do that badly.

But Stan Webb had a secret: after a while, WOAI didn't care that much about ratings. Truth was, it didn't really need ratings when it had something better: a personal relationship with advertisers who were also listeners. Indeed, using news personalities like Henry Guerra to draw in new business was working like a charm. And, having few other options, Webb began to push the envelope.

One day he informed John Barger that he was trying to pitch Handy Andy. So Barger would tell Henry Guerra to do a story on Handy Andy during the next day's business report. And nobody (including Guerra) complained, because it was a matter of survival. Since Barger gave the okay, there were no programming guys to claim that the news was tainted by commercialism. "We were in the business of sales; we were not in the business of programming," says Webb. "And I think that's what made us different from the very get-go."

Any lofty notions of culture, objectivity, and public access were promptly tossed out the window, foreshadowing the issues that would plague Clear Channel decades later. Never mind that these notions embodied for many Americans what it meant to be American. In the eyes of Barger and Webb (and, by inference, Lowry Mays), making money in the most efficient manner possible was the purest expression of patriotism. Coming from a small, struggling radio operation, such brazenness and bluster seemed almost charming (or at worst tacky). But applying the same perspective to the workings of the multinational media conglomerate Clear Channel evolved into would one day seem downright boneheaded.

At the time, though, the sales-at-any-cost approach was employed mostly out of necessity. These weren't some young revolutionaries looking to reinvent radio. The guys at WOAI really wanted good ratings because good ratings meant higher ad rates, which meant making payroll. And making some real money. It's just that those ratings weren't happening, not with an all-news-talk format in San Antonio.

Stan Webb went through a long list of salespeople before he began finding the few folks he really needed, the kind who understood the new hybrid being developed at WOAI. It was a confusing notion to some, the idea of an all-advertising-based model where every minute of programming was fodder for a sale. But for those who got it, it sang. And the money started rolling in.

One day Barger and Webb came up with a concept for a show called the *Morning Magazine,* which ran from nine to noon every day. The whole show was devoted to putting clients on the air and turning them into local news ("So, Charlie, tell me how Handy Andy got started?"). It worked because most of the local businessmen were already listeners. And it really, really worked. Before he knew it, Webb was fielding calls from local ad agencies trying to place their clients on the show.

Even Barger was amazed: "As Rex Tackett used to say, 'We did it honestly because they didn't let us use a Smith & Wesson.' We just went in and took the money. We just found the right people to call on. We didn't call on their agencies, we called on the principals, particularly those who liked us, toward people over the age of forty-five, and it was simply, 'Hey, Charlie, you're a listener, aren't you? Well, your goddamn agency doesn't buy us.' That was the pitch."

Many took issue with the drastic format change, but in that case Clear Channel had history on its side. After all, its sales reps could say, "We're just taking the station back to what it used to be. Don't you remember Henry Guerra and the news?" Turned out the station had its die-hard listeners who had tuned in even when the station had turned to Top 40.

A revealing indicator of Clear Channel's rabid local following: For about five years, Barger recalled having to hold job interviews with the college-age children of virtually every family who lived in the Alamo Heights neighborhood of San Antonio, where Mays resided, as a courtesy to his boss. "Many of them were very ill suited for radio," says Barger. These well-to-do families wanted their kids to stay in San Antonio but still have a decent job. And working at Clear Channel, probably for the first time, was considered decent.

As for Lowry Mays, he maintained his reputation as a hands-off manager. Every day at five in the afternoon, he would call in to Barger and ask what was going on. Barger would tell Mays in advance if he was going to fire somebody or hire somebody, but more because Mays had been in San Antonio a lot longer and might know something about the employee that Barger was not aware of.

Meanwhile, Barger took an aggressive business stance that at that point was rare in the radio business, raising his advertising rates as high as he could as soon as he could. Often, WOAI's rates would go up even though its ad inventory was only 85 percent sold. The way Barger saw it, if he wasn't losing 10 percent of his advertisers due to his rates, he wasn't doing his job.

He also developed a healthy aversion to the Arbitron ratings, an inherently flawed system that required pollsters to call families in the evening at their homes and convince them to maintain a diary of their listening habits. Barger figured the system didn't accurately account for the very poor and the very rich, both of whom generally

have unlisted phone numbers and don't do well with telephone so-
licitors. "The very poor think they're bill collectors," says Barger,
"and the very rich think they're trying to sell them something."
Those well-to-do listeners were the same ones that ultimately
made WOAI successful. Barger estimated that WOAI went on to
have a listenership two or three times that attributed to it by the Arbitron rating book. Consequently, he canceled the station's Arbitron
subscription, a radical move in the radio world of that era, when
Arbitron's expensive weekly reports were the sole means of demonstrating listenership numbers to advertisers.

It took a lot of nerve to sell clients on a station with inferior ratings, especially when it came time to raise rates. When Barger and
his crew took over WOAI, some ads were selling for as low as $4 a
spot. Barger felt no self-respecting radio station could sell ads for
less than $25 a spot. So he made his sales force raise prices on
those same ads to $30 a spot.

Dismayed by this development, the one holdover from the original sales force pulled Barger aside and asked him, "What about integrity?" After all, how could the same old spots suddenly be worth
seven and a half times what they had sold for a day earlier?

"Fuck integrity," Barger responded firmly (and perhaps jokingly) while pointing to the clause in WOAI's standard contract that
said the station had the right to adjust its rates on twenty-eight
days' notice. Barger soon enough got a call from the manager of
KTSA, a crosstown competitor, thanking him for raising his rates
and letting him know that they would be raising their rates to $40 a
spot. Now WOAI could comfortably charge as much as the market
would bear.

By the end of 1976, WOAI could claim billings of $3 million, a
remarkable number when considering the station had begun at
number twenty-six in the ratings.

Barger had pulled off a miracle—a poorly performing radio sta-
tion that made money. Stan Webb was in awe. "I credit Johnny
Barger as being the most important person in the success of Clear
Channel to this day," Webb says. "I think if it had not been for

Johnny—and me, to a degree—that company would have never survived."

Yet for all of its cold-blooded salesmanship, Clear Channel was shaping up to be a pretty eccentric, go-your-own-way kind of company. Webb's and Barger's oddball McLendon roots seemed to show even when they didn't intend them to. Aware that they couldn't peddle stations filled with plugs for their advertisers forever, they soon were straining to find new programming to bolster their stunning turnaround. Progressive-rock radio, which found an engaging if small home on FM from the late 1960s, had grown into something more mainstream and profitable by the mid-'70s. And that meant Clear Channel would soon be interested in prog rock in a big way.

Of course, Clear Channel's entry into the FM rock market would be every bit as unconventional and cataclysmic as its previous ventures. And, as usual, the company's success was far from assured.

4.

WAR STORIES

By 1978, WOAI had established itself as the dominant radio station in San Antonio. For multiple years after that, it had the highest annual revenue of any broadcast radio operation in the area while (somewhat miraculously) never rising above number eight in the ratings. "After a year, we really began knocking it out of the park," says Stan Webb. "After three years, we were the top-billing radio station in the market."[1] More astoundingly, for much of that same period, 60 percent of Clear Channel's business was placed through direct billing with the advertiser. The typical radio station today might have about 15 percent direct billing.

WOAI's close relationships with its clients and the heads of advertising agencies made its financial stability even stronger. The station's salespeople didn't bother taking media buyers out to lunch, since they already knew they weren't interested; instead, they schmoozed the advertisers. The station even mailed out a weekly newsletter to all of its clients and other ad professionals, detailing the success of the station and its advertisers. And by using its on-air personalities to make pitches, it developed even deeper relationships with the station's clients. Barger began coaching the station's hosts on how to better deliver ads, and Webb began paying the editorial staff talent-appearance fees on top of their regular pay to acknowledge their contribution to WOAI's advertising content. Giving commentators a piece of the ad-sales pie created a station-wide incentive to produce better ad spots. As a consequence,

WOAI's customers became very loyal. The station's renewal rate was nearly twice the industry average.

That isn't to say there weren't some missteps. In an effort to drum up new advertising categories, John Barger launched a show called *War Stories*, catering to the large number of military veterans living in the San Antonio area. The idea was to get vets to come on the air and tell their old tales of military bravery. Listeners were bored by the show, and advertisers showed little interest.

But constant brainstorming produced some unlikely hits as well. For a while, Barger and Webb did their own show on Saturday mornings called *Tradio*. Essentially an on-the-air version of a newspaper classified section, it soon became one of the most popular radio shows in San Antonio. One could easily attribute the sheer simplicity and nerve of the idea to two old McLendon cohorts pushing the envelope (and keeping things low-budget). A listener might call in to offer up a rocking chair owned by her great-grandmother in Fredericksburg for $50. Then the hosts would ask her to describe it, and inject a little comedy as well.

Religious programming also became a big revenue source during those years, thanks to another Barger brainchild. His idea was to sell time to religious broadcasters late at night, when many other area stations went dark. The result was another $30,000 to $40,000 per month in billings, thanks in part to WOAI's big, booming signal, which held great appeal to ministries trying to spread the word.

It was around that time that the company earned the nickname Cheap Channel. Later used by its critics as an attack on the company, the moniker was actually regarded as something of a badge of honor by some of its earliest managers.

Rex Tackett, who served as WOAI's general manager from 1978 to 1989, recalls the environment in which the company earned the name: "Most broadcasters had grown up in the business and sold some advertising, and all of a sudden they're running multiple stations, maybe they're buying them. You saw a lot of people expanding in the broadcasting business in the '80s, and the banks and the lending companies ended up owning them. They were people who were novices at high finance. Well, Mays was no novice. Investors loved that about him. Because they knew he was taking business seriously. There was no hanky-panky in any of these stations. Every day was business."[2]

Whether Clear Channel was buying another station or simply buying a transmitter for an existing station, it was a good bet that Lowry Mays would try to talk the price down as low as it could go. Clear Channel was also one of the first radio companies to try to reduce the sales commissions earned by the national advertising rep firms that sold national ads to stations in local markets. Mays taught his managers to be concerned not just with the top line but with the bottom line as well. As far as what was in the middle, the man at the top couldn't care less. Clear Channel executives didn't waste their time talking to him about the disc jockeys they were hiring or the color scheme of station logos. As far as he was concerned, none of that was his business.

"A lot of radio people [at that time] viewed themselves as being in the entertainment business," continues Tackett. "Barger and Mays were never delusional about that: they were in the money business and building assets, and they never forgot that. They started out that way and they ran the company that way. And when you worked there, that's what it was about. They weren't cheap— they just ran a good business."

Tackett says most of the radio business back then was not unlike the old 1970s sitcom *WKRP in Cincinnati*, starring Howard Hesseman and Loni Anderson as employees at a folksy, by-the-skin-of-its-teeth radio station. The TV show portrayed a station as a fun place to work where all anyone wanted to do was sell a few spots, play some music, and do some remote broadcasts. Then, of course, there was the Felliniesque cast of characters. On the show, the general manager, played by Gordon Jump, was running the station for his demanding mother, the station's owner—a representation not far off the mark, as many stations in those days were family affairs.

And nearly every station, Tackett says, had its Johnny Fever, the groovy DJ played by Hesseman; and a geeky news reporter like Les Nessman; and "li'l ole girlie secretaries" like Jennifer Marlowe (Anderson). There were no women salespeople. "The only real difference was that the sales managers never answered to the program director," he says. "That just didn't happen."

Tackett, a native of the tiny West Texas town of Cross Plains, had been on the other side of the fence and knew which side he liked better. Having briefly worked for WOAI as an ad salesman in its revenue-challenged Avco days, he much preferred the new regime. Tackett later worked across town at KITE-AM and KEXL-FM, then owned by Doubleday. When the stations were suddenly sold, and he was asked to relocate to Denver to manage other Doubleday stations, Tackett refused. When KEXL's new owner offered him the general manager spot, he tentatively said yes.

Then, one night at ten, he got a phone call at home. The man on the other end barked, "This is Barger, what do you want?"

"Who is this?" Tackett asked.

"Barger, Barger. What do you want?"

"I don't want anything, John," he told the man he only knew in passing. "What are you talking about?"

"What job do you want over here?" Barger said impatiently.

Tackett explained that he had just accepted a job with KEXL's new owner.

"Where do you live?" Barger insisted. Tackett timidly explained he lived about twenty-five miles out of town. "Give me directions."

A half hour later, Barger showed up at his house wearing jeans, penny loafers, white socks, and a white dress shirt, untucked. With little introduction, he sat down and tried to make a deal with Tackett to become general manager of WOAI. Tackett was impressed: Barger was making him an offer that would net him nearly twice his salary, around $100,000 per year. After a little waffling, he took the job. He later concluded that Mays and McCombs "couldn't have hired anybody better in the United States" than Barger to help structure their fledgling radio operation.

While the thrill of working at San Antonio's biggest radio success story was almost immediately exhilarating, Tackett recalls the typical Clear Channel budget meeting as a somber affair. The budgets regularly consisted of around seven hundred line items. A station's general manager would sit down with Mays and go over the budget line by line. Mays would stop at an item such as trade publication subscriptions and ask, "Well, what are they?" And the manager would have to tell him the titles, why they were needed, whom they were for, and how they helped the station make money. Determining employee compensation demanded another bull session with Mays, who didn't believe in automatic raises—for anyone.

Some of Mays's practices may rightly have earned him the "Cheap Channel" name. He didn't, for example, like to buy coffee for the staff. But the rules applied to everybody, employees proudly pointed out, and both Mays and Barger earned high scores from employees for their straightforward manner and truthfulness—though Mays was decidedly hands-off and Barger most certainly wasn't, quickly earning himself a reputation as a hard-driving, difficult boss.

Certainly it was no WKRP. "At least it wasn't at WOAI, where Barger was," says Tackett with a chuckle. "No sir, it didn't operate that way."

In the often dodgy world of radio, Clear Channel had an impressively ethical reputation. Unlike other radio companies that would occasionally sell spots and never run them, Clear Channel ran every ad it sold, say employees from that era.

Overall, Clear Channel stood out for its then-revolutionary notion that a radio station should operate like any other business, breaking with the typical mom-and-pop operators who had no idea whether they were even turning a profit.

"If you look back at some of the great owners, they were pretty much drunks," says Robert Unmacht, former editor of a prominent radio industry trade journal, *M Street* (he later sold his stake to Clear Channel). "They came up through radio sales, got their own stations, and drank heavily," most likely a result of too many boozy lunches wooing clients and the long hours that traditionally accompanied radio station life.[3]

Not that Mays didn't have his colorful side. "I remember back then Lowry used to ride a motorcycle and was a pretty wild guy," says Ralph Guild, chairman and chief executive of the leading radio ad rep firm Interep.[4] "He had an accident and broke a leg or something."

An old friend also recalls Mays battling something of a drinking problem himself in those days. "He's very nicely overcome it, commendably," says Guild, who has known Lowry since 1970. "But I think in those days, he was a handful."[5]

Regardless, Clear Channel's operational triumvirate was beginning to shape up nicely. Mays worried about the financial end; Barger was the programming guru; and Webb was the sales visionary who could do no wrong.

But Barger soon took on a more crucial role. Early on, he exhibited a knack for finding stations in trouble and convincing Mays to buy them. Some jokingly suggested it was Barger's ploy to make things too complicated for Mays and Red McCombs to back out of the radio business. "There'd be no Clear Channel if it wasn't for Barger," says Rex Tackett.

In 1977, Clear Channel bought a couple of distressed stations in Port Arthur, Texas, that would provide an early blueprint of how the company would acquire properties to grow. Barger and Webb would drop in to town and reprogram the radio station. Barger would hire staff and determine its new format. Webb would organize the sales force. Next on the list was a station in El Paso. Oklahoma City, New Orleans, and New Haven, Connecticut, were soon to follow.

The message from the top was clear. There was plenty of cash flow, and the point was to invest it wisely. "Growing up in Clear Channel, it was all about how much profit we could make," says Webb. "It was all about the margins." And those margins were formidable by anybody's measure—in the 50 percent range, by some estimates, putting Clear Channel in its first few years in or around the ninety-eighth percentile of profitable radio companies in the nation.

Webb would never again work at a Clear Channel news station, returning with his next move to his true love, music radio. But his time at WOAI had left a strong impression. Radio wasn't just about selling commercials. It was about selling commercials that worked. Never mind the average cost per point, it was about groceries and Fords. It was about creating the right environment for the right advertiser. Clear Channel had no choice. If ads didn't get results on WOAI, then the agencies would blame the performance on the station's ratings and try to steer their clients elsewhere.

Three years to the day that Stan Webb had been hired at WOAI, Lowry Mays offered him a new assignment in Tulsa, Oklahoma. Mays's two Tulsa stations, still owned under the San Antonio Broadcasting Company umbrella, were not performing well. Mays wanted Webb to fix things. On Webb's last day in San Antonio in June 1978, he, Mays, and Barger had lunch at the St. Anthony Hotel, and then he and Mays boarded a plane to Tulsa, where he became the general manager of KMOD-FM, an album-rock-format station, and KXXO, an AM station that had changed formats so many times it didn't have an identity at all.

Webb was just thirty-four years old. But his success at WOAI gave Mays the confidence to let him repair matters in Tulsa. And Mays didn't ask too many questions. "Mays had zero interest in programming," says Webb. "It was all about how much are we going to collect? Not bill, but how much are we going to collect this month?"

KMOD was a new kind of challenge for Webb. The station's programming mix of Lynyrd Skynyrd and similar hard-rock fare did well ratings-wise, but in a Bible Belt town like Tulsa a lot of advertisers considered it an unappealing commercial environment.

Webb's first priority was to set up KMOD as a more traditional business. "It was a wild rock-and-roll radio station," he recalls, lacking in basic professional standards. Within ninety days, and after a few personnel changes, the station was operating with Clear Channel's signature efficiency.

The AM had been converted to a WOAI-like news-talk format that so far proved unsuccessful, and its poor signal ensured a similar future. So Webb decided to simulcast KMOD on KXXO, thus cutting expenses dramatically and capitalizing on the popularity of the FM station.

A year and a half later, KMOD was the third-highest-rated album-rock station in the country—in a metropolitan area of only about half a million people. Webb and his staff had doubled the ratings in about eighteen months. How did they do it? Webb imagined the average KMOD listener was "some kid with a bunch of hair hanging out of a gimme cap driving a pickup truck." But he also figured there were some potential listeners out there who were wearing ties and jackets.

So Webb did a little research and unleashed a string of wholesome-seeming promotional events. One Memorial Day weekend, the station sponsored a soapbox derby race, in which listeners were encouraged to build their own soapbox derby cars to coincide with the Indy 500. On the air, as a cross-promotion the station featured the Rock and Roll 500, a countdown of the top 500 rock songs of all time. The race was held in a local park with a gently sloping hill and fifty or sixty participants. KMOD salespeople invited clients to the race to show that the station's listeners weren't a bunch of "out-of-work deadbeat hippies," in Webb's words. The event also helped put a human face on the station, allowing listeners to meet the on-air talent in person.

The strategy worked. In time, one of the station's biggest clients was Getty Oil Company, which was based in Tulsa. Until then, buttoned-down Getty would never have advertised on a local rock station. But with Clear Channel in control, the oil giant became the largest spender on KMOD.

Soon, KMOD had nudged its competitors to switch to other formats and became one of the top four stations in Tulsa. More important, from Clear Channel's perspective, it began churning out profits at a 50 to 55 percent margin. "Radio's the only business in which you can sell widgets without having to produce widgets," marvels Jim Smith, who succeeded Stan Webb as KMOD's general manager. "Radio is the true conceptual non-tangible."

And more profits meant more money to spend on promotion, to make more money. Inspired by seeing the San Diego chicken mascot for the Padres baseball team on television, Webb dreamed up a mascot to help soften KMOD's image, called the Dallas company that provided character costumes for the Six Flags Over Texas amusement park, and thus the KMOD Rainbow Rabbit was born. Dressed in a top hat and tuxedo, the Rainbow Rabbit, usually played by a local teenager hired part-time, toured Tulsa in a mobile home (paid for with Getty dollars) dubbed the Rabbit Hutch. The Rabbit Hutch became a familiar site at everything from high school football games to grocery store grand openings.

Webb also hired Gailard Sartain, a tubby Tulsa-born actor who played the Big Bopper in the 1978 movie *The Buddy Holly Story* and was also a talented illustrator, to create a series of colorful promotional posters for KMOD.

The two-thousand-plus-capacity Caines Ballroom, a faded Tulsa landmark where Bob Wills had played in the 1930s, was revived as a rock venue and played host to many a KMOD-sponsored concert. Webb would pitch the local beer companies to co-sponsor certain shows, which meant kicking in some money for on-site promotional opportunities. Soon, KMOD was the beer companies' number-one ad buy. Such cross-promotional tie-ins, the norm in today's concert business, were rare in the early years of FM radio's heyday.

As for programming, Webb's main initiative was to make the on-air environment less hip-seeming, so as not to limit the station's potential audience.

The lesson for Clear Channel's employees was clear. Profits

were to come before matters of taste whenever possible. Anything was possible as long as a station was profitable, preferably extremely profitable. Without profits, there was nothing.

In June 1981, a former rock-and-roll DJ named Jim Smith answered an ad in a radio trade magazine looking for a general manager with management experience. The ad had been placed by John Barger. Clear Channel needed someone to run its new pair of stations in Port Arthur, Texas, KALO-AM and KHYS-FM. "He wanted an entrepreneur, someone who had gotten blood on their sword," Smith recalls. "He wanted someone who could make his own decisions and live or die by the decisions he made. If you had been in the war and had survived, that was a guy he wanted on his staff." Smith fit the bill and got the job.

Like Stan Webb, Smith had been bitten by the rock-and-roll bug as a 1950s teenager, getting hooked on his older sister's 45s by performers like the Everly Brothers and Elvis. He attended Southeast Missouri State University on a trumpet scholarship and graduated with a degree in music. Like Webb, he'd gigged with a lot of local rock bands, usually playing guitar or keyboards. He was also a radio junkie—he liked to say his earliest childhood memories were of wanting to be the man talking on the large console radio his mother listened to all day.

His résumé proved it. Smith was only thirty-two in 1981, but already he had an astonishing amount of radio industry experience under his belt. A native of Jackson, Missouri, ten miles from Cape Girardeau, Rush Limbaugh's hometown, he began his career in the late 1960s at KGMO, the station where Limbaugh got his start. He worked as a disc jockey on morning and midday shifts; Limbaugh, still in high school, had the late-afternoon slot.

After a management stint at a station in Paducah, Kentucky, Smith returned to his hometown of Jackson in his late twenties to help start a station he eventually owned with three other partners.

When his partners decided to sell, Smith started looking for a job. He felt he knew the business inside out, and rightly so. "In that period of time, working in smaller markets like Cape Girardeau and Jackson, markets of sixteen thousand to twenty thousand people, you were able to be a news director, a disc jockey, a manager, a sales manager, you sold spots, you did your own production, you weren't departmentalized," says Smith. "When you're working in small-market radio, when the transmitter goes on the blink, you go figure out how to get it going again."

From the moment Smith made contact with Clear Channel, he knew it was the place for him. A place where you were given every opportunity to do things your way. Not that he had many dealings with Lowry Mays in those days. As far as he could tell at first, John Barger seemed to be running the show. Barger flew him down to San Antonio, interviewed him, and became convinced he was the man to run Port Arthur. Before Smith got the job, Barger took him to see Mays. Clear Channel's top exec asked Smith "about four questions," and he was hired.

At Clear Channel, there was no babysitting for new general managers. Smith learned quickly that Barger expected him to do his own budgets, make his own income, and make his own bottom line. As a former owner-manager, he loved it. "You could drive your station right into the dirt, and if you did," Smith says with a laugh, "you got fired."

Smith was intoxicated by the free rein Barger offered him. He would have the opportunity to make big programming decisions on his own, knowing full well that if the stations bombed, he'd take the fall. It was a lot of pressure, but Smith loved the feeling of controlling his own destiny.

That was until he arrived in Port Arthur. KHYS-FM was being run by a former Xerox salesman without any radio background. The market consisted of twenty-two radio stations and was 62 percent African-American, and yet there wasn't a single urban-formatted station. Within sixty days, Smith changed the format to urban rhythm and blues; and within six months he'd turned around KHYS-FM's fortunes. By 1983, it had become the number-one-rated urban station in the country. "It wasn't any magic," says Smith.

Smith had little time to rest on his laurels. Barger made it clear very early in Smith's tenure that Mays intended to sell the Port Arthur stations—formerly failing properties that had been purchased for cheap—as soon as they were profitable. Smith got used to the "tire kickers" stopping by the station, potential buyers checking out the operation.

So Smith was running Port Arthur, Webb had Tulsa under control, and Barger had turned WOAI in San Antonio into a cash machine. One other Clear Channel station, KELP in El Paso, had been lagging, so Mays decided to sell it. And Clear Channel was beginning to look an awful lot like a successful radio company. "All of a sudden we had three little radio stations that were smokin'," says Smith. "And that was really, I think, the first time that Mays stopped to say, hmm, this could be all right."

Until that time, Lowry Mays, by most accounts, had subscribed to the Willie Sutton approach to radio. Sutton was the thief who famously responded to the question "Why do you rob banks?" with the answer "Because that's where the money is." Mays liked being in radio because that's where the money was, especially if he and his staff could identify distressed stations in smaller markets, buy them at a discount, make them financially accountable, and then turn them into successful businesses.

The pattern was becoming clear: WOAI had been bought at an estate sale; KMOD in Tulsa was purchased out of bankruptcy; KPAC was acquired from Port Arthur College, which was divesting itself of its broadcast properties due to financial difficulties. Mays's original intention was to generate revenue by selling each station in three years or so at a tidy profit.

But during a six-month period in 1982, Mays shifted gears. All of Clear Channel's stations were throwing off a lot of cash. And it finally occurred to Mays that maybe this radio business was a good thing after all. For the first time since he founded the company, Mays began to act like he was in the broadcasting industry.

John Barger helped get his boss on the board of CBS Radio, officially to give Mays a taste of the big leagues in the business he had wandered into. Others at the company suggested that Barger didn't want to cede power to Mays and was looking for ways to keep him distracted.

In early 1982, Stan Webb began to get homesick for Texas and requested a transfer down to Austin, where Clear Channel had just purchased KMEX, a Spanish-language-programmed station. When Webb moved on to Austin in June, Jim Smith immediately lobbied to have Webb's old job in Tulsa, but there was some concern that the Port Arthur stations would collapse if he left. A year later, the Tulsa job was available again, and Smith got it.

Crisis greeted Smith almost immediately upon his arrival in Tulsa. One Monday morning, only a month after he started as general manager of KMOD, he came to work to find a message from the building's landlord urging him to come see her immediately. Smith was worried maybe the rent check had been late, but the problem was much graver. The landlord informed him that some remodeling on a lower floor of the building the station was housed in had revealed walls caked with asbestos. The station would have to evacuate the building.

Smith explained that his business was a radio station and evacuation was not that easy. How much time did he have to clear out? he asked. The landlord told him they needed to be out that day.

Impossible, thought Smith. Nonetheless, he raced into action. The station owned an old studio at its former location in downtown Tulsa. It also had an old remote broadcast unit that had two turntables built into it. Smith had his technicians wire the remote unit directly into the transmitter at the old facility. Four hours later, the station was up and running in the new location. The station's employees ended up scattered in five locations for the next year until Smith secured a new facility. Miraculously, the station set ratings records in three Arbitron books in a row, despite the decentralized nature of the operation.

Early in 1984, Lowry Mays offered one of the first clues that he had a bigger plan than most third-tier radio broadcasters. It was around then that he hired the New York investment firms of Blyth Eastman Paine Webber and Schneider, Bernet & Hickman to arrange an initial public offering for Clear Channel Communications. At the time, there was only one other pure radio company that had gone public. There were larger radio companies, but all were privately owned. The radio divisions of CBS, NBC, and ABC were all owned by public companies, but those companies were essentially television operations.

Those close to Mays in that era say they suspect he was scheming to go public nearly as soon as Clear Channel was profitable. "That was his background," says Webb. "Lowry had little to no interest in how to make the wristwatch; he just wanted to know what time it was."

What had started out as a strategy for survival had evolved into a prudent corporate philosophy that Mays could easily pitch to Wall Street. "I think Lowry thinks that he came up with the idea that we were a real client-driven company," says Stan Webb. "And we were, but it wasn't something we developed in a focus group. It was just necessity."

On April 19, 1984, 750,000 shares of common stock in Clear Channel were put up for sale at $10 a share on the American Stock Exchange. Clear Channel stated it intended to use the proceeds to pay off bank loans and operational expenses. Mays, in typically low-key fashion, claimed the transition was no big deal. "Being public means a way for employees to own and participate in a company," he said. "For our managers, there's a stock option program. The only disadvantages are living in a public fish bowl and having to produce a costly [nearly $20,000] annual report."[6]

But within months the company made its biggest push yet to

expand. All of its stations were humming, and its cash flow was superb.

Around that time, Mays observed that radio broadcasting was a "highly fractionalized" business that might consolidate into much larger companies if not for FCC ownership restrictions.[7] Since 1953, the FCC had decreed that no company was permitted to own more than seven AM stations and seven FM stations.

In October 1984, Clear Channel owned twelve radio stations, in nine different formats, thanks to its $26 million purchase of Broad Street Communications of New Haven, Connecticut, headed by Richard Geismar and Fred Walker. Broad Street included KTOK-AM and KYJO-FM in Oklahoma City, WQUE-AM and -FM in New Orleans, and WELI-AM in New Haven. It was the company's first foray into the Northeast. Broad Street also owned the Oklahoma News Network, a statewide radio network with forty-seven affiliates.[8]

Despite the company's increased size, Mays remained adamant about Clear Channel's recipe for success. He saw the company's decentralized structure as its biggest strength. "The market is the important thing for us," he said. "Once we are in a market, we feel that we can run any type of format and be good."

As new stations were welcomed into the fold, longtime executives tried to prepare new station managers for the intense, adversarial scrutiny they would encounter with their new boss. They were warned to be prepared to explain every line item in their budgets. They were told such scrutiny would take at least half a day. "A budget meeting with Lowry Mays was truly a religious experience," jokes Stan Webb.

But most new Clear Channel execs eventually became converts. Even those lacking strong accounting backgrounds became solid numbers guys. Other radio companies turned DJs into programmers. Clear Channel turned DJs into accountants. From a purely objective standpoint, this was a much more impressive feat.

Then came the Louisville deal, Barger's Waterloo. And Clear Channel would never be the same.

In the first few days of 1986, word trickled out of Louisville, Kentucky, that the Bingham family planned to sell off its fabled media empire.[9] True Southern patricians and social progressives, the Binghams, often called the Southern Kennedys, had endured a tragic and tragically public period of multigenerational unrest. In 1918, Robert Worth Bingham, Louisville's mayor and a circuit court judge, had purchased a majority interest in *The Courier-Journal* and *The Louisville Times* for $1 million. A devout supporter of President Franklin D. Roosevelt's New Deal, he established the papers as liberal bastions in the conservative South. After Judge Bingham's death in 1937, his son, Barry Bingham Sr., took charge of the company, which by then included WHAS, an AM radio station, and a commercial printing business, Standard Gravure.

Under Barry senior's control, the company thrived while espousing liberal causes. Its newspapers supported labor unions and lambasted strip-mining companies for destroying the landscape. In the civil rights era, the company remained staunchly anti-segregationist. The Binghams were respected statewide, but that respect came at a cost: by the 1960s, family members had been branded as liberal elites, and the papers had been deemed out of touch with the common workingman.

During that time, two of Barry senior's sons also died in shocking accidents, triggering what became known as the Bingham curse. In 1964, Jonathan, twenty-two, was electrocuted while climbing a utility pole to wire a barn; two years later, Worth, then thirty-four, was killed in a bizarre car crash on Nantucket involving a surfboard propped inside the car that swiftly broke his neck. (In 1999, Worth's son, Robert Worth Bingham IV, an up-and-coming novelist of note, would die of a heroin overdose in his downtown New York City loft at age thirty-three.)

Barry junior, Barry senior's youngest son, would ultimately take over the newspapers in 1971 and, later, WHAS Inc. and the printing business. Under his care, profits at the Bingham companies dipped below 10 percent of revenues in the 1970s, and though they rose to 12.6 percent in the mid-1980s, they remained below industry averages at all the companies. On the other hand, the papers won three Pulitzer prizes and became renowned for their reporting standards and integrity.

Around that time, one of Barry senior's two daughters, Sallie, became harshly critical of Barry junior's management skills and what she claimed to be an intra-family sexism that restricted the women in the family from making serious business decisions. Tensions rose; Sallie was voted off the company's board and in 1984 expressed a desire to sell her share in the family's holdings. Barry junior ultimately offered $26.3 million for Sallie's stock, an offer she refused as too low. Growing animosity between the siblings soon made a family truce unlikely.

On January 9, 1986, in an effort to bring closure, Barry senior, then seventy-nine, announced he had decided to divest the family of its newspapers; its commercial printing business; and WHAS Inc., which by then included a television station and two radio stations. Barry junior immediately resigned, citing his father's betrayal. "In my proprietorship here," he told a few hundred co-workers in a meeting held in the company cafeteria the next day, "I've tried to operate these companies so that none of you would be ashamed of the man you work for."

On May 19, the Binghams announced they had sold the papers to Gannett, one of the country's largest newspaper chains, for around $306 million. Standard Gravure was sold on May 23 to the Atlanta businessman Michael Shea, who paid $20 million. A week later, on May 30, the Providence Journal Company purchased WHAS-TV.

Clear Channel became interested in WHAS-AM and WAMZ-FM as soon as its executives learned about the fragile family culture and benefits surrounding the stations. The stations had a reputation for paying their employees very well. They had a day-care center in the building. But they were also the two biggest, highest-profile, and highest-billing stations in Louisville. Clear Channel smelled blood.

After battling Katz Radio, Clear Channel won the stations with a bid of $20 million for the pair. At the time, it owned and operated six AM stations and six FM stations with revenues of $26.27 million.[10] Clear Channel's obvious advantage was its huge reserves of cash, acquired from its money-spewing, high-margin stations.

And for the first time, Lowry Mays got involved in the nitty-gritty of the deal, the biggest in Clear Channel's decade-plus history. Prior to the sale, some radio station employees circulated a petition requesting the Bingham family to be mindful of potential buyers. Their concern was that Clear Channel and some of the other bidders would reduce their benefits and eliminate jobs.

On Monday, June 9, the day the deal closed, Mays met with employees for over an hour to address their concerns. "If I was an employee of this station, I would have signed the same letter of concern," he said, referring to the stations' strong reputation. "We want to continue that." He noted that WOAI in San Antonio had seventy-three employees while WHAS operated with far fewer employees in comparison, only sixty-three between the two stations.

Within the company, Mays expressed concern that, as profitable as they were, the Louisville stations came with some risk. "I don't know how they make so much money, but I perceive Louisville to be like a carton of eggs," he said. "And if you shake 'em too much, it'll break."

After hashing out the details, Mays left on an anniversary cruise with Peggy. In his place, he assigned John Barger, Clear Channel's chief operating officer, to Louisville to tie up any loose ends. According to company legend, Barger showed up at station headquarters in his typical tough-guy mode, clearly unaware of Mays's egg analogy, and reportedly told the employees in a meeting that everything they knew was about to change. One account has Barger telling those assembled that he was getting rid of their prized day-care facility and that anyone who was driving a company car should throw the keys on the table. His message, in plain English, was: You're going to be run like the rest of the company. But his tone and timing couldn't have been worse.

Unfortunately, unbeknownst to Barger, the deal was not entirely finished yet. Distraught employees went straight to Barry senior and said they would all quit if he sold to Clear Channel. Bingham promptly called Mays via satellite phone on the ship and told him the deal was off. In a panic, Mays hired a helicopter to get him off the ship and back to Louisville to smooth the feathers Barger had ruffled. Among the terms he agreed to was, no matter what happened, John Barger would not be in charge of the Louisville stations.[11]

The incident resonated: Lowry Mays was in charge, and from now on he would be taking a much larger role in operations and acquisitions.

Still, entrepreneurship remained a core company value. Bob Scherer, who had been hired by WHAS Inc. in 1963 as an account executive and worked his way up to general manager, was named a vice president at Clear Channel after the purchase and was permitted to run his operation much the same way he always had.[12] Scherer himself had devoted his life's work to the company, and though he lacked the shoot-'em-up verve of the San Antonio wing, he was highly respected in Louisville. "Bob was a gunfighter, but not like the rest of us," quips Jim Smith. "He kind of had a velvet hammer."

So the Bingham culture at WHAS prevailed, to a point. Though the WHAS stations were number one in terms of billing in the Clear Channel universe, they were number seven when it came to profit margins. As long as Scherer kept making money, he was allowed to run things pretty much his way. And Clear Channel's executives learned there was more than one way to skin a cat.

Scherer, for example, was known for his meticulous way of interviewing job candidates. In his mind, each employee was an employee for life, so he spent more time getting to know each applicant and communicating the seriousness of taking a job with his stations. As a result, the stations had an extremely low employee turnover rate.

WHAS also employed two full-time copywriters to generate advertising copy. Clear Channel didn't have a single copywriter in the company, preferring to leave the task to its ad salesmen because they were the ones interacting with the customers. But Scherer informed his new bosses that that's the way things were done in Louisville. Indeed, many of the company's customs went back to its origins in the 1930s.

The lesson of Louisville was an instructive one for Clear Channel, especially as it continued its expansion. Different markets around the nation had different cultures and demanded a new flexibility that most of the company's executives acknowledged was a welcome change. John Barger, by most accounts—including his own—was not one of those executives.

Clear Channel's strategy in Louisville was something new. Instead of jumping in with a raft of cost-cutting measures, the company successfully made changes to WHAS's expense structure gradually over the next five years. "They had monstrous billing, but they also had monstrous expenses," says Stan Webb. "So those stations went through several bumpy years of trying to get into the Clear Channel exercise program."

After the Louisville near debacle, Lowry Mays asked John Barger to step down from his position as chief operating officer and become Mays's administrative head in June 1986. He was permitted to stay on the board. "He just told me he wanted to take a more active role in the company," says Barger.

In his new role, Barger ended up doing most of the same things he had done before. He exited Clear Channel in July 1988, along with his heavy-handed management style. He remained affiliated with Clear Channel as a consultant and board member until he went into the station brokerage business a few months later. His legacy, however, of controlled costs and sales-motivated expansion would cast a long shadow at the company.

"Barger is a genius, he is literally a broadcasting genius," marvels Jim Smith, adding with a sly chuckle, "That is, if you can withstand the torrent of bullshit that comes at you and you're able to extract the pearls."

Meanwhile, back in Austin, Stan Webb was channeling his inner Gordon McLendon again. His first gambit was changing the call letters of KMEX to KPEZ and reformatting the station as EZ 102, an easy-listening station, an affordable and usually surefire format. Unfortunately, the change met with lackluster results in Austin, the youngest and most musically sophisticated city in Texas. While ratings and billings were steady, the overall financial picture was gloomy.

In early 1986, Webb caught wind of a few stations trying a new format freshly coined as "classic rock." So he jumped on a plane to Houston to listen to one of the first stations to play the format, a regurgitation of hits from the Rolling Stones, Led Zeppelin, and other big groups from the 1960s and '70s—the stalwarts of album-rock radio who no longer notched mammoth record sales but still had major, if aging, fan bases.

He liked what he heard, so he spent a night at Lowry Mays's house in San Antonio and made his pitch for switching KPEZ to a classic-rock format. Mays agreed to the plan. But all acknowledged a stealth operation was required to topple the number-one rock station in Austin, KLBJ. So Webb plotted the format change out of Tulsa—all the audio equipment and music were purchased there to avoid a local tip-off. Then Webb invited Jim Smith and a couple of his programmers down from Tulsa and put them up in an Austin hotel to cook up Clear Channel's own brand of the classic-rock formula. He even borrowed a few of the Tulsa DJs to appear on the air. "We had to sneak up on them," says Smith. "We couldn't be found out before we did it."

In preparation for the changeover in mid-1986, Webb devised a promotional stunt to coincide with Willie Nelson's Fourth of July picnic, a massive concert event that Nelson hadn't held in Austin since 1980. Some 20,000 to 30,000 fans were scheduled to show up at an old racetrack. "I knew there would be 100,000 nitwits out there drinking beer and listening to Willie," says Webb, "and 90,000 of them would be potential listeners to my station."

So Webb hired an airplane out of town, had a sign made up calling the station Z 102, Austin's Classic Rock, so he didn't have to change the call letters, put the sign on the back of the plane, and flew it all around on the Fourth of July, particularly in the vicinity of the Willie Nelson concert.

Smith instructed all of his part-time DJs at KMOD in Tulsa to report to the station on a particular Friday with clothing for a week and he would have plane tickets for them. He refused, however, to say where they were going until then, but that they would be working shifts at a radio station. "We literally went in and fired everybody in the station, shut it down, and overnight redid the entire control room, put in all new consoles, CD players," providing the studio with a much-needed upgrade, recalls Smith.

On the night before the format change, the station's studio was filled with anticipation, as well as a fair number of Clear Channel's top executives, including John Barger, Lowry Mays, Jim Smith, and Stan Webb. Randall Mays, then a student at the University of Texas and a gofer at the station, was sent over to the Best Buy electronics store to buy the CDs and off-the-shelf CD players that constituted the new station's makeshift studio console. The format switched to classic rock that same morning and was an overnight success.

Even Lowry Mays had a blast that night, Smith recalls. The normally reserved boss ran out in the middle of the night and, upon his return, ordered everyone to stop working and take the elevator to the parking garage. What they found was Mays's big black Fleetwood Cadillac set up like a fast-food buffet. "It had Wendy's hamburgers and French fries and malts and Cokes down the fender, over the back of the car, and down the back fender," says Smith. "That was his way of contributing. He was a real part of that project."

The "Cheap Channel" taunts, however, now grew louder among some of the company's competitors, meant to mock its penny-pinching ways. The funny thing was, Clear Channel's executives continued not to mind. They almost seemed to flaunt the gibe. There was a good reason: Most radio companies in those days shot for a 15 percent profit margin. Anything left was spent on company cars, country club memberships, and all manner of perquisites. But Clear Channel set the bar higher. A lot higher: Mays and Barger now expected margins of 45 percent, at a minimum.

Clear Channel's executives, it seemed almost instinctively, were prone to save money. For example, its stations were much more likely to hire bright but less experienced salespeople at a lower salary, with the hope of training them.

With profits so high, Clear Channel station operators also developed a certain arrogance about running their businesses. Building on its track record in Port Arthur, Tulsa, Austin, and San Antonio, the company was confident in its new model. Since most of the company's general managers were former DJs used to doing it all at small, understaffed stations, they were less intimidated by troublemaking employees. "If a disc jockey wanted to quit on me and thought he was going to hold me hostage because I couldn't finish the radio program, he had another think coming," says Jim Smith. "I could sit down and finish the radio program and have fun doing it because I'd done it all those years.

"And all of us were like that. Stan was on the air. Barger was on the air. I was on it. We all had held virtually every job in the radio station. Some news guy comes to me and says I'm not going to read the news at three o'clock if you don't give me a raise now, it's hit the door, pal, I'll read the news. It was a different paradigm."

Indeed, there was a whiff of the Wild West that emanated from the Clear Channel command center. The managers liked to view themselves as gunfighters, ready at a moment's notice to charge and conquer. "Give me a signal and I will show you how to win," says Smith, describing the mentality, "almost a chip on your shoulder."

Still, the atmosphere at Clear Channel was anything but corporate. In some ways, it had an almost soulful, down-home quality to it. Each week, Jim Smith, Stan Webb, Rex Tackett, and John Barger regularly consulted one another by phone on strategy matters or just to chat. They had a warm rapport and a strong team mentality but weren't afraid to get blood on their swords. They all also regularly put in sixty- to seventy-hour weeks. And, as a matter of course, winning meant everything.

In the midst of all the passion and profit taking, though, there was little talk about the future of radio as a medium. This motley bunch of sales guys and tacticians was revolutionizing the way the radio business operated, yet the content itself remained eerily irrelevant. Radio's famously high profit margins had begun drawing a new breed into the business—cunning, bloodless, and unerringly focused on the burgeoning bottom line.

5.

ANARCHY ON THE AIRWAVES

By the late 1980s, Clear Channel was arguably the best-run radio company in the country. It was simply more prepared to handle its markets than its competitors, at least purely from a business standpoint. Clear Channel stations weren't always number one in the ratings, but they generally billed more than their competitors. They generally kept expenses lower than their competitors and were run locally by managers who had an exceptional understanding of the communities they were serving.

Meanwhile, Lowry Mays kept one foot on Wall Street, earning extra points by staying on message. What had once been a sales strategy built on sweat and desperation had blossomed into a company-wide guiding principle that he could sell to investors. Mays would regularly head to New York to make presentations to the analysts. With his broad, beaming face and his fatback Texas drawl, he would explain in plain English the company's emphasis on sales, as opposed to programming. He would explain its attention to expenses and its preference to push responsibility out to the local managers. In some cases, he would even present these ideas as philosophy he had engineered on his own. The reality was irrelevant, since the philosophy he presented was a classic corporate strategy in the Graham and Dodd mode, something Ivy League MBAs of Wall Street felt comfortable with. Oh, and one more thing: Clear Channel quickly developed a reputation for never missing its quarterly projections.

Indeed, the only barrier limiting Clear Channel in the early days of 1985 was those pesky radio ownership caps enforced by the FCC. No one company was allowed to own more than seven AM stations and seven FM stations. Clear Channel already owned six and six. From where would the fledgling public company's future growth emanate? The answer was still hazy, but possibilities lurked.

By 1988, Clear Channel was on a roll. Thanks to the relaxed ownership caps, it claimed a portfolio of seventeen radio stations. With gross revenues of $37.16 million in 1987, the company could boast a 36 percent increase over the previous year. More impressive, after-tax cash flow reached $5.98 million, up from $3.83 million in 1986.[1]

And thanks to Mays's prudence, the company's debt-to-operating-income ratio was astounding, a paltry 2.8 to 1, compared with the broadcasting industry average of 10 to 1.

In 1985, Dan Sullivan was working as an executive at a small start-up television company in Houston called Southwest Multimedia when he bumped into Lowry Mays at a meeting of the Texas Association of Broadcasters. The two relatively small-time media men chatted for about an hour, though Mays did most of the talking. Sullivan recalls that Mays had "a lot of questions about television."[2]

Certainly the native of Nashville, Tennessee, who had spent his whole career at second-tier small-market television companies, was impressed with what he was hearing. To Sullivan, Lowry Mays—considering he had no experience in television—seemed awfully savvy about the business. "Our views of the broadcast business were very similar," says Sullivan. "His previous take on people in the television business was that they were all 'show-business people' and that they didn't really understand about marketing and sales."

Sullivan, Mays gauged accurately, was all about sales. They

both shared a philosophy about television that sounded strikingly similar to Clear Channel's approach to radio. "Lowry said many times that we're not in the broadcasting business," Sullivan says. "We're in the business of selling tacos, burgers, beer, soft drinks—whatever products our advertisers are selling, that's what business we're in." If anything, Sullivan's prognosis was even dourer than Mays's: "My philosophy has always been, there's no 'show' left in show business. And if we don't sell products, we're going to be out of business."

In addition, Mays communicated his fear of the risky television business to Sullivan. Apparently, all the television execs he had met previously had talked about the integrity of their news and how great the networks were. But here was Sullivan talking about independent stations that weren't associated with a network. This was a guy who was more interested in selling advertising than in going to network meetings.

Flattered by Mays's interest, Sullivan explained matter-of-factly about the glut of independent UHF television stations that had recently flooded the market due to the difficult advertising climate. In the old days before cable television's dominance, UHF channels resided on the higher numbers of the television dial, a viewers' no-man's-land dominated by local public TV outlets and religious broadcasters. They generally had weak broadcasting signals and competed badly with local network affiliates, who had stronger signals, first-run programming, and a sturdier corporate infrastructure to carry them through tough times.

Sullivan mentioned he had been trying to buy some of the independents out of bankruptcy in his job at Southwest Multimedia. But his current scenario did not favor his business strategy. His employers, he explained to Mays, didn't have much equity and were trying to buy stations almost solely with borrowed money.

Sullivan's advice to Mays was that if the radio owner was ever interested in getting into television, he should take a look at these independent stations. "There's a lot of them for sale," Sullivan explained, "and I think there's a future there."

Mays responded, without missing a beat, "If you ever have a station you need a partner on, give me a call."

About a month later, Sullivan called Mays and told him about a station Southwest had been looking at. Mays eagerly asked Sullivan to come to San Antonio to make a pitch, which he did. Afterward, Sullivan felt like the meeting had gone well. He figured he had himself a new partner.

The week after, Mays called him back.

"I thought about your deal. But I think we're going to pass."

"Why?" Sullivan asked.

"Because we've got financing in place, we've got equity in place. The only thing Southwest Multimedia brings to the game is you."

After a pause, Mays added, "I'd rather just buy you."

Then Mays made him an offer: If Sullivan came to Clear Channel, Mays would secure $25 million in equity and $25 million in debt financing, for a total of $50 million available to buy TV stations. And Sullivan would be the head of the resulting company.

It took a while for him to decide, but Sullivan eventually said yes. In September 1988, he became president of a new independent company, Clear Channel Television, based in Houston. Mays pleaded with Sullivan to come to San Antonio, but Sullivan had the sense he'd be better off in Houston, far enough away that Mays couldn't meddle with his start-up operation and yet close enough that he could hop on the hourly Southwest Airlines flight for a meeting in San Antonio.

Sullivan began kicking the tires at about ten TV stations a week—new stations that were failing, old stations that were failing. If there was trouble, Dan was there. In Sullivan's estimation, most of them were overleveraged and paying way too much for their syndicated programming, the lifeblood of UHF channels.

The first station Sullivan bought for Clear Channel, in October 1988, was WPMI-TV, Channel 15, in Mobile, Alabama. He purchased the small station, recently orphaned by the Michigan Energy Resources Company, for $8.9 million, chicken feed by television standards.

The next was KDTU-TV, Channel 18, in Tucson, Arizona. KDTU was the bargain-basement kind of deal Sullivan became known for. KDTU had been the first commercial TV station in the nation owned by the Catholic Church. The local diocese was having financial trouble, and KDTU was in bankruptcy proceedings and scheduled to be shut down a week before Clear Channel made a formal offer. The price? A mere $5.9 million.[3]

Sullivan sold Mays on KOKI in Tulsa, that city's first independent UHF channel, which found itself struggling against its network competitors. WAWS in Jacksonville, Florida, was snatched up from Malrite Communications, another radio company that had made a foray into television—and met with nothing but trouble. Wall Street analysts generally looked askance at radio companies that delved into TV. Malrite, controlled by its founder, Milton Maltz, had gone public in 1984, too, but unlike Clear Channel, its stock had plummeted, forcing the company to return to private ownership in 1988. In July 1989, Sullivan nabbed WAWS, an early Fox network affiliate, for $8.5 million plus some liabilities.[4]

Sullivan also had several unusual ways to repair these stations once they were owned by Clear Channel. For one, he stated bluntly that Clear Channel's TV stations would not have local newscasts, a feature he regarded as too costly and unnecessary. Then there was his strategy to acquire syndicated programming, the off-network sitcoms and drama series that typically fueled smaller independent stations. In Sullivan's view, the Hollywood studios that owned the syndication rights to such series often held smaller stations hostage. Fearing for their existence, the stations got into a mentality that they absolutely needed, say, *Magnum P.I.* reruns to survive. "The studios have been notoriously successful at creating false demand and an auction hysteria over program buying," says Sullivan. "My position was, every time they started telling me how great their programming was, I would ask them if they understood the definition of television programming."

The question would often prompt a quizzical look from a studio representative. "Well, I think I do," the rep might respond. "What's your definition?"

"Programming," Sullivan would retort with a smirk, "is the shit we run between the commercials."

Even in television, which rarely touted the same lofty free-speech ambitions of radio, most executives believed that a station's goal was to acquire programming that audiences wanted to watch and then the advertisers would follow. Sullivan and Mays simply didn't agree with that assessment.

Instead, they were prepared and willing to purchase less popular programs—old *Happy Days* reruns as opposed to recent episodes of the top-rated *Wheel of Fortune*—at a steep discount and settle for lower ratings. Then they put their muscle into selling ads. Television sales reps traditionally were far less aggressive than radio reps, acting as if they were in the commodity business. The better a station's ratings, the more they could charge for an ad. The high profile and bragging rights of working for a top TV station were formidable. But Sullivan and Mays didn't care about any of that stuff. Instead, Clear Channel Television put the heat on ad sales. Poor ratings, paired with high margins, were almost a source of pride within the company.

And for the most part, the strategy worked.

In the first few weeks of his tenure, Sullivan tagged along with Mays to New York for a meeting with representatives from the Bank of New York, Clear Channel's lead lender for much of its early history. Mays gave the pitch for Clear Channel Television and requested the $25 million line of credit he had promised to Sullivan. The bank said yes to the deal but only if Clear Channel Communications was the guarantor. Lowry said no way, either you like the deal or you don't; we appreciate your interest. The meeting lasted fifteen minutes.

Without missing a beat, Mays and Sullivan jetted off to Dallas and, the next day, presented the same offer to Bank of America. Bank of America said okay, and didn't require a guarantee from the parent company. Within a year, Bank of America was Clear Channel's leading lender, and Bank of New York was out. Unlike most radio owners, Mays knew how to play hardball with the bankers.

But for all his financial bravado, Mays remained the fiscally conservative force he had been from the start. Every new acquisition prompted a stream of questions and demands for information and rationale. Still, within five years, Clear Channel would own ten television stations, mostly in Southern and Midwestern markets.

While Sullivan was impressed by Mays's financial acumen, he also found him to be something of a controlling eccentric who often lost sight of the big picture. According to Sullivan, Red McCombs, who remained a board member and major shareholder, often pushed his partner to take more risks.

In 1993, Sullivan, who was not on the board of directors but nonetheless attended every board meeting for the ten years he was with the company, recommended that Clear Channel buy a Fox affiliate TV station in Minneapolis from the Nationwide insurance company. The station had $3.5 million in cash flow, and the purchase price was $35 million, a straight ten-times deal. But when Sullivan made the presentation at a board meeting, Lowry expressed reluctance. The amount was three to four times more than what Clear Channel had ever spent on a TV station. Mays felt the deal was out of the company's sweet spot due to the purchase price and the existence of major competitors.

At that moment, Red McCombs stood up and castigated Mays for his doubts.

"Lowry, Sullivan has done ten or twelve television deals, and every deal has worked so far," said McCombs. "If he likes the deal, I like the deal. I think we ought to do it."

The rest of the board immediately concurred.

Mays shook his head and said, "Well, if the board wants to do it, I'll go along, but I just want you to know this is a pretty big risk."

It took three months, but Clear Channel ultimately did the deal. In the first year of owning the station, it reaped a cash flow of $7 million, twice the amount of the previous year. The second year cash flow reached $12 million. At the year-end board meeting in 1995, Mays went on and on about how much he adored the Minneapolis acquisition, then turned to McCombs and said, "Red, I'm sure glad I dragged you over the finish line on that deal, because I know you didn't like it."

McCombs didn't mind having a laugh at his own expense, especially if he'd profit in the end. He was "all about the money," according to Sullivan, and in favor of any move that would drive up the company's stock price. But Mays persisted in his frugal ways, often turning station budget meetings into excruciating daylong sessions in which he would ruminate over each line item, no matter how small, and use virtually any excuse to challenge the manager responsible.

In one such budget session, debating costs for KSAS-TV, a Fox affiliate Clear Channel purchased in Wichita, Kansas, it was determined that the station needed six new translators, broadcast devices that receive a television signal, then strengthen and rebroadcast the signal on a different frequency. Translators were crucial in thinly populated rural areas like Kansas. The cost for the new ones was $350,000. Another item on the list was a $150 membership to the Chamber of Commerce in nearby Salina, Kansas. Mays fingered the $150 expense and asked the station manager, Rip Riordan, why it was needed. The manager responded that he was planning to assign a salesperson to Salina and he wanted to demonstrate that Clear Channel was part of the community. Mays scrunched his brow and said, "Why don't you wait till we do some business over there before you join?"

After about a half hour of heated debate, Sullivan suggested that if the strategy didn't work, he'd take the $150 out of Riordan's salary. Riordan agreed to the plan, and, finally, so did Mays.

The next item on the agenda was the translators. Sullivan handed Mays a presentation book two inches thick filled with contour maps and population densities. Mays thumbed through it and looked at Sullivan and said, "Have you read this?"

"Every page."

"Do you think it's a good idea?"

"Yes, I do," Sullivan responded.

Forty-five seconds later, Mays said, "Okay, then let's do it."

Concerns about wasting money clearly were an obsession with Mays. But such minute financial wranglings were also a way of testing his employees' mettle. He wanted to know their level of commitment; he also intended to emphasize the culture of Clear Channel. It was easier to save a dollar than to sell a dollar, in Mays's thinking.

While even loyal employees found Mays's tightwad ways irritating at times, financial analysts would positively swoon at his regular road-show presentations. In a roomful of young MBA types, Mays would often start his talks by saying something like, "Let me make one thing perfectly clear, I've got 95 percent of my personal net worth tied up in the stock of this company. I'm never going to put that at risk. Every time my leverage gets over about two and a half or three times, I get very nervous. I don't sleep at night. So I'm never going to put this company at risk."

In September 1995, Sullivan got an offer from ABRY Partners, a Boston-based equity fund, to run Act III Communications, which the firm had just purchased from Norman Lear for $520 million. In exchange for a significant personal investment in the new partnership, he would become the company's president and change its name to Sullivan Broadcasting. It was the chance of a lifetime for the TV veteran to run his own show.

One morning over breakfast in a hotel suite before an analyst presentation, Sullivan told Mays about the exciting opportunity and that he was leaving the company. After a few minutes, Mays said, "Well, I don't think this is something we want to do."

Sullivan was stunned: "What do you mean?"

"This isn't in the best interest of the company, and we're not going to do that."

At first Mays threatened to hold Sullivan to his contract. But as time passed, he acquiesced. Though the two men ran into each other at broadcasting conferences, Mays wouldn't speak to Sullivan for almost a year. Though Sullivan says Mays eventually forgave him, he was shaken by his former boss's cold maneuvering.

By 1995, Clear Channel owned nine television stations and had ties to five others through local marketing agreements.[5] Most of the stations, all in large or midsize markets, were affiliated with Fox. Sullivan had built the TV group into one of the strongest in the industry, with cash flow increasing by more than 80 percent annually and revenues increasing by almost 50 percent during his time with the company. Television by then represented almost 60 percent of the company's cash flow.

Sometime in 1988, Stan Webb got an urgent call from Lowry Mays asking him to take over as general manager of the country-music station KAJA-FM in San Antonio, which was experiencing stiff competition from a new entry into the market, KCYY-FM, owned by Cox Media. Webb was still based in Austin, ninety miles away, and decided he didn't want to do it. Webb loved Austin, and his two sons were still in high school there.

Finally, under pressure from Mays, he agreed to manage KAJA, but only if he could remain in Austin. For the next two years, Webb spent a lot of time driving I-35, back and forth between the two cities.

Webb didn't make many personnel or operational changes at KAJA. Mostly what was required was instilling a renewed confidence in the sales staff. Still, it was a challenge to manage a portfolio of stations in two cities. The traditional radio model dictated that each station had its own general manager to fine-tune programming and sales strategies to a particular market. Managing stations in more than one city meant spreading that expertise a little more thinly. Though Webb was able to bolster KAJA, the ratings battle between it and KCYY would persist for years to come.

In his own little way, Webb had gotten a taste of the future of radio. The country-radio gunfight in San Antonio was a glimpse at radio's future as a duopoly, a market system in which it became advantageous to own multiple stations in the same city in order to compete against one other major competitor who also owned multiple stations. It was the broadcasting industry's version of the arms race, and Lowry Mays was an innovator and leader in the practice.

Webb also got an early glimpse of what was evolving into Mays's master plan when his boss approached him in late 1995 to take a bigger role in future business arrangements. Mays wanted him to run the radio group with an eye toward deregulation. Webb was named president of operations but was told to "keep my mouth shut" for at least six months about what the company's agenda was in light of a probable easing of FCC radio ownership caps. "Lowry told me we wanted to be poised and ready to jump all over this," he says.

Clear Channel also got a head start on the Spanish-language market in May 1995 when it purchased a 26 percent stake in the Dallas-based Heftel Broadcasting, later known as the Hispanic Broadcasting Corporation, for $20.5 million, making it the biggest stockholder of the leading Spanish-language radio company.

Reed Hundt vividly recalls the moment when he realized he had lost his battle against the radio industry. Indeed, describing that moment in his cramped but well-appointed office at a major consulting firm's Washington, D.C., outpost nearly a decade after the fact, Hundt, who served as chairman of the Federal Communications Commission from November 1993 to 1997, still wore a faint smirk of defeat. Dressed in a pale yellow polo shirt, khaki pants, and brown tassel loafers on a steamy summer afternoon, he looked like a graying, rumpled version of the actor William H. Macy. His Midwestern accent was even some approximation of that used by Macy playing the folksy rube in *Fargo*.

Planted under a photo of himself arm in arm with his old pals Bill Clinton and Al Gore (he was a law school classmate of Bill's and a high school buddy of Al's), he wearily recounted the events that resulted in the elimination of the radio ownership caps that occurred with the passage of the Telecommunications Act of 1996.[6]

"To me, the story of Clear Channel is the story of Lowry Mays, and there were two or three other people who had generally the same idea, that's it," says Hundt. "This is not about hundreds of thousands of people wanting to be entrepreneurs. It's got its own distinctive traits. It's not the same as the telephone company mergers; it's not the same as the Disney and ABC merger. In very high-level generalities, I suppose you could say it was the story of convergence, but mostly it's the story of the radio industry wanting to organize itself in a certain way and the Republican Congress deciding to give them exactly what they wanted."

Hundt, formerly an antitrust litigator, was nominated to his chairman post by President Clinton and set out to imbue the FCC with a renewed commitment to the public interest. One of his biggest initiatives during his tenure was getting a statute passed that required television station owners to broadcast three hours of educational children's programming each day. Another of his plans involved promoting Internet access in public school classrooms, an idea slightly ahead of its time. But Hundt, a civic-minded Democrat, created conflict at the FCC from the start of his tenure by insisting that the agency's primary goal was to serve the public, a situation only exacerbated in November 1994, when Republicans took control of both houses of Congress.[7]

Despite being described by *The New York Times* as a "protégé and soulmate" of Al Gore, Hundt brought a distinctly free-market approach to his job as chairman.[8] In early 1994, the FCC received positive public feedback for a plan to auction off more than two thousand licenses for various devices, including cell phones, paging units, wireless computers, and other personal communications equipment. But vehement disagreement within the agency over the educational programming proposal created a rift that only got worse over time.

This was not only unfortunate but also a case of extremely bad timing.

As the original electronic mass medium, radio had long been saddled with more regulations than other media businesses. There was a good reason for this: from its very beginnings, radio advertisers in the United States held much more sway than those in newspapers and magazines, since commercial broadcasters made all their revenue from advertising. As early as the late 1920s, advertising agencies produced about one-third of all radio programs.[9] Another 20 percent were created by individual sponsors. Radio networks at that time accounted for only 28 percent of the available programming; the rest was supplied by special-project producers. Within a few years, the agencies controlled almost everything except the programs the networks ran during periods without a sponsor. Sensible people, meaning anyone who was not part of the advertising industry, concluded that radio could easily be used for nefarious purposes.

Ironically, in those days, cultural conservatives were some of the biggest proponents of radio regulation, along with the socialists. The FCC, created by the Communications Act of 1934 with the mandate to regulate radio, telegraph, cable, and telephone, was often branded a New Deal agency, but in fact it was President Hoover, not President Franklin D. Roosevelt, who had shaped and framed the substance of the legislation.[10]

The reasons for Roosevelt's support were obvious. In the 1932 election, six out of ten newspapers went against him; radio networks, on the other hand, gave Roosevelt access to the airwaves whenever he wanted, allowing him to appeal directly to the public. Later in his presidency, Roosevelt became known for his fireside chats, casual speeches lasting usually less than a half hour, broadcast on radio for the American people. By 1940, forty-two New Deal agencies were generating programming for radio.

Still, from its beginnings, the FCC retained a healthy suspicion of propagandistic radio broadcasts. A 1941 case involving a Boston station, WAAB, that, according to testimony, aired editorials disparaging local politicians without grounds resulted in an FCC ruling banning radio editorials entirely. In 1949, the FCC repealed the ban and instated the Fairness Doctrine, which permitted stations to broadcast political opinion but required them to offer reply time to opposing viewpoints. A longtime point of contention for conservatives, it was abolished in August 1987, during the Reagan administration, with the support of most broadcasters, though the proposal was initiated by Charles Ferris, FCC chairman during the Carter years.

Also in 1941, in response to the blossoming RCA, the FCC ruled that it violated the public interest for any organization to own more than one radio network and for any network to own more than one station in an area. No ownership caps were stipulated at the time, but the agency stated no license would be granted to a station in any area where there were so few options that ownership would substantially hurt competition. The concern was that established networks would prevent new networks from starting as well as prevent other stations from serving the interests of their local communities.[11]

The role of the FCC until the 1980s was that of industrial supervision.[12]

The original spirit of the FCC rules guiding radio encouraged multiple owners in each market with the notion that radio was a relatively low-cost and easy-to-launch medium, compared with newspapers and, later, television. But the unintended effect over time was the buildup of program syndication firms that could distribute content to stations nationwide. Howard Stern, Rush Limbaugh, and the other megawatt radio personalities who emerged in the 1980s were a direct result of the FCC's regulation of radio ownership since syndication firms were in the business of promoting talent as opposed to radio stations.

By the time the 1990s rolled around, deregulation had gained two staunch and powerful supporters, Mel Karmazin of Infinity Broadcasting and Lowry Mays of Clear Channel. The basic idea was that there were huge financial incentives to control both content and the means of distributing that content. By owning the whole distribution channel, a media company could ensure that none of its profits would be siphoned off as its content was being delivered. The business pros call this strategy "vertical integration." The merger of the Walt Disney Company and Capital Cities/ABC in 1996 was built on this principle. So was the whole oil industry.

If you had asked virtually any media analyst in the mid-1990s whether such a strategy would work, he or she would have said most certainly.

The problem was, the media industry bore little resemblance to the oil industry. Content distribution was an inherently local business, whereas content businesses knew no boundaries. More troubling, in the vertical integration model, the content creators tended to sell to the distributors they owned and not market much to those they didn't. And the distributors tended to favor content provided by their own company, not necessarily the best or most appealing to their customers.

In reality, the only way a media company could make vertical integration work was if it held a virtual monopoly on both ends. Lowry Mays seemed to have figured this out before any other radio executive. Clear Channel understood that to make vertical integration work, it needed a larger scale operation, much larger-scale.

It was the wrangling of Mays and virtually every other good-sized radio company that helped make the legislative process leading up to the Telecommunications Act of 1996 one of the most complex and inscrutable. As a former chairman of the National Association of Broadcasters, and a member of its executive committee, Mays was present at many of the negotiation sessions, according to sources, giving him the added competitive advantage of knowing exactly what the likely changes would be prior to the act's passage.[13]

In fact, the bulk of the act focused on the deregulation of phone services. Local phone companies, the "Baby Bells" that resulted from the breakup of AT&T in the 1980s, would be allowed to offer long-distance service in exchange for permitting long-distance companies and start-up companies to use their local lines to compete for customers. The idea was that consumers would benefit from increased local competition, allowing them to choose not only their long-distance carrier but their local phone company as well.

"The radio industry, through the National Association of Broadcasters, had been lobbying for that kind of activity for a long time," says Robert Unmacht. "They had tried in the '70s to open up the Telecom Act and it was such a hot potato; they cracked it a little bit, but then they put the lid back on."[14] The advent of the Internet in the mid-1990s, a disruptive technology that threatened to change the equation, was the first legitimate excuse to reopen the discussion.

Despite the potential benefits, the average person on the street had little incentive to follow the proceedings. Politics was the main thrust of the Telecom Act. The staunchly pro-business Republicans were represented by Representative Tom Bliley of Virginia, a solid backer of AT&T; and Representative Billy Tauzin of Louisiana, the chairman of the Commerce Committee's telecommunications subcommittee, a key ally for the regional Bell companies. With Vice President Gore at the helm, Democrats imagined the act as a way to reinvent themselves as the pro-business party.

In a speech he gave to radio broadcasters at the World Media Expo in New Orleans on September 8, 1995, Chairman Hundt preached the dangers of consolidation. "I am sure that the House and Senate bills propose to lift radio ownership because of the view that radio competes with other media for advertising dollars and, therefore, that the current national radio ownership limits are too strict to permit radio groups to compete effectively for those dollars," he told expo attendees at the Ernest N. Morial Convention Center. "I agree with that. Even if no reform emerges from the legislative process, I would raise the current national cap of twenty AM and twenty FM stations. I also think there is room to raise the local cap of two AM and two FM stations, certainly in medium and large markets.

"But the House and Senate would allow a few companies to buy all the radio licenses in the country. And if you think that's far-fetched in practice, it is just as disturbing—and more at odds with the theory underlying the FCC's 1981 programming deregulation—to see that in a local market Congress may allow a single company to buy all the radio licenses."

On that same visit, Hundt shared a rich meal in a New Orleans hotel dining room with a small group of radio executives, including Lowry Mays, Infinity's Mel Karmazin, and Entercom's CEO, Jeff Smulyan, presumably those who were most interested in having the ownership caps lifted. Their message was simple: the radio market was ridiculously fragmented, where nobody had more than 2 percent of market share, as measured by ad revenue. Hundt agreed but said he simply did not believe that eliminating the caps completely was the solution. His opinion was received with polite smiles. That past May, the Progress & Freedom Foundation, a conservative think tank with connections to the Republican Speaker of the House, Newt Gingrich, had publicly called for the abolition of the FCC.

President Clinton reportedly was dismayed by two proposals in the law laid before him relating to media ownership. One involved eliminating the number of radio stations a company was allowed to own, and the other erased the prohibition of owning television stations and a newspaper in the same city. But Clinton was apparently more bothered by the TV and newspaper provision since, as he liked to say, if the anti-Clinton *Arkansas Democrat-Gazette* and the television stations in Little Rock had been owned by the same folks, he would never have become president.

Legend has it that Clinton therefore agreed to support lifting the caps on radio ownership as long as the law keeping television and newspaper ownership restricted was preserved.

The radio provisions were unusual in the statute because they were not phrased in the form of a directive to the FCC. They were instead phrased as a direct order. There was no regulation to pass. There was no regulatory procedure to go through. There was no secondary debate about the details surrounding the changes. There

were no public hearings. The Republican-controlled Congress simply ordered that the law be changed.

"My impression is that this was kind of an afterthought," says
the current FCC commissioner Jonathan Adelstein, who did not
participate in the passage of the legislation. "The primary focus of
the bill was the long-distance versus the local Baby Bells. It was a
masterful job of lobbying on the part of the broadcasters—they
kind of just slipped in there when there was a lot of noise surrounding it about other issues that were much more publicly debated."[15]

Blair Levin, who served as Hundt's chief of staff at the FCC,
praises his former boss for speaking out against raising radio's national ownership caps at the time, though Hundt's words clearly
had little effect. "He understood that to eliminate the national cap
meant that you would get a certain kind of consolidation in the industry that has proven problematic," says Levin. "What he had predicted would happen, did happen. And I think there were a lot of
people in Congress who didn't want that to happen, both Democrats and Republicans."[16]

But Stan Webb discounts the notion that Mays had any over-
bearing influence on what was going on in Washington. "The one
thing we were prepared for more than anybody else was that deregulation," he says. "Because when the whistle blew, Mark Mays and I
were on airplanes and stations started falling like dominoes."

6.

A BRILLIANT IDEA

The Telecommunications Act of 1996 was passed by Congress on February 1, and Bill Clinton signed it a week later— twice—with a gesture indicative of the new media era dawning. The first time was with several regular pens, including one used by President Eisenhower to sign the Federal Aid Highway Act; the second time was with a digital pen that posted his signature on the Internet.[1] The world was changing, and big media would be forced to change with it.

Within a month of President Clinton's signing the Telecom Act, the radio business nearly went off the rails. By March 1996, more than $1.8 billion in radio deals had been announced.[2] In the first week of that month alone, at least five station mergers or acquisitions totaling more than $630 million took place. Five of the ten largest radio companies purchased eighty-two stations in that same period of time. The Wild West atmosphere on the one hand was perfectly understandable, given the seventy-five-year-old restrictions that had been lifted, but on the other hand was legitimately rattling. There were 10,200 commercial radio stations in the country with about fifty-two hundred individual owners. It went without saying that the ranks of owners would soon be thinning.

Andrew Schwartzman, president and chief executive of the Media Access Project, a liberal-leaning public interest law firm in Washington, D.C., recalls the prevailing mood as somewhat ominous. "The conventional wisdom at the time, which people repeated to each other endlessly in the year or two after the '96 act, was that radio was going to consolidate a great deal," he says. "Almost everyone in the radio industry was now going to have to be a buyer or a seller. And Clear Channel set out to be buyers in the most aggressive way possible—but they were not alone."[3]

The insanity was dominated by young, previously obscure players, a group that in addition to Clear Channel included Infinity, Evergreen, Jacor, and SFX Broadcasting. Of all of the upstarts, Jacor, based out of Cincinnati, was initially the most aggressive. Controlled by the eccentric real estate mogul Sam Zell, Jacor slurped up twenty-six radio stations and two TV stations during a ten-day stretch that February, spending a whopping $926 million. Overnight it became one of the largest radio station owners in the country.

Though Clear Channel showed a certain level of preparedness in the early days of deregulation, the company was by no means on its own in the battle to bulk up.

But while the ultimate winner of the vast radio buildup remained unclear, anyone who knew anything about the radio business knew who the big losers were. "It was probably good for the shareholders and senior executives of these companies," says the radio industry veteran Lee Abrams, "and it was the worst possible thing for listeners."[4]

Mid-level station programmers weren't thrilled, either, particularly after stations began changing hands multiple times within a single year. Not only did they worry about the frequent changes to their health-care benefits, but they feared the worst: that their services would not be required anymore. And indeed, as radio groups got larger, they demanded less and less creative input. Radio executives became far more interested in quantitative research than in the opinions of any one programmer, regardless of that person's level of experience. For that reason, radio quickly got a case of the doldrums. "A lot of people were not doing what they got into radio for in the first place," Abrams says.

———————

By 1990, Mark Mays was playing a much larger role at Clear Channel than most outsiders realized.[5] "Mark was running the company," says Rex Tackett, who returned to the company that same year to salvage a station in Oklahoma City. Tapped by his father to be the company's treasurer and head of finance a year earlier, Mark until then, by his own account, felt a strong push to go his own way. Still, Stan Webb recalls joking around with John Barger when Mark and Randall were still in middle school about when the boys would take their jobs. "It wasn't a matter of if," he says. "It was simply a matter of when."[6]

Lowry's eldest son, born in 1963, grew up around Clear Channel and took his first summer job at the company as a teenager doing construction work on one of the San Antonio stations.[7] But his upbringing was largely a privileged one spent away from San Antonio.

Mark spent his high school years at the Hotchkiss School in Lakeville, Connecticut, and then attended Vanderbilt University in Nashville, graduating in 1985 with a degree in economics. After college, he briefly worked for Eppler, Guerin & Turner, a Dallas-based investment-banking firm, and for Capital Cities/ABC, now part of Disney. After earning an MBA at Columbia University in New York, he was considering offers from Wall Street when his father called and offered him a position at Clear Channel in 1989 as company treasurer and head of finance. His official job would be to build relationships with banks to finance new acquisitions.

In reality, he toiled as an underling in the bowels of Clear Channel's accounting department, though his access to top company executives was nonpareil. "I can remember doing budget presentations and Mark sitting in those meetings and being a real observer," says Webb.

Others recall Mark and Randall's attendance at informal management cookouts at their father's ranch, even while they were still in school. "We'd play horseshoes and barbecue burgers and ride horses," says Jim Smith. "So I knew both the boys since they were really little."

Within a few years, Mark was named vice president of operations and soon enough was named president and chief operating officer in 1993. That same year he offered a job to his younger brother, Randall, as treasurer and chief financial officer. Randall Mays, born in 1966, had also attended Hotchkiss, moved on to the University of Texas at Austin, and then got an MBA from Harvard Business School.

From the start, close associates noticed a certain team mentality between the brothers. There was no sibling rivalry revealed in the business environment; to the contrary, the two formed a consummate partnership, somehow complementing each other with their various strengths and deficiencies. Yet neither possessed the home-spun likability and common touch that got their father so far, associates say.[8]

Mark earned a reputation as being open and easygoing, a real communicator with strong social skills and a natural tendency toward leadership. Randall, younger, leaner, and sometimes meaner, became known as something of a mysterious darker force. A born financial whiz with little interest in societal niceties, he happily deferred to his brother as the heir apparent, content to work in the shadows and offer broad-based strategies.

"Randall is really the brains behind it all, and I think most people don't even know that," says Bob Turner, who ran a turnkey media ad rep firm for Clear Channel out of Interep's New York offices in the 1990s. "And he's comfortable in that role. He's the numbers guy behind the scenes, but he's doing all the work from the numbers point of view."[9] But Rex Tackett describes how many in the company viewed him: "Randall had that banker, bean-counter mentality."

Insiders sometimes formed a radically different impression, though—as if below the surface, the brothers' personalities were the direct opposite of what they appeared externally. "Mark would seem to be the more gregarious of the two, can crack a joke, make you feel real comfortable like you've known him a long time, and yet I can tell from the experience of observing him in situations, there is ice water in that man," says Jim Smith. "Nothing bothers him."

Randall, on the other hand, says Smith, could seem aloof and hard to know. "And yet he probably has the biggest heart of the family," he continues. "He's very sensitive about what people think and that kind of thing."

The cloaked roles of both apparently came in handy during heated negotiations. "Mark would slit your throat and wouldn't miss a meal," quips Smith. "But you'd think it was Randall who was going to do it."

The debate is still open as to which son more resembles his dad. Randall, by most accounts, has the same low-key relatable quality, combined with a similar sense of emotional distance. But Mark was regarded by some as closer to Lowry in terms of leadership skills and making quick and decisive resolutions.

Turner recalls the close, almost playful relationship between the sons and their father when he first flew down to San Antonio for a meeting in 1994. "They were a perfect team, a perfect fit, a perfect match," he says. He and Interep's chairman, Ralph Guild, showed up one day at the Clear Channel offices to pitch the Mayses on the notion of a dedicated national advertising representation firm.

In the radio business, most radio groups do their own local ad selling. Ad rep firms like Interep get hired to sell national spots. At the time, the leading radio rep firms were Interep and Katz Media, owned by a Clear Channel competitor, Tom Hicks's Chancellor Media in Dallas.

Based on a hunch, Guild came up with the idea of creating a Clear Channel–branded rep firm, even though Clear Channel only had about thirty-five stations at the time. At that point, Clear Channel split its national business between Interep and Katz.

During a four-hour meeting at Clear Channel headquarters, Guild and Turner tried to sell the Mays clan on the merits of the deal. Also in the room were Stan Webb and two other Clear Channel general managers, Dave Ross and Bob Cohen. After the fourth hour, Turner and Guild were asked to leave the conference room while the others considered the deal.

After the two retired to Lowry's office, something extraordinary happened: unbeknownst to his sons, Lowry slipped in the football-field-sized office through another door and coached the duo from Interep on how to clinch the deal. The decision to go with Interep would be Mark Mays's first major one as the company's leader; his father didn't want to give the impression he was making it for him. And yet Lowry knew the outcome he wanted—and was determined to make it happen in any way he could.

By the time Guild and Turner reentered the conference room, the two sides had an agreement: Turner and Guild would travel to every single Clear Channel station and make the same pitch they had made to Lowry, Mark, and Randall. In the next week and a half, the Interep team visited all thirteen Clear Channel markets. At least half of the stations initially didn't want to go with Interep, most notably the Louisville stations that had been with Katz Media for decades.

After Turner and Guild returned to San Antonio, Mark Mays took a silent vote via voice mail as to whether Clear Channel should go with Interep. But he had already tipped his hand to Turner, making it apparent that he liked the arrangement. The outcome of the vote was never revealed, but Interep was hired that same day. The five-year deal included exclusive representation by Interep on a sliding scale beginning at 10 percent (instead of the usual 12 percent) and moving up to 14 percent—the more billing Turner did, the higher Interep's commission became. And under the contract, every new radio station Clear Channel bought became an Interep client. It was the first deal of its kind in the business, and a very lucrative one for both partners.

By 1993, the two brothers as a team were, for all intents and purposes, running the company. Turner, who became close to the family over his six years running Clear Channel Radio Sales, spent many Sunday night dinners with the family at Lowry Mays's San

Antonio home; the gatherings would often include the Mayses' eldest daughter, Kathryn Johnson, who for a long time headed Clear Channel's corporate communications department. Turner was impressed by how closely knit the family was. He recalls Mark and Randall's mother, Peggy—"she's the boss," he says—telling him how their personalities weren't that different from when they were children.

He also noted how at that time the boys often wore identical suits and even shoes. "They are the nicest billionaires you'll ever meet," says Turner. "They are so unassuming, almost like they don't have any money."

Turner, who frequently visited the homes of everyone in the Mays family, was also struck by how modest the family's residences were. Mark's home was large but only because he had expanded it to accommodate his and his wife Patty's six sons. Even Lowry's two-thousand-acre ranch on the northwestern edge of town had a very reasonable-sized ranch house on it, nothing lavish or flashy, according to Turner.

Turner recalls that once, at a black-tie event, Peggy Mays took home six of the flower settings from the tables afterward. "They were all rolling their eyes, saying, 'Oh, that's Mom.' "

But Turner also witnessed the tough business side of Lowry, even as he had begun relinquishing control to his sons. Turner's Clear Channel–branded ad sales firm was underperforming in a certain market in 1995. "He was very frank and very direct on his unhappiness with me and in no uncertain terms didn't want any excuses," he says. "He wanted to know, 'How are you going to fix it?' and 'When are you going to do it?' " No yelling, no bullying, but also no compromise.

George Sosson had sweated it out at CBS Radio for twenty-one years when he decided it was time for a change. A native of Philadelphia, he got his first job out of college in the early 1970s at WCAU, a CBS-owned FM station in his hometown, when FM was nothing, financially speaking, and thus was populated with young college grads who couldn't get jobs in AM.

After two decades, Sosson had worked his way up to become CBS's vice president of FM stations. But by 1990, he was ready for something a little more entrepreneurial. With advertising in a slump, Sosson had the idea he could acquire some FM stations in small to medium markets for a song. At first he had a tough time finding financial partners, but he found an unusual supporter in GE Investments, the division of General Electric that managed the company's pension fund.

By mid-1992, he had $54 million in the bank, thanks mostly to GE, and put together a group called Radio Equity Partners.[10] When more opportunities arose, GE ponied up another $100 million. Within three years, Radio Equity Partners was thriving and included fifteen FM stations and four AM stations in places like Greensboro, North Carolina; Memphis; Oklahoma City; Columbia, South Carolina; New Orleans; Springfield, Massachusetts; Providence; and Fort Myers, Florida.

"My investors, the General Electric pension fund, really didn't want to pay to get into the big, top markets," says Sosson. "So the medium markets at the time were priced quite reasonably. These were all pretty good solid-performing stations. They basically wanted cash-flowing stations; they really didn't want to do any turnarounds."[11]

Sosson had received a call from Mark Mays in 1995 to arrange a meeting at the New Orleans National Association of Broadcasters convention at which Reed Hundt had made his anti-deregulation speech. He had met Lowry in passing over the years but had never met his son. "I thought what he wanted was a swap," says Sosson, "that we would swap New Orleans and Oklahoma City so that we'd both wind up with more clustered stations than we originally had in one or the other of those markets, because that was where we had overlapping markets."

When they finally met in New Orleans, Sosson was floored by what Mays told him. Clear Channel wanted to buy his whole radio group. Two other things about the meeting surprised Sosson. The first was Mark's age: still in his early thirties, Mays was tall and personable like his father, but very young-looking. The second was Mark's aggressiveness. "It was clear, even at an early age," says Sosson, "that his dad had given him the authority to do the deal." Mark was clearly in charge and had the power to get something done.

Sosson was also impressed by Mark's charm, and the two men clicked immediately. The older man returned to investors and described Clear Channel's interest in the stations. Since the Telecom Act had not been passed yet, they decided to wait. Sosson had a hunch they could bump up their asking price substantially once it did.

When the Telecom Act of 1996 passed in February, Sosson began getting lots of phone calls from larger public radio companies, including SFX and Clear Channel. But Clear Channel was particularly enamored with Sosson's properties because it already owned stations in New Orleans and Oklahoma City and liked his other markets, since they were small and mostly in the South.

By May 1996, the contracts had been signed. Clear Channel agreed to pay $235 million in cash to Radio Equity Partners for nineteen radio stations in eight markets, pending FCC approval.[12] It was the biggest deal Clear Channel had ever attempted. By August, the deal had been done and done cleanly. "There was no changing when we got to the closing table," says Sosson. "They paid exactly what the contract said. It just went down perfectly." Clear Channel now owned and/or operated ninety-two radio stations.

Sosson says he did the deal with Clear Channel based almost solely on comfort level. He guesses he could have squeezed a few more dollars out of someone else but didn't even pursue the other offers he received.

When Clear Channel took over Radio Equity Partners, it changed very little about the stations it now owned. Every general manager that Sosson had hired remained in place after the deal. He says his employees fit in well with the existing Clear Channel culture because he himself was a very cost-conscious manager. When it came to extras like retirement benefits and medical insurance, Clear Channel came up way short. At the time, it took a virtually unheard-of seven years to become fully vested in the company's 401(k), and its health-care program required filling out forms for every single claim.

Indeed, Sosson seemed almost impassioned about the new relationship, so much so that one night over dinner in New York with Mark Mays, he suggested that Clear Channel hire him. "As we got toward closing," he says, "it became apparent to me that I needed something to do." Though hardly in need of a job, Sosson suggested to Mays that as the company grew, it could use someone on the sales end with his experience. Mark Mays apparently liked the idea and soon agreed to hire Sosson as senior vice president of Eastern operations.

But Sosson got a dose of reality as soon as he began to negotiate his salary. "This was the first indication I had that Clear Channel was a little bit on the tight side," he jokes. The base salary he was offered was nearly $100,000 less than what he was being paid to run Radio Equity Partners. Still, Sosson said yes. Since he had been amply compensated by the Radio Equity deal, he could afford the pay cut. The job also came with stock options, which Sosson didn't have to be a genius to figure might be worth something someday soon. Besides, at fifty years of age, he figured it would be hard to come by a suitable senior position in the radio business.

In an arrangement struck with Mark Mays, Sosson worked primarily out of his home office in southern Connecticut—though he was on the road more than at home in those heady days of 1996.

By the time Sosson was hired, Mark was calling most of the shots at Clear Channel, at least in terms of being the go-to guy for acquisitions. From the day the Telecom Act passed, Stan Webb and George Sosson would get daily phone calls from Mark Mays, instructing them to jump on a plane to a new market to introduce themselves to the staff. The idea was to give the staff a pitch about what great stewards Clear Channel was going to be for the radio station. That they would be joining the Clear Channel family.

It would usually take about ninety days for each purchase to be cleared by the FCC. But in typical Clear Channel fashion, the company would often strike its own operating sub-deal with new stations, known as an LMA, a local management or marketing agreement.

LMAs first showed up in commercial radio in the early 1990s, when ownership restrictions limited companies to only one AM and one FM in a market and fourteen AM/FM stations nationally. LMAs were a legally viable contractual tool manufactured expressly to address what these commercial broadcasters saw as a regulatory environment that blocked them from maximizing profits. Capstar, later to become AMFM, was the first radio company to use such arrangements.

The most common use of the LMA was to circumvent FCC ownership limitations to operate multiple stations in a single market by entering into a contract to program, sell advertising for, and manage other stations without actually acquiring the license. LMAs usually ranged from one year to five or six years—timed to coincide with the owner's license renewal date.

Clear Channel's use of LMAs was at the point of entering into a contract to sell a station. The interval between the filing of a sale/ license transfer and its final FCC approval (usually four to six months) was a risky operational period for both the buyer and the seller. Since the impending sale of a station was public information during this period, advertising sales often dropped, staff sometimes left, and ratings sometimes faltered. Short-term LMAs provided an opportunity for buyers and sellers to enter into brief management agreements that enabled the buyer to operate the station until the final sale and transfer were approved by the FCC. This type of LMA was generally a year or less in length.

"We would take over operations immediately," recalls Webb. "And you had to be delicate with how that was done so that you did not interfere with what the licensee was really wanting."

Most remarkably, Webb and Sosson had near-total autonomy. With his corporate background, Sosson was unaccustomed to making major decisions without notifying higher-ups, but Mark Mays quickly assured him that he should call all his own shots. "I had had twenty-five years of experience at high levels, and I knew what I was doing," says Sosson. "And Mark knew I knew what I was doing and let me do it."

Sosson theorizes that one reason Clear Channel employees were so loyal at the time, despite the subpar pay and benefits, was the commitment from Lowry and Mark Mays to let executives do their own thing.

Even in the blur of the acquisition snowstorm, though, Clear Channel made every effort to stick to its tried-and-true operational style. "One of the real strengths of Clear Channel in that particular period," says Stan Webb, "was that we're not going to come in here and bring some sort of Big Mac approach to operating."

General managers were usually not replaced at new stations after they were acquired. And those managers largely continued to control their own destinies by being allowed to hang themselves or flourish based on their executive decisions.

7.

SUCCESS (THE NEW RADIO UNIVERSE)

The consolidation of the radio business was the big news that nobody really heard. That is, the sea change in radio ownership was barely a blip on the cultural consciousness. But while having made little or no impact on the average radio listener—at least at first—for the small-time station operator the Telecom Act of 1996 was nothing short of colossal in its effect.

One of those small-time owners, Ed Levine, was typical of the breed. Levine, now in his early fifties, had spent his formative radio years in upstate New York, first as a rock disc jockey at WAQX-FM in Syracuse and later as a programmer in Albany, Houston, and Washington, D.C. Levine fell in love with the dramatic aspects of radio as a teen, energized by the legendary New York progressive-rock station, WNEW-FM. He dropped out of Syracuse University's Newhouse School of Public Communications in 1978 to work full-time at WAQX. "Radio just fascinated me," he says, "the 'theater of the mind' aspect of it, and the use of words, and the creativity—and of course the music, too."[1]

His ultimate dream to become an owner began in 1990 with a small station built on a brand-new signal in Utica, New York, WKLL-FM. He and a partner purchased it for $165,000 while Levine still held down a job as programmer for Albany-area stations owned by Infinity. Despite the ongoing ad recession, Levine opted to leave Infinity the next year in a fit of adventurousness, choosing his lowly struggling station in Utica over a secure middle-manager job with a nice salary and stock options.

Fueled by his passion for radio, Levine envisioned running a station brimming with the kind of creativity he had fallen for as a kid. But the reality was the business of programming had changed quite dramatically since the early 1970s free-form radio he grew up with. "The cookie-cutter approach to formats had started happening all over the country," says Levine.

Because Clear Channel eventually became the largest radio chain in the country, it is often blamed for the lack of variety on today's music stations. But while Clear Channel may have perfected the art of synchronized programming and enabled its spread into some of the smallest markets, it certainly did not create the notion of radio formulas.

Much of the blame for the McDonald's approach to radio programming, as surprising as it may seem, can actually be laid at the feet of just one man: Lee Abrams. Abrams was the inventor of the first FM radio rock format, known as album-oriented rock, or AOR. A native of Chicago, he works today as the head of programming for XM Satellite Radio, ironically one of the two companies currently creating a challenge to traditional "free" radio with satellite radio's subscription-based business model.

When I meet Abrams one afternoon at XM's sleek, hipster-ish Washington, D.C., headquarters, ensconced in a converted warehouse building near the entrance to the highway, he appears anything but threatening. Overweight and lumpy, with shaggy white curly hair and a mustache, Abrams looks like an aging rock-band roadie, especially dressed as he is in an oversize black T-shirt with a security card dangling from a lanyard around his neck that very much resembles a backstage concert pass. The walls of his compact office are festooned with framed gold and platinum records by rock musicians such as Warren Zevon, Iron Maiden, and Ozzy

Osbourne, recognition for his role in those smash hits as a radio programmer. A Gibson Les Paul rests on a stand next to his desk, as if he were about to pick it up and carry it onstage.

Abrams, who is in his mid-fifties, got a precocious start in the music business, playing guitar in garage bands in the mid-1960s. He later managed bands and started his own record label while still in high school. Abrams would routinely survey fans as they came out of the shows he promoted, asking them about their musical tastes. Though still in his teens, he gleaned some extremely valuable business insight from the surveys.

"An amazing thing started to happen around '65 and '66," he recalls. "The Top 40 audience really started to fragment. In the early 1960s, a hit record kind of reached everybody. But now there was a real break, mainly among guys fifteen to twenty years old, just rejecting some of the mainstream stuff and really aligning themselves with the Yardbirds and the Byrds and the Animals and the Rolling Stones."[2]

By the time 1969 rolled around, the intricacies of the musical tastes of the Woodstock generation were hardly a mystery to Abrams. Fortunately for him, they were, by and large, to most of the established radio business.

In 1970, at age eighteen, he scored a job as music director at a Top 40 station in Miami; soon after, he took a job at a free-form underground rock station in Detroit, WRIF-FM. He found the Top 40 station too constraining and the free-form format too undisciplined and "bizarre." Some of the disc jockeys in Detroit, for example, had ties with underground organizations and spent their days talking about politics and revolution instead of what music they were going to play.

Convinced there was a market for a radio station somewhere in the middle, "for people who liked every fifth song on Top 40," Abrams axed some of the insurrectionist DJs and began crafting his own mix of music in Detroit and gained some real ratings success, especially among male teens. He tried pitching the format to other stations, but few showed much interest.

Around Labor Day of 1972, at the ripe old age of twenty, he decided to form his own consulting firm, recruiting a more established partner, Kent Burkhart, a former radio group head and AM radio consultant based in Atlanta.

Abrams considered himself something of an FM radio expert and suggested to Burkhart that together they'd have AM and FM covered. Thus Burkhart/Abrams Consulting was born.

Over the next two decades, the firm signed up more than one thousand clients, including radio stations and bands, and later expanded into product placement deals with advertisers such as Swatch. Along the way, Burkhart/Abrams invented a new industry.

Abrams's mission, he says, was never bland, repetitive programming. In the early days, he did plenty of research, but it was very unorthodox research that sought to get to the heart of the matter. The result was a very raggedy, eccentric version of today's focus groups. In addition to his concert exit polls, Abrams came up with the "callback card," a card that music fans would pick up at their neighborhood record store, fill out with their address and phone number, and drop in a box at the store. A few weeks later, Abrams would collect the boxes and call the customers back to find out which cuts off an album to play on the radio.

This in itself was a radical notion at the time. Record companies traditionally decided which tracks got designated as singles, the songs pitched to radio for their perceived hit value. In the post-Woodstock rock era, mining albums for hidden gems such as Fleetwood Mac's "The Chain" and Pink Floyd's "The Great Gig in the Sky" that were never issued as 45 rpm singles and playing them on radio helped enhance the careers of many big 1970s groups. The archetypal non-single that became hugely popular thanks to radio was "Stairway to Heaven" by Led Zeppelin. Abrams dubbed his new baby the Superstars format, though it later became known as AOR.

Perhaps Abrams's most memorable research strategy was the hitchhiking study. He would leave home in the morning and try to get picked up by as many cars as he could throughout the day. Once he had a ride, he would discuss with the driver his or her radio and music tastes. In the early 1970s, says Abrams, "almost 100 percent of the listeners who picked me up were the kind of listeners we'd target."

Abrams's grassroots research uncovered some fascinating stuff that would help shape his programming ideas going forward. He found that many of the tried-and-true practices of radio programming were despised by many listeners. For example, DJs in that era loved to "talk up" the record, keeping their patter going through the beginning bars of a song, only stopping a split second before the vocal came in. "But listeners hated that," says Abrams. "They'd tell me, 'I want that asshole to shut the fuck up.' "

Certainly his methods were highly unscientific. The sampling groups were very small, and he could never convince fellow employees to do the hitchhiking study. But the spirit of Abrams's methods began to influence his clients' stations rather dramatically. A series of Burkhart/Abrams talk-show-style bull sessions, at which a host would rev the audience up about certain music topics, helped spur the Disco Sucks movement on rock radio in the late 1970s. "We were always aware of disco and figured some people liked it and some people didn't," says Abrams. "But we found out, no, some people really hated disco and thought it was an attack on the culture."

Soon, rock stations Abrams worked with were taking an aggressively anti-disco stance on the radio. Some even held anti-disco rallies and destroyed disco records on the air.

As time went on, Abrams shaped some general concepts for Superstars stations. The goal was to be commercial without losing a progressive edge. DJs on Superstars stations talked about the records they were playing and hyped them with genuine excitement. More important, they never talked over the music. Stations promoted themselves with "image enhancers" such as "Two for Tuesday" promotions and midnight album hours, where full albums were played cut by cut. On Superstars stations, new music would be played more than once a day. And once favorite artists were identified, the stations would play lots of different songs by those artists, moving the focus away from individual songs to the artists themselves. It was almost like free-form radio, only a lot more profitable.

Next, Abrams applied this approach to different radio audiences. Out of that research came some of the best-known formats in today's radio. Soft rock. Classic rock. Adult contemporary. Smooth jazz. And over time, the playlists became as bland-sounding as the format names.

Competing research firms also sprouted up, though most employed more traditional research methods that Abrams avoided. Calling people at dinnertime to ask them what their favorite song was didn't cut it, as far as he was concerned, since his research showed that people needed to hear songs over and over before they really formed an opinion of them.

The creative programmers of the 1960s and '70s were slowly replaced by what Abrams calls "rocket science" programmers who programmed based on spreadsheets rather than what they had a feeling for. "We always believed in a balance of science and emotion," says Abrams. "Everything starts emotionally, and then you use the research to see if you're full of it or not." Great programmers, in his mind, had a creative batting average.

At its height, Burkhart/Abrams accounted for the programming choices on about one thousand stations across the country. Gradually, the proliferation of the more rigid formats began to take its toll on what was playing on the radio. Abrams theorizes that even some blockbuster groups of the early 1980s, such as the Police, who didn't become stars till their third album, would have found it difficult to break through on radio just a few years later. U2, perhaps the most successful rock group of the 1980s and '90s combined, actually had trouble getting on American radio for their first few albums, because, says Abrams, they didn't "test" well. "I actually remember asking one program director, 'Heard any good music this week?'" he recalls. "And he looked at a spreadsheet and said, 'No, there's nothing good this week.' What he was basically saying was,

'I haven't listened to anything, so I'll just go straight by what the re-search says.' " Radio companies were becoming more corporate, and rather than make arguments based on matters of taste, pro-grammers simply found it easier to justify their decisions with hard numbers.

By Abrams's standards, today's radio programmers are batting .000 since the rewards for making creative programming choices are considered nil. Most commercial stations these days measure their success primarily by advertising revenue, not listenership. That means there may be a big audience for a particular format of music, but if that format doesn't translate into ad dollars, it is at im-mediate risk. A good recent example of this phenomenon is the de-mise of one of the most popular and most beloved oldies stations in the country.[3] In June 2005, with no warning, New York City's WCBS-FM, for thirty years a refuge for legions of fans of 1950s doo-wop and other nostalgic fare, switched to a new format called Jack, a DJ-less mix of hits from the 1970s to the present.[4] When the station's general manager was asked to explain the switch, he re-sponded, "We did a lot of market research and found a hole in the market that wasn't being served by any other station." In July 2007, WCBS returned to the oldies format, presumably because of poor ratings.

The 2005 results of the "Power Ratio" survey, compiled by Miller, Kaplan, Arase & Co., a Hollywood-centric accounting firm, may shed a little light on the reasons why a station might drop a popular format.[5] The power-ratio formula attempts to show how different radio formats convert listeners into advertising revenue by taking the market revenue share of each format, the percentage of total radio revenue it garnered, and dividing it by the average quarter-hour audience share. The median power ratio is 1.0, and anything below that is regarded as underperforming. The 2005 power ratio for the oldies format was 0.97, a slight decline from a year earlier. The Jack format, in contrast, had a power ratio of 1.13; blander formats with shorter playlists like adult contemporary (1.44) and classic rock (1.50) score much higher, whereas more organic formats like gospel (0.55) and classical (0.58) fall way below the norm.

The idea that a radio group would make a drastic format change at a station after thirty or so years based on nothing more than a slight decline in a somewhat arbitrary financial ratio seems absurd. The reality is such data are often used to justify boneheaded management decisions that later prove to be ill conceived. With WCBS-FM, the changeover appeared to be a case of chasing after a younger demographic, though after the switch to the Jack format, the station's ratings plummeted drastically and never fully recovered.

In addition, the flaw in programming by such measurements, beyond the harsh reality of meting out culture by the dollar, is the way it reinforces the status quo while ignoring potential growth areas. For example, all Spanish-language and urban formats, except Regional Mexican, fall below 1.0, even though they represent some of the fastest-growing populations and economic bases in the country.

The proliferation of Abrams's approach to radio programming arguably spawned FM radio's growth in the late 1970s and the '80s. "It just got out of control," Abrams says. "What it needed then was actually 180 degrees from what is needed now—back then, it needed discipline, now it needs art."

Ed Levine felt the brunt of Burkhart/Abrams in the early 1980s with his earliest station in Utica, primarily because he swore off consultants as a policy. So Burkhart/Abrams went across town to his competitors and beat his ratings handily. Truth was, from a business standpoint, it was hard to resist the pack mentality that was sweeping radio nationally.

Levine remembers the moment in 1982 when one hundred of the big rock stations in the country got rid of all their Beatles and Phil Collins albums and began playing a "modal" format, meaning blocks of music communicating a similar speed and energy. That meant that glammed-out heavy-metal bands, so-called hair bands such as Twisted Sister and Quiet Riot, soon dominated the airwaves. "Suddenly everything was hard-driving, up-tempo," says Levine. DJs were called on less and less to rely on their own personal tastes. Modal formats were designed to please advertisers, not listeners. Radio programming was evolving from an art to a science.

Every industry has its consultants. In most cases, they serve their purpose as long as their recommendations are kept in perspective. But in the radio business, the effects tended to be swift and numbing. One consultant came up with the phrase "kick-ass rock and roll," and in a matter of months anywhere from twenty-five to fifty radio stations around America were touting "kick-ass rock and roll" on the air.

Nonetheless, Levine eventually made the numbers in Utica go up, thanks in part to a successful morning show. And in 1993, he found another investor with a failing FM station in Syracuse, and money to spend, allowing his tiny radio company to grow. Within a couple of years, Galaxy Communications, as the company became known, owned six stations in Utica and Syracuse. In 1995, Levine added two more stations in Syracuse, "and that's pretty much where we stayed for much of the '90s," he says. "We sat out the consolidation craze, unfortunately."

From 1996 to 2000, Galaxy purchased no new stations, in part because Levine's financial partner was loath to take on corporate debt. In 1999, Levine bought out his partner and found some new financial backers in Boston. But he never thought of the radio business as a commodity business. "We were in it to be legitimate broadcasters and to be there for the long term," Levine says. "I never aspired to own three hundred radio stations."

Levine also didn't intend to compete with a company that did. In February 1999, Clear Channel announced a station swap with Cox Radio, based in Atlanta, of stations in Louisville and Tampa for five Syracuse-area stations, WYYY-FM, WBBS-FM, WWHT-FM, WHEN-AM, and WSYR-AM. Virtually overnight, Clear Channel was a player in Syracuse.

When Clear Channel tried to add two more stations in Syracuse in 2001, Levine filed complaints with the FCC, both of which were summarily dismissed. Levine attributes Clear Channel's success to the acumen of Randy Michaels, who knew the market so well that he also knew how to work around the local limitations by buying WPHR-FM, which he claimed was going to be in Ithaca, New York, and WVOA-FM, a Hispanic-oriented station. The FCC accepted the explanations and okayed the purchases. "They're supposed to only own four FM stations," says Levine. "They own five 50,000-watt stations, which is a blatant violation of what the FCC intended the law to be."

Suddenly Levine was in a tough spot, since all of his FMs in Syracuse were 6,000-watt stations, "because that was all that was left" of the stations allotted to the city by the FCC when he was making his purchases.

Guessing that Clear Channel would move WVOA's headquarters from Ithaca to Syracuse (which it wasn't able to do) and then switch it to a rock format (which it eventually did), Levine tried to protect himself by filing to move one of his stations to a neighboring town where he would face a less competitive advertising environment. Thankfully, Clear Channel's station never got more than a 1.5 share of the radio audience due to its weak signal in Syracuse.

While Lee Abrams admits that Clear Channel was hardly alone in pushing for more uniform playlists, the company's size and worldview made it particularly susceptible to criticism. "The kind of radio they do I think created an opportunity for XM and other media to come in, because the focus is so advertising-driven and listeners are almost secondary," says Abrams.

But Abrams observes that with its bulk also came a historic opportunity for Clear Channel to take the medium to the next "freedom level, but they haven't," he says. "You'd think that they could be a little more adventurous and take the opportunity of their size to kind of rewrite the playbook for today. You look at the radio playbook, the way radio sounds, it hasn't been updated in thirty years."

Abrams is talking principally about the hokey kinds of promotions that still populate the airwaves, such as "Two for Tuesday" or "Block Party Weekends" or when a DJ heatedly announces that the "ninth caller to the station" wins a pair of concert tickets. "That was very clever at the beginning of the touch-tone phone era," he says, "but again, that was thirty years ago."

Today, listeners are motivated—and genuinely excited—by choice. Or at least the perception of choice. Satellite radio, iPods, Internet music sites—these kinds of listening options put the consumer in a position of increased control. Interactivity no longer refers to cheesy call-in contests (though maybe cheesy text-messaging contests via cell phones). It more often involves listeners exchanging their musical preferences in real time online. If those preferences happen to be as bland as the offerings of Top 40 radio, then so be it. But at least the option to broadcast more musically diverse programming exists, whereas before it simply did not.

8.

BILLBOARDS AND
BEYOND

Nearly everyone knows about the famous Burma-Shave signs
that populated the highways of America from 1925 to well
into the 1960s. At their peak, there were about seven thousand red
signs with white letters scattered across the country in sequential
groups of four, five, or six, with clever (or corny) verses. A typical
series read: "SHE EYED / HIS BEARD / AND SAID NO DICE / THE
WEDDING'S OFF / I'LL COOK THE RICE / BURMA-SHAVE."

Sitting in the conference room of his downtown Phoenix office
suite, Karl Eller recalls the impression those signs left on him as a
nine-year-old boy in the 1930s on the long drive from Chicago to
Tucson, where he and his family relocated shortly after his father
fled the family. "These were two-lane highways; and they were small
signs, they were in order, and they always had a rhyme to them,"
Eller says. "As a kid you're aware of everything. I'd see these darn
signs, and I kind of fell in love with the Burma-Shave signs. We
used to make up our own slogans."[1]

Eller—a fit-looking man in his late seventies with twinkling
blue eyes and a humble way of carrying himself, clad in dress slacks
and a striped oxford shirt—had no idea at the time that he would
later become one of the architects of the modern billboard industry. In 1997, he sold his billboard company, Eller Outdoor, for
$1.15 billion. Within four years, he had decided to leave Clear

Channel, realizing that Mark and Randall Mays and he would never see eye to eye. Today, his office suite is right across the hall from Clear Channel Outdoor, Clear Channel's billboard division, which is run by the staff he built from scratch. "I just moved over here," he says. "That was my baby," he adds, pointing across the hall.

Indeed, early in his career, there was little reason for Eller to strive to be a leader in the billboard industry. In those days, billboards weren't exactly a big deal. Prior to the 1880s, outdoor advertising had the highest revenues of any media.[2] But by the end of the nineteenth century, magazines had overtaken billboards. Billboards never really recovered, at least in terms of the popular perception. The outdoor advertising industry, as billboards became known, did well, but nobody outside the business cared. Eller's boyhood dream was to be a football coach. Later, he imagined a career in advertising but walked out of a job at J. Walter Thompson in Chicago after realizing he'd be slaving in the trenches for decades.

He got his first job in the billboard business in 1952 as a lease man in Tucson with Foster and Kleiser, the biggest outdoor firm in the West. Eller's job was to negotiate leases with landowners on which the company's signs would eventually stand. Turns out he had a knack for it. He switched to ad sales for Foster and Kleiser in Phoenix and later moved to California to work for the San Francisco–based company, both in its San Francisco and its Los Angeles offices.

Foster and Kleiser was bought by W. R. Grace in 1952, and in 1959 it was sold again, to John Kluge's Metromedia. In a fit of extreme confidence, Eller approached the billionaire Kluge, whom he describes in his memoir as "the Warren Buffett of media investors," and asked to be president of Foster and Kleiser.[3] Kluge said no but offered some encouraging words. Eller's bravado eventually paid off in 1962, when out of the blue Kluge called him up and offered to sell him his billboard plants in Phoenix and Tucson, as well as in Fresno and Bakersfield in California, for $5 million. All Eller had to do was come up with the money in ninety days. Thanks to some friends and family, he did, and Eller Outdoor Advertising was born.

Outdoor advertising shared some similarities with radio—it started out as a mom-and-pop industry run mostly by small local firms. Revenue was 70 percent local and 30 percent national. In the days before television, billboards were the only true national advertising medium, making them a natural buy for Wrigley's gum, Coca-Cola, Marlboro, General Tire, and Budweiser, among others.

Even after TV's rise, outdoor advertising maintained its reputation as the most affordable way to reach a mass audience. Today, the typical cost per one thousand viewers, otherwise known as CPM, is about $2 for billboards. In contrast, the CPM for drive-time radio is around $5; for magazines, $9; and for newspapers and prime-time television, $10 to $20.

It was profitable, too. Eller says he operated with 50 percent margins from the day he opened his doors. "The business is an occupancy business," he tells me. "If you run it at 100 percent occupancy, you make a fortune; if you run it at 80 percent occupancy, which is the average, you make 50 percent margin; if you operate at 50 percent occupancy, you probably make 20 percent margins."

Yet from the 1960s on, outdoor advertising didn't get much respect, due to its low glamour quotient. Unlike television, radio, and print, billboards had no content other than the message put forth by the advertiser. In the television age, oversize, hand-painted signs propped up over the highway seemed tragically quaint.

Still, Eller prospered, despite weathering some of the pitfalls that came with erecting huge signs with your name plastered on the bottom. When Lady Bird Johnson initiated the Highway Beautification Act of 1965, which limited billboards on federally funded highways, many in the business worried, but Eller held his ground. In fact, he bought a lot of billboard companies that wanted to cash out. While his children paid the price at school with jeers from classmates, their dad publicly fought the restrictions, and the soft-spoken but resolute businessman made a killing. The Highway Beautification Act actually made existing sites more valuable. "It ended up being a very good deal," says Eller.

While community leaders in Phoenix would complain about

billboards, nobody wanted to eliminate them, since they were an integral part of the local community. "People that couldn't afford to do other advertising could do billboards," Eller explains.

Even as an owner, Eller prided himself on contributing to the creative vision for various ad campaigns. His enthusiasm for media helped him build Combined Communications in the 1970s, which eventually included billboards, fourteen radio stations, seven television stations, and two newspapers. Eller says it was the world's first true media conglomerate. It was certainly the largest billboard operation in the United States.

Eller prides himself on having experimented with synergy decades before it became a buzzword in the late 1990s. "We tried that one time in 1968 when we first got into the radio and television business," he says. "It never worked."

A few years later he sold Combined to the Gannett newspaper company for $373 million plus $250 million in debt. The plan was for Eller to become Gannett's president, but a clash with the company's chairman, Al Neuharth, caused Eller to leave his post within six months. Under Gannett, the business went into a tailspin.

A call from a friend, the financier Herb Allen, in 1981 gave Eller a shot at the movie business as president of Columbia Pictures. Eller's mission was to expand Columbia's television portfolio; instead, he ended up helping sell Columbia to Coca-Cola in January 1982.

Soon Eller encountered an even bigger setback after becoming chairman and chief executive of Circle K convenience stores in 1983. For the first time, he was in a business he didn't really know, and the effect was disastrous. The original plan, formulated with his business partner at the time, Carl Lindner, was to bulk up on individual stores, improve operations, and then sell the company to one of the major oil companies. Most of the growth was enabled by junk bonds. Eller engineered a series of acquisitions and racked up $1 billion in debt. After five years, he couldn't find a buyer; inflated oil prices only worsened the situation.

In the billboard business, debt was not a big issue, because the number of sites is limited by law and therefore each one almost always increases in value. In seven years, Eller grew Circle K from eight hundred locations to five thousand, just in time for the recession of the late 1980s. In early 1990, Circle K filed for Chapter 11 bankruptcy. Eller, who had invested his own money in the company, was down $100 million. It was a devastating situation for the self-made mogul. Few businesspeople of any means recover from such blunders. Even in Phoenix, where Eller was regarded as a hometown hero, old acquaintances condemned him, refusing to look him in the eye.

Shareholders booed him at one meeting in 1990 after he was introduced as a director of Pinnacle West Capital Corporation, the parent company of Arizona Public Service, holding him responsible, rightly or wrongly, for the company's ill-fated forays into banking and real estate. One of his best friends stood up and made a speech saying he thought it would be better if Eller stepped down from the board. "Nobody told me they were going to do it," he says.

Eller stood up and made his own speech in his defense, and then left the room and headed upstairs to his office. Then the sixty-five-year-old man broke down in tears.

After some soul-searching, he did the only thing he could imagine: he decided to start over. In a miraculous rebirth, Eller dove back into billboards in 1992 by convincing Gannett to sell him a piece of his original business in the Phoenix area. He made the purchase with $20 million provided mostly by a local competitor, Arte Moreno, CEO and president of Outdoor Systems.

In his new life, Eller learned to appreciate the advantage he had over more corporate outdoor operators. He was an entrepreneur, and the billboard industry favored entrepreneurs. "You've got to know the best location—how to pick them, how to lease them—you have to be creative as hell," Eller says. There is an art to knowing which locations work best and knowing all the local zoning and regulations governing those locations. Ninety-five percent of billboard locations are leased from whoever owns the land, but the 5 percent that a billboard company owns itself are extremely profitable. As a result, says Eller, "you've got to know the community like the back of your hand."

Eller's reemergence also coincided with a revolution in the billboard business, mainly due to the introduction of computer-generated images on a weather-resistant vinyl. Until 1993, most billboards were painted by hand, and most outdoor companies employed fleets of painters. The cost reduction allowed by the new printing technology was dramatic and helped Eller build up the business faster than he had before. Soon Eller Media had amassed more than fifty thousand displays in fifteen major markets in eight states, including Los Angeles, Chicago, San Francisco, Dallas–Fort Worth, Atlanta, and San Antonio.[4] The company had revenues of $352 million in 1996 and was the second-largest billboard owner in the nation after Outdoor Systems.

Late that year, Eller made plans to take Eller Media public in a $220 million initial public offering. But other forces were at work: Hellman & Friedman Capital Partners in San Francisco controlled 73 percent of Eller Media after financing most of Eller's acquisition of Patrick Media Group in 1995. Eller Media had been performing so well in the previous eighteen months that Hellman & Friedman now wanted to cash out.

So just weeks before the scheduled IPO, the game plan changed.

Near the end of 1996, Lowry Mays paid a visit to Eller's office in Phoenix and made him a pitch in person. Clear Channel wanted to buy him out. Clear Channel owned radio stations in many of the same markets that Eller owned billboards, in places like Texas, California, the Midwest, the Southeast, and the Southwest.

The two entrepreneurs immediately hit it off. Eller admired Mays's plainspoken style, as well as his hands-off style of corporate governance. A few other large media conglomerates had also approached Eller, but he says he hadn't been familiar with Clear Channel until its offer came through. Still, he added, "I was sort of impressed."

Within three months the two men had a deal. On February 25, 1997, Clear Channel announced it had agreed to buy Eller Media for $750 million in cash and $400 million in stock.[5] At the time, Eller Media owned more than fifty thousand display faces, most of which were billboards, including, not incidentally, about twelve hundred of the nearly two thousand billboards in the San Antonio area. The company was only four years old.

According to the agreement, Clear Channel would take full possession of Eller's company; Eller would remain in place as the division's chairman and chief executive. He would keep his same staff and run things as he always had. Mays, who had no experience in outdoor advertising, trusted that Eller knew his own business. The billboard king retained all the freedom he enjoyed as an entrepreneur. The only differences were a lower risk profile and access to Clear Channel's deep coffers.

Whatever the mitigating factors, the deal fundamentally changed the composition of Clear Channel. Prior to acquiring Eller, Clear Channel had 70 percent of its holdings in radio and 30 percent in television. Afterward, the company was divided somewhat differently, with 55 percent in radio, 25 percent in outdoor advertising, and 20 percent in television.

It also spurred rapid consolidation in the outdoor advertising industry. A few months later the number-one player, Outdoor Systems, spent $1 billion to buy the number-three player, National Advertising Company, from 3M.[6]

There were early signs that the merger would not go smoothly. For one, Mays talked about synergy from their very first meeting. Eller says he was candid about his own failed experiences trying to cross-sell billboards with radio and television. But Mays had his mind made up, and Eller decided he wasn't about to try to change it.

Though Lowry made the deal, Eller reported to Mark Mays,

who had recently been made president of Clear Channel, and Randall Mays. His first impressions of the Mays boys were less than positive. Both struck him as arrogant and unreceptive to new ideas. No doubt the wide age difference between the older employee and his new bosses was a factor, but more grating to Eller was their lack of experience. Eller mostly recalls Mark Mays making swift decisions and then begging him for strategic advice.

To make things worse, both younger men often met Eller's proposals with skepticism. "It was hard selling those guys," he says. "Now they think outdoor is the greatest thing alive."

As part of Eller's arrangement with Clear Channel, he became a director and began attending all board meetings. But he soon realized he had made a big mistake. The first issue that came up was the company's name. The company began pushing to call it Clear Channel Outdoor. Eller, trying not to sound too egotistical, explained that his name had real credibility in the billboard business and he thought it brought real value to the product.

It didn't help that the roles of Mark and Randall had grown enormously shortly after Eller joined the company. Around that same time, the brothers also became board members.

Eller's earliest memories of Mark Mays were not strong ones, simply because Mark usually sat in the corner of the room during negotiations while his father did all the talking. When it came to doing due diligence, Mark usually asked a few questions, but rarely any of much significance. Randall struck Eller as far more outspoken—though he never got a strong sense of him as the financial whiz others had described. "We had some arguments," Eller admits.

Eller recalls Randall as the one who proposed acquiring SFX Entertainment, the patchwork company of all the top rock concert promoters created by Robert F. X. Sillerman. Mark gave Randall his unerring support.

Mark Mays also proved difficult to challenge. In one instance, the company had bought Universal Outdoor, and Mark claimed the newly acquired firm employed only two men and a truck to install rotating vinyl billboards, instead of a crane and a larger crew, at a substantial cost savings. Eller, though, with his fifty years' experience, knew that it was not a safe and reliable installation technique and said as much to Mark and Randall. But Mark called a meeting with Eller and his team anyway to discuss the implementation of the new process, which involved hoisting the gigantic ads up to the site with a pulley system. Eller's son, Scott, who was Eller Media's president, was so upset by the tenor of the debate that he walked out of the meeting.

The next morning Eller visited Mark Mays in his office, where the younger man asked him for some advice. Eller shook his head. "I'd told you fifteen times before you'd gotten to this meeting that what they're doing is bullshit," Eller responded. "You can't do it that way—it's not efficient and it's dangerous."

But Mays was determined to have it his way. "He just wouldn't listen," says Eller now. "That was just his personality."

To be fair, Eller's view of media consolidation seems a hair more disciplined and commonsensical than that of the average media mogul. As far as consolidation goes, he's all for it—just as long as each division is run separately. The norm for media consolidators is to merge and then scramble to cut costs and double up duties, particularly on the business end. "You've got to sell your own medium, you've got to fight for every dollar you can get, instead of trying to spread it out," he says. "Once you go into a situation where you try to package things up, all you do is lower the rates and lower the impact."

While Eller was at Clear Channel, he did help engineer one large deal, the October 2001 acquisition of the Ackerley Group, a Seattle-based outdoor advertising firm that also owned radio and TV stations, for around $500 million in stock.[7] The Ackerley deal paid off handsomely for Clear Channel Outdoor, but by then Eller had all but lost his enthusiasm for the new operation.

Karl Eller left Clear Channel on January 1, 2002, and started his own outdoor consulting firm, the Eller Company, whose main client is Coca-Cola. His former general counsel, Paul Meyer, became Clear Channel Outdoor's president and chief operating officer and carried on business in a largely uninterrupted manner.

On our second day together, Eller began by thrusting toward me the November 14, 2005, issue of the trade magazine *Advertising Age*. It was folded open to an interview with Mark Mays. Clear Channel had recently announced plans to sell off 10 percent of Clear Channel Outdoor to investors. Over time, Outdoor had become the company's most profitable division. As television and radio had suffered declines in advertising spending due to audience fragmentation—too many options with no mass favorites—good old-fashioned out-of-home advertising had gained a new luster. And Clear Channel Outdoor remained the market leader.

So in the name of raising some cash for the other foundering divisions, Clear Channel had begun slaughtering the fatted cow.

"Read the article," Eller says irritably. "It says it all. It says the opposite of what's really going on."

The article claimed that Lowry had long been the company's deal maker and Mark was the "strategy wonk," the one who knew how "to better grow the businesses organically."

"That's bullshit," sputters Eller. "The kids are the ones who brought in the entertainment business, brought in Chancellor." Now he was steaming. "If it was anybody else but those two kids, they'd be fired."

If there was one external figure who helped launch Clear Channel headlong and helpless—albeit unintentionally—into the mainstream media's fray, it was Michael Powell, a Republican member of the Federal Communications Commission who later became chairman. Appointed by President Clinton in November 1997 and elevated to chairman by President George W. Bush in January 2001, the son of the former secretary of state Colin Powell rocketed into the media deregulation debate at the very time when the opinions of a pro-capitalism regulator could have the most impact.

Given the power to regulate the whole of the nation's telecommunications sector at the unlikely age of thirty-eight, Powell quickly gained a reputation for unerring self-confidence and bipartisan appeal. A former army officer sidelined by a jeep accident, he left the military in 1988, attended law school at Georgetown University, and went on to carve one of the most stellar career arcs in communications policy history. In Howard Stern's final months on terrestrial radio, he relentlessly mocked Powell as having gotten his job through his father's connections.

Though well credentialed, Powell, prior to his FCC tenure, indeed had no media business experience. After law school he clerked for Harry Edwards, the chief judge of the U.S. Court of Appeals for the District of Columbia. He followed that with a stint at the prestigious D.C. law firm O'Melveny & Myers, where he represented Conoco Oil in dealings with the government. In late 1996, he joined the Department of Justice's antitrust division, ironically, where he worked as chief of staff for the assistant attorney general Joel Klein.

A mere two months later, Senator John McCain of Arizona, an old pal of Powell's father, put the younger Powell up as a candidate for a Republican post at the FCC. Swept in as one of four new commissioners, Powell spent his earliest days at the federal agency treading an uneventful path, characterizing himself as "moderate" rather than a "blind ideologue" to Republican Party views.[8]

His media mettle would almost immediately be tested when WorldCom and MCI Communications announced their historic merger just a few weeks prior to the start of his tenure. Asked at the time by a reporter for his reaction to what later became one of the most notorious cases of corporate fraud, Powell refused to comment specifically. He did acknowledge, however, his concern for rapid acceleration of telecommunications and media mergers since

1996: "The pace is scary."[9] On the other hand, he observed that deregulation required a complex understanding of the media landscape with a statement that became something of an omen: "I don't accept blindly the proposition that a consolidated company necessarily means you won't get more diverse programming."

As time went on, however, Powell's perspective shifted rather radically into the media-consolidation camp. By the time he became FCC chairman in 2001, he was billing himself as a self-styled technology czar.

A free-market libertarian, Powell was as good a messiah as Lowry Mays and the boys could have hoped for. The advent of the Internet, he argued, warranted an updating of media ownership rules. Telephone-era regulations were simply insufficient, in Powell's view, in the newly cluttered telecom marketplace.

In his first comments as chairman, Powell distinguished himself from his Democratic predecessors by questioning the commission's responsibility to bridge the digital divide, the much-talked-about notion that each new technological innovation further isolated the poorer segments of society if it was not evenly distributed in a democratic fashion. In one roundly criticized passage, Powell delivered a let-them-eat-cake rebuttal that signaled to media bigs that everything was going to be all right—for them. Instead of a digital divide, he said, "I think there is a Mercedes divide. I'd like to have mine."

The flip tone of the comment stung those who took radio's public mandate seriously, among others, including some members of Congress. But as far as the Telecommunications Act of 1996 went, Powell was a true believer. He stated that the competition that the act was intended to spur was in fact occurring but that it would take some time for it to reach its full potential.

The former FCC chairman Reed Hundt contends that, in the end, all Powell's talk about deregulation was just that—all talk. "He didn't really do anything significant in that respect," says Hundt. "He just used the word to make himself seem appealing to *The Wall Street Journal*. At the end of his four-year term, you'd have to say it was 99.9 percent about rhetoric."[10]

Yet Powell helped set the tone in a media business environment that increasingly favored mass over class, with less and less thought given to the quality of the content. The rapidly expanding Clear Channel was blissfully in tune with the times, simply by applying continued discipline to the business approach that had always served it well in the past.

9.

THE MERGERS
THAT TRANSFORMED
CLEAR CHANNEL

Jacor Broadcasting began innocently enough when Terry Jacobs, a veteran insurance actuary based in Cincinnati, bought three religious-themed daytime-only AM radio stations in 1981. Jacobs had worked for the American Financial Corporation for decades, but he knew he was never going to become chief executive of the family-controlled company. So he decided to start his own. He settled on radio, he says, because he had watched the dramatic growth of American Financial's stake in John Kluge's Metromedia (which owned radio stations).

Jacobs says he had absolutely no interest, or previous experience, in the industry to which he was about to devote all of his waking hours. But he certainly liked the cash-flow potential and the simplicity of the business. "You didn't have supplier problems, you didn't have major labor problems, there was no manufacturing process you had to learn, there were no major distribution issues," he says. "It was basically a people and cash business—I thought it would be an easy business to learn."[1]

With the ownership caps still in place, Jacobs's original plan was to trade smaller stations in smaller markets for bigger stations in bigger markets. The plan largely worked; and with Jacobs's financial acumen, Jacor became the first radio company in the country to hold an initial public offering, in the summer of 1982. At the time, the company had only six radio stations, in Ohio and West Virginia. Soon after, Jacor bought more stations with the more than $4 million it raised—stations in Jacksonville, Florida; Cleveland; Atlanta; and Cincinnati. Then came Tampa, Nashville, and Knoxville. In a few years, Jacor was the eighth-biggest radio broadcaster in the United States, larger than Clear Channel. Unlike Clear Channel, though, Jacor made its mark mostly with AM stations.

Jacobs recalls meeting Lowry Mays in the mid-1980s at a broadcasters' convention. The two former financial types hit it off immediately. Neither, after all, was one of the industry's countless radio geeks. They recognized each other as two genuine adults in an industry populated with overgrown adolescents.

But it was the acquisition of WLW-AM, a 50,000-watt clear channel in Cincinnati, as part of Jacor's acquisition of Republic Broadcasting in 1986 that would point the way to the future for the rapidly expanding operation. Republic was run by Bobby Lawrence, Dave Martin, and a former radio engineer and DJ named Randy Michaels, previously of Taft Broadcasting. Lawrence became Jacor's vice president of sales, and Michaels was named head of programming.

Randy Michaels quickly emerged as the salient force in the operation. Born Benjamin Homel, the rotund and puckish Michaels made his name as a wildly creative programmer with a lifelong affection for radio technology. When Jacobs first traveled with Michaels, he recalls Michaels sitting on the plane leisurely reading the *Broadcasting* magazine yearbook, essentially a telephone-book-sized reference guide to the year's mergers and acquisitions activity.

Michaels also proved one of the more controversial DJs of his era. Credited with helping invent the modern country radio format in the 1970s at WDAF in Kansas City, Missouri, with a faster-paced Top 40–ish style, he later became far better known for farting on the air, making antigay jokes, and describing women in vulgar ways.

In at least two incidents in the 1980s, he also became associated with alleged unethical work practices. In 1984, soon after

Michaels left Taft to work for Republic's WLW in Cincinnati, the program director at its competitor WKRC-AM, Michaels's former home base, discovered during a staff meeting that the room was bugged. Though nothing was ever proven, and Michaels later denied it, many suspected him as the culprit.

In September 1988, the parent company of a radio station in Jacksonville, Florida, WCRJ, filed a lawsuit against Jacor, owner of WQIK in Jacksonville, after one of its employees allegedly sent a fake confidential memo on station letterhead to WCRJ staffers outlining bogus station format changes and the firing of key talent. The case was later settled out of court. The suit accused both Jacor and Michaels, then the company's senior vice president of programming, of theft of trade secrets, stealing an intracompany document, and libel, for false statements about a format change.

Also around that time, Terry Jacobs recalls an incident at a management meeting at a Tampa conference center, where Michaels presided over a team of programmers making presentations about their stations. One station manager took the entirely unprecedented step of hiring totally nude strippers to strut through the meeting, much to the consternation of other hotel guests who witnessed the parade. Jacor and its guests were immediately asked to leave the premises. "That was at least the second occasion when I should have fired him," says Jacobs.

At a Radio & Records conference in 1990, Michaels—while discussing the importance of being outrageous on the air—ripped off the shirt of a woman planted in the audience. Ironically but perhaps not surprisingly, at the group's next gathering two years later, the main topic was sexual harassment.[2]

Then matters went from bad to worse. In February 1992, the ABC newsmagazine *20/20* aired a segment titled "What a Place to Work!" about the office environment at WFLA-AM and WFLZ-FM in Tampa. The damaging report detailed a variety of sexual harassment complaints and civil suits filed against Jacor and Randy Michaels by the former WFLA talk-show host Liz Richards.

One former WFLZ music director described Michaels walking up and down the office hallway with a long rubber penis wrapped around his neck as he salaciously greeted female staff members. The *20/20* story also broadcast audio of Michaels on the air describing "nubile, incredibly horny, wet and ready" women. Another female employee alleged Michaels mooned her twice in the office, pressing his rear end against a glass partition.[3] Richards testified that she was the victim of numerous unwanted sexual comments.

Richards later dropped the charges, many of which Michaels nonetheless publicly acknowledged in an industry journal. "People have different senses of humor," he said, attempting to explain his actions. "The radio business isn't IBM, and it's not an insurance company. The audience has to think we're having fun."[4]

Still, there were real financial consequences. On the Monday after the *20/20* report ran, Jacor's stock dropped three points. The lawsuit, later settled out of court, was a huge cash drain and created a terrible image problem for Jacor that eventually affected the company's profile on Wall Street. Jacor's board of directors pushed Jacobs to fire Michaels after the fallout, but he refused. "Randy was brilliant," Jacobs says, "and I always thought his brilliance would overcome the difficulties. And I think from a financial standpoint, it did. Because of the good things he was able to create for us in our markets and our stations. The financial performance was always much stronger than if we had not had him."

Ironically, in 1993, Michaels oversaw an on-air tirade against Clear Channel as the executive in charge of "The Power Pig," an outrageous Jacor-owned Top 40 station in Tampa. When Clear Channel purchased its fierce rival Q105, the Pig attacked, lampooning Lowry Mays with prerecorded comedy routines that referred to him as "Lowry Mayonnaise" and "Low Rent Mayonnaise." Mays was portrayed as a philandering "evil Texas banker" who ordered a black disc jockey to wax his Cadillac and fanatically "cut costs" at the station.[5]

On the more bankable end of his abilities, Michaels reportedly

helped save big AM stations like WLW by beefing up news operations. He was one of the few senior executives in radio who had
come out of programming and thus was more comfortable with
content-based growth strategies. "He was one of the only operators
out there who believed that news was a value," says Robert Unmacht. "He knew the value of programming as opposed to just cost-
cutting."[6] Colleagues marveled at how Michaels could visit any
market in the country, listen to the stations, and predict which ones
would be successful and which ones wouldn't be. He could also rat-
tle off what the unsuccessful ones needed to do to be successful.

Still, Michaels's strengths were as an engineer, not as a dyed-in-
the-wool programmer. "Musically, I think he relied on other people," says Lee Abrams. "I didn't see him as a real music kind of
guy."[7]

Solely from a station's call letters, Michaels would recite from
memory where it was located, what format it was in, who owned it,
what the tower height was, what the power of the radio station was,
and when it was put on the air. "I once asked him, 'How do you
know all this?' " says George Sosson. "And he said, 'When kids
grew up with baseball knowing Mickey Mantle's batting average, I
knew radio stations.' "

Prior to an acquisition, he would arrange a set of radios programmed to every frequency in the relevant market, listen to each
one, and explain to his fellow Jacor executives what their strengths
and their deficiencies were. If Jacor was buying a troubled station,
Michaels would recommend the best format change for success
based on audience share—and usually made the right decision.
"Randy Michaels was the smartest guy in the radio business—
probably still is," Jacobs says, adding that pairing Michaels, a programming whiz, with Lawrence, a radio-sales expert, was a terrific
combination.

Using a software program called RadioSoft, which plots radio
signals nationally, Michaels mapped out his dream radio empire
with a skill equaled by few. "He'd use it like three-dimensional
chess," says Unmacht. "He'd think twenty or thirty moves out."

At the same time, he fostered a frat-house-style office environment everywhere he went. "I liked to say he was a forty-year-old eighteen-year-old," says Jacobs, "and now he's probably a fifty-five-year-old eighteen-year-old."

Within the industry, Michaels earned a reputation as an amiable blowhard always eager for attention. At one industry gathering, he showed up in shorts and sprayed water on the audience; at another, he made his entrance on a throne carried by six well-endowed women. Comparing Michaels with the culture at Clear Channel, Stan Webb says, "We were at absolute opposite ends of the spectrum."

Unlike Clear Channel, Jacor in the late 1980s staggered under extreme debt. By 1990, its shares were trading for seventy-five cents as it grappled with bankruptcy.[8] "The thing about the Mayses that was amazing to me," says Jacobs, "was that they were always very conservative and had a strong balance sheet, and when everybody else got into trouble and had to start selling stations or had debt problems, Lowry was able to make some fantastic acquisitions because he could finance it and nobody else could."

Then, only a year after the *20/20* imbroglio, Michaels engineered something of a coup. He recruited the mercurial Chicago mogul Sam Zell to infuse Jacor with $70 million. Zell, a so-called vulture investor and erstwhile motorcyclist with his own club known as Zell's Angels, specialized in purchasing troubled companies.

Jacobs, uninterested in working for someone else again, decided to bow out. So Randy Michaels was left minding the shop, ultimately becoming the company's chief executive.

Under Michaels, Jacor radically transformed itself from a relatively staid, sales-oriented operation in the Clear Channel mold into an aggressive programming-driven beast. Michaels had little interest in ad sales, priding himself instead on what he believed was his ability to discern the needs of radio audiences.

The first big opportunity for Jacor was the Telecommunications Act of 1992, which allowed radio companies to own up to thirty AM and thirty FM stations nationwide. The previous limit was twelve of each.

More important, the 1992 act allowed duopolies, meaning all of a sudden radio companies could own two stations in one market. The FCC formerly allowed only one AM and one FM per market. Cincinnati became duopolized more rapidly and heavily than most. In June 1993, Jacor bought top-rated WLW's main competitor, the local news-talk station WKRC-AM. It later roped in WIMJ-FM.

In August 1994, Chancellor (later to become AMFM) out of Dallas bought two Cincinnati FM stations and an AM. Citicasters, a local Jacor rival, grabbed a second FM. A local lawyer also picked up two AMs and an FM around that time.

The cumulative effect was astounding. By 1995, thanks to the duopoly rule, most of Cincinnati's radio business had been consolidated into the hands of just a few owners. Jacor cleaned up with 44.3 percent of radio ad revenues, as well as an additional 5.6 percent due to advertising it sold for stations owned by another company. Chancellor had 15 percent; and Citicasters garnered another 12.6 percent.[9]

"We're big. We're bad. We're back. We're rich," Randy Michaels famously boasted to Cincinnati's *Enquirer* in 1994. Station owners, Jacor included, began mining the benefits of duopoly in other ways, by slashing jobs and by various other cost-cutting measures. Soon radio companies were moving multiple stations into the same building, sharing office supplies and often employees.

Soon, Michaels began developing a hub-and-spoke operating system similar to the one used by the airline industry. In the wake of the Telecom Act of 1996, Jacor bulked up from 26 stations in 1995 to 149 stations in June 1997. In typical fashion, Michaels ruled over the proceedings with an equal mix of technical expertise and bravado.

When Jacor hoovered up the ten-station Noble Broadcast Group in July 1996 for $152 million, Michaels showed up at KOA in Denver, where the engineer had an old transmitter. The engineer told him, "Great, you're a radio guy—now we can replace this old thing." Michaels responded jovially, "Replace it? We're going to re-build it. I've got the parts at home!"[10]

A key post-1996 megadeal for Jacor was the acquisition of Citi-casters for $770 million. Indeed, the purchase stirred enough dust to pique the interest of the Justice Department, which for the first time began investigating the possibility of antitrust activities in radio. Jacor emerged relatively unscathed this time, ending the investigation by selling just one station, WKRQ-FM, cutting the company's revenue slice by just a few percentage points.

All the while, Randy Michaels maintained that Jacor's advertis-ing revenue increases were due mainly to formatting changes he had implemented, such as creating a nostalgia format for listeners over fifty, which in turn attracted new advertisers wanting to sell to those listeners. In addition, he and other radio executives argued that the Justice Department's main concern—that companies like Jacor could raise advertising prices indiscriminately—was entirely unfounded, primarily because advertisers could always bolt for other media such as newspapers, television, or billboards. "Justice is concerned about nothing," Michaels protested. "I can't mention a single advertiser who didn't have options. Indeed, we couldn't name one advertiser who uses radio exclusively." By the end of 1996, Jacor owned about 130 radio stations in twenty-seven markets.

Next, Michaels went shopping for content. In March 1997, he ac-quired EFM Media Management, the program syndicator that employed the alarmingly popular conservative commentator Rush Limbaugh for $50 million. On the same day in April, Jacor an-nounced it would pay $165 million for Premiere Radio Networks, another program syndicator, and $11 million for NSN Network Ser-vices, a company that manufactured two-way satellite and Internet audio transmission technology for the radio industry.[11]

Within a matter of weeks, Rush Limbaugh's provocative talk show was beaming out to more than six hundred stations around the country. And with the addition of Premiere, suddenly a host of radio personalities, including Dr. Laura Schlessinger, Michael Reagan, Casey Kasem, and Leeza Gibbons, were all under one roof at Jacor.

In the fall of 1997, Jacor announced its plan to buy seventeen stations owned by Nationwide Communications, a division of the Nationwide Mutual Insurance Company of Columbus, Ohio, for $620 million. The Nationwide deal launched the company into five new markets, Dallas, Houston, Minneapolis, Phoenix, and Baltimore, while strengthening three of its existing markets, San Diego, Cleveland, and Columbus.[12]

Michaels's hub-and-spoke idea was to develop programming in local markets that could then be syndicated and marketed to nearby metropolitan areas. The result was programming with costs that could be distributed over a series of small stations, which then could sell advertising for a larger combined audience. These small networks would ideally deliver an audience similar in size to that of a large local newspaper or television station, but at a substantially lower cost to advertisers.

"He believed that you could have a quality product and do the things that Wall Street wants," says Robert Unmacht. "He actually built a company that was a pretty good radio company in addition to being an economic force."

From a business standpoint, the strategy smacked of brilliance, if only for the fact that it perfectly exploited the new universe created by deregulation. It linked a farm system for talent with a cost-saving distribution structure. For numbers guys like Mark and Randall Mays, Michaels's big-picture thinking no doubt held unparalleled appeal.

As the industry began to consolidate, content—never Clear Channel's strong suit—was going to become important. "I think one of the reasons they looked toward Randy Michaels and Jacor was they saw someone who was assembling the soft goods—Premiere Networks and Rush Limbaugh and the other things Randy was assembling," says Unmacht. "They must have thought, we've got this great asset base and they've got the content, it should be a great fit."

Executives at Clear Channel can recall when rumors started circulating that Sam Zell wanted to cash out of Jacor.[13] Mel Karmazin's Infinity and Clear Channel were reportedly the two main suitors. Then, in May 1999, the deal was struck. "I'll never forget the phone call," says George Sosson. "Mark Mays called me and told me that they had bought Jacor."

Sosson's immediate response to Mays was that his days at the company were probably numbered. Everybody in radio knew about Randy Michaels and what a character he was. He was known and feared as a man who would do anything, absolutely anything, to get ahead. There were rumors that when visiting stations doing music tests, he would go through the trash of that station and look for discarded results he could pore over for missed data trends.

But Mark reassured Sosson, promising him he would retain his autonomy. Yet the Mays family offered few details, even to longtime executives, as to how the corporate structure would shake out. When Mark Mays announced that Randy Michaels would head the combined radio divisions, it was obvious to Clear Channel's top brass that the world as they knew it was about to change for good.

When the Clear Channel–Jacor deal was announced in October 1998, it stunned the radio industry. The price, $3.4 billion in stock and $1.2 billion in debt, in itself was an incomprehensible wonder. Still, with the price at about fourteen times cash flow, it was dramatically lower than the twenty-times multiples that radio stocks had seen that past summer.

As the rumors had grown, people had begun assuming that Jacor would hold an auction and that Clear Channel would stay out of the way, given Lowry's dislike of auctions.[14] Most industry watchers had predicted that if any company were to snare Jacor it would be Karmazin's CBS. CBS would most likely have paid in cash, but Zell agreed to settle for Clear Channel's stock deal instead. Zell and Jacor's other shareholders would end up owning about 25 percent of the new company.[15]

Then again, it was the season for big shocks in the radio business. In August 1998, Chancellor Media acquired Capstar Broadcasting in a then-record stock-for-stock deal worth around $4.1 billion.[16] The new entity consisted of 463 stations in 105 markets, creating the largest radio company in the country in terms of revenue, cash flow, number of stations, and listenership. Overnight, it seemed, CBS Radio, the urbane industry leader for decades and drenched in radio history, had been knocked from its perch by, ironically, a bunch of upstart Texans, namely Tom Hicks, chairman and chief executive of the Dallas investment firm Hicks, Muse, Tate & Furst; and his younger brother, Steve Hicks, who headed Chancellor and, later, the resulting company, AMFM.

Michaels was characteristically cocky from the moment the Clear Channel–Jacor deal was announced. "It doesn't feel much like a takeover to us," he told one reporter. "We rather actively sought this merger out. We're very enthusiastic about it. It feels like a partnership."[17]

Once the initial shock subsided, most radio folk marveled at the brilliance of the merger. In many ways, the idiosyncratic Clear Channel was a much better fit for the go-its-own-way Jacor than CBS, which was much more of a pure bottom-line operator. Then there was the realization that the two companies' growing empires hardly even overlapped. The resulting company would cover about seventy of the top one hundred markets in the country with a few problem areas, such as Houston, where Clear Channel already owned seven stations and Jacor owned three (Heftel, a Spanish-language radio company of which Clear Channel owned 26 percent, owned another six). Cleveland, Tampa–St. Petersburg, Jacksonville, and Louisville also posed some regulatory problems.

Then there was the happy notion of vertical integration, thanks to Randy Michaels's acquisition of Premiere Radio Networks, by then the third-largest provider of syndicated radio programming in the country, and Clear Channel's recent acquisition of Eller Media.

Analysts noted approvingly that 40 percent of Jacor's revenues came from markets in which its new parent had large numbers of billboards.

Radio media buyers, however, hated the deal—or rather they feared it. The theory was that the combined behemoth would erode the agencies' ability to negotiate affordable rates for their clients. Ad rates would skyrocket, and Clear Channel's aggressive sales force would go after advertisers directly on a national scale.

Though Mark and Randall were the deal's biggest boosters, even they had some reservations. Shortly after the Jacor purchase was initiated, Terry Jacobs recalls getting a call from Lowry Mays, who invited him down to San Antonio for an information session. Over dinner, the three Clear Channel leaders grilled Jacobs about the personalities of Jacor's top brass. "They knew of Randy's reputation, they knew of Bobby's reputation, they knew of Jacor's reputation at the time," says Jacobs. "But it was an acquisition that they were very excited about." The Mayses were primarily concerned with how they could manage the personalities involved and motivate them to do what they wanted them to do.

Randall Mays, in particular, adored Michaels and his shtick. "They really were kindred souls," says Gary Stevens. "He liked that act; he bought it all the way."

Jacobs told them that Michaels and Lawrence together made a great team, as long as Randy was kept in check. He also had high praise for Jacor's chief financial officer, Chris Weber, whom he described as a prudent financial manager and as the glue that held the operation together. Unfortunately, Weber refused to move to San Antonio (though, ironically, so did Michaels and Lawrence) and shortly left the company.

Many in the industry were amazed that Clear Channel had bought out Jacor, rather than the other way around. "I think people were surprised that Sam Zell wouldn't be the consolidator," says Terry Jacobs. "The speculation was that he would provide the wherewithal to Jacor to be the survivor and the acquirer." But Zell clearly saw an opportunity to sell high and take his money off the table. The sharp billionaire, having bought at one of radio's lowest ebbs, saw an opportunity to exit at its top.

Within the radio industry, the rise of Michaels within Clear Channel was something of a puzzle. "Everybody assumed that was just part of the deal," says Interep's Ralph Guild. "He was just not part of their culture at all."[18] But Michaels's Jacor team emerged clearly in charge of the radio division. Longtime Michaels cohorts, notably Marc Chase—a former DJ and program director at Jacor's notorious Power Pig—thickly spread Jacor's bad-boy ethos over the relatively staid Clear Channel framework. Some Clear Channel execs from the time pinpointed Jacor transplants like Chase—who eventually became a regional vice president of programming—as particularly harsh reminders of the crudeness and cruel culture that came to hold the power.

It didn't take a rocket scientist to guess the partnership would create heat, though. "I thought putting the Mayses and Randy together was going to be unbelievably weird and volatile," says Dave Allan, who worked for Clear Channel in Philadelphia.[19]

In direct opposition to Clear Channel's decentralized management model, Michaels demanded that all programming decisions funnel through him. Rather than relocating to San Antonio, he remained ensconced at Jacor's Covington, Kentucky, headquarters, in the Cincinnati area, and demanded that all senior Clear Channel executives fly to him for regular meetings. He also quickly implemented the principles of what Stan Webb liked to call "seagull management." He explains: "Randy's programmers would swoop in and shit all over everything and then swoop out."

Indeed, the first power Clear Channel's local general managers lost under Michaels's control was the right to program their stations in the best way they saw fit. Programming consultants, previously considered an unnecessary expense by Clear Channel, became the norm under Michaels. "Randy has one of the largest egos ever," says Jim Smith. "And Randy thought nobody could program like he could."[20] Even while running Jacor, Michaels had begun implementing technology that would allow him to program all of the company's stations from his Cincinnati perch. By the time Clear Channel made its purchase, Michaels's automated system was nearly in place.

Though Clear Channel had purchased Jacor, Michaels made it clear who was running the show. "Randy was a control freak," says Robert Unmacht. "The Clear Channel guys were financial control freaks, and Randy was a radio-content control freak."

Once in charge, Michaels forced Clear Channel's top managers to submit to a weekly ritual humiliation. "All the senior vice presidents would have to fly to Cincinnati on Mondays to have lunch," says Webb. "It was just lunch, which was an hour's worth of Randy sharing his philosophy and view of life."

Michaels then would encourage the men (as a matter of course, the group was all men) to stay in town for a big dinner and cigars. Mostly, though, the San Antonio–based execs would rush to catch a 2:30 flight home in hopes of getting some work done for the day.

Those who valued their independence at Clear Channel soon vowed their days there were numbered. Stripped of their authority and creative power, they got the message as to where the power in the organization now lay. As Webb puts it, "It was all focused in that one office."

"When Randall and Mark, who have never worked at a radio station in their life but who are brilliant businessmen who were sent to the best schools in the country, saw the opportunity presented by all of these lines going to all of these stations, the dollar signs just started to flash in their eyes," says Jim Smith. "Unfortunately—and I've got to be careful here because if it got quoted they'd probably send a hit man for me—their lack of knowledge of how important localism is caused them, I think, to make not a great decision in their investing of all of this money. And the ratings of the stations start down, and the revenue starts down because of the lack of ratings, and then they start cost-cutting because the revenues are starting down so they have to really cost-cut and they cut out more personnel. You see how it can just start snowballing."

Smith recalls a showdown with Michaels over the stations

Smith commanded in Tulsa. Clear Channel's rock stations kept two Tulsa-area artists who made it big, Leon Russell and J. J. Cale (writer of the Eric Clapton hit "Cocaine"), in regular rotation long after both musicians had generated their biggest hits.

Russell, a long-haired hippie eccentric who penned 1970s FM radio staples such as "This Masquerade" and "Delta Lady," recorded many of his early albums in a converted church in downtown Tulsa. "Leon Russell is part of the integral fabric of Tulsa," says Smith, "as is J. J. Cale." Russell still tests well on Tulsa stations to this day.

But when Jacor took charge, the programming structure immediately changed. Formerly independent program directors now reported to a regional program director who in turn reported to Randy Michaels. Soon after the merger, the regional programming director stormed into KMOD in Tulsa and demanded to know why there were five Leon Russell tracks in heavy rotation. The local programmer explained that it was still the highest-testing music in the area because Russell was from Tulsa. "I don't give a shit where he's from," responded the regional manager. "Get that crap off this radio station."

Smith, who oversaw KMOD, among other stations, called Randy Michaels and related what had happened. Michaels told Smith, "Listen, until you get that shit off that station, we can't get it to where it needs to be. You have to trust us, we know what we're doing." Today, after a decade as the market's number-one station, KMOD is consistently rated fifth.

Michaels instead pushed to use more voice tracking, a technological concept in play since the McLendon days that allowed programmers to pipe the same content into multiple markets with a single DJ who would drop a few regional references to give the impression he or she was broadcasting locally.

Some say increased voice tracking was an industry-wide trend that Michaels used on a larger scale out of necessity due to Clear Channel's rapid expansion. "It was not something, from my conversations with him, that he did because he thought it was better," says

Robert Unmacht. "It was his desire to try to keep programming up to as high a level as could be done and still meet the demands that Wall Street and others were putting on the broadcast groups."

While at Clear Channel, Michaels bought a company called Prophet Systems that made voice tracking easier and more user-friendly, theoretically enabling more creativity. Still, he was not totally won over by the notion of voice tracking, according to Unmacht: "It was his attempt to mitigate it as much as possible by doing the next best thing."

Michaels's taste ran toward male-oriented formats. He didn't like adult contemporary, smooth jazz, and other formats geared toward female listeners. As a result, many Clear Channel stations shifted to a classic-rock format, as long as research backed up the move. Michaels also believed in developing recognizable radio brands such as KISS, for Top 40 radio stations, and the Beat, for dance hits, around the country in the coming years.

Next came an overhaul of the company's sales strategy, a process particularly galling to the sales pros who had helped found the company. After all, they regarded Michaels as an unreconstructed novice in the area of advertising. "All that the senior vice presidents were really going to be," says Webb, "were conduits for massive amounts of data, and not so much seasoned managers of people."

While the future of Clear Channel was at stake, the issues being wrestled over were classically American ones and had universal repercussions. Had American culture been homogenized to such an extreme that regional tastes in music, talk radio, sports coverage, and news could be satisfied with a nationally calibrated McDonald's-like menu? Or did localism still matter? Was the Deep South different from the Midwest? Were urban stations in Chicago any different from urban stations in New York and Los Angeles?

While the answers to many of these questions could be endlessly debated, particularly from a cost-structure perspective, the response from the hard-nosed, budget-minded Clear Channel old-timers was surprisingly passionate and united. "Barbecue in

Texas is beef and sausage; barbecue in Memphis is pork and ribs,"
says Webb. "And you know what? I like both, but they're both really different." Webb and the other senior vice presidents felt that
radio should offer a similarly diverse menu, not necessarily for cultural variety but for bedrock financial reasons.

Shortly before he left the company, Webb was approached by
Mark Mays to be the company's "synergy manager." Webb's response was measured but not altogether positive. He told Mays how
unlikely it was that he would be able to get the head of Clear Channel's outdoor division to work with Randy Michaels at the radio
division to sell joint advertising. "Ain't going to happen," he explained to Mays. Webb knew that Mark had never been out on the
street making a sales call in his life.

Mays also appeared to have no idea what hurdles lay in front of
the ad reps who would have to do so. For one, each medium had its
own media buyers. Budweiser, for example, had one person buying
its outdoor advertising in Phoenix and another buying its radio advertising. Webb argued that if he approached Budweiser trying to
sell it radio, television, and outdoor as a package, the company
would say it was already buying all three and what could Clear
Channel offer in addition? The only possible answer seemed to be a
volume discount.

And why, Webb wondered aloud to Mays, did Clear Channel
want to discount its products? "There just wasn't an advantage and
there isn't an advantage," says Webb. "Wall Street hated it, everybody hated it—except Mark."

Few top Clear Channel executives at the time disputed the fact
that the Jacor deal was Mark Mays's baby. The theories about why
Mark was so enthusiastic about the union, however, varied. Some
suggested that he and Randall, with their gold-plated upbringings
and Ivy League educations, didn't like the idea of running a company known, even in passing, as Cheap Channel. By that mark, the
Jacor merger was an opportunity to change the culture of the company from within, somehow making it more impressive-seeming,
white-collar, and, well, corporate, which presumably meant consol-

idating the content end of the business and creating a more hierar-chical management structure.

Another theory was that Mark understood that drastic change was the key to the media business's future. "Mark was very enam-ored with every next new thing that he bought," says George Sos-son. "He loved change—he even had a general managers' meeting one year where the whole theme was how to adapt to change." The question was whether it was change for the sake of change alone that he was embracing.

A third possible motivation was that Mark instinctively knew that Randy Michaels would be a much different kind of manager from the kind he was. If this theory was correct, the implication was that everything the Mayses had heard about Michaels attracted them rather than repelled them from Jacor. Emboldened by the tête-à-tête, Mark would have emerged confident that, as long as he could keep the wild side of Michaels in check, he'd have a real radio innovator on his staff to catapult Clear Channel to the next level.

"Where I saw it really, really change with Clear Channel," says Galaxy's Ed Levine, "was when they bought Jacor. That's when it went from this little, sleepy, gentlemanly Texas company to all of a sudden this snarling, nasty saber-toothed tiger." While the average radio listener probably noticed little change in the wake of Clear Channel's acquisition of Jacor, small-time radio owners like Levine felt the heat almost immediately. "Clear Channel bought Jacor, but Jacor took over the company. The key players were all Jacor guys. And they didn't want to just go in and compete, they didn't want to go in and win—they wanted to go in and destroy you."

George Sosson, who still worked for Clear Channel at the time, agrees. "The most accurate quote I can give you is, when we bought Jacor it was as if Jacor bought us," he says. "It was absolutely bizarre."

Even Bob Turner at Interep, who had such a warm relationship with the Mays family, saw a shift in the way the company began to do business post-Jacor. Prior to the deal, all new stations that Clear Channel bought were directed to Turner and Interep for their national ad buys. Because the Jacor deal was so large, suddenly Turner wasn't automatically getting the new business. "Before we got to a new contract to figure out the Jacor issue," he recalls, "they bought AMFM, which was even bigger than Jacor."

AMFM owned Katz Media, Interep's main competitor, which snuffed out any chances for a new negotiation. Turner was lured to work for Clear Channel's Katz for a brief period, bringing much of his Interep staff with him. But within months, he regretted the decision and returned to Interep.

At the end of 1998, Clear Channel announced plans for a brand-new world headquarters in the Alamo Heights area of San Antonio to be designed by the Overland Partners architecture firm. The edifice would be a stunning glass and limestone creation overlooking the Quarry Golf Club.

In retrospect, many observers wondered what possessed Mark and Randall to become so enthralled with the "genius" of Randy Michaels, considering the potential pitfalls of the partnership. "Mark and Randall, in particular, were raised to be real thoroughbreds," says Jim Smith. "And I believe that their early experience in the company and their exposure to people referring to the company as Cheap Channel and such detracted from what they considered to be the thoroughbred type of company that they wanted to run." Starting with the Jacor deal, the younger Mays generation saw an opportunity to adopt a different corporate culture.

"Randy Michaels is as likable a guy as I have ever been around," adds Smith. "If I were going to dinner, if I wanted to laugh, if I wanted to talk radio, there is no one on this planet that I would rather be with than Randy Michaels. But he was so driven by technological advance—and in his mind, he was the greatest programmer alive. And until every radio station in the country was playing what he thought they should be playing, they weren't going to be as good as they could be."

10.

THE WORLD'S BIGGEST RADIO COMPANY

By the time 1999 rolled around, Tom Hicks, nearly a decade younger than Lowry Mays, had earned a reputation as the second-biggest radio man in Texas. It didn't hurt that he was known as the man who made George W. Bush rich when he bought the Texas Rangers from an investment group that included the soon-to-be governor, boosting Bush's heavily leveraged $600,000 investment to $14 million practically overnight. Though his main avocation was running one of the most voracious leveraged-buyout firms in the country, Hicks, Muse, Tate & Furst, out of his Dallas office, Hicks in some ways was far more steeped in the culture of the radio industry than his business-minded San Antonio counterpart.

Born into relatively modest means, Hicks got his start in radio while still in junior high school. His father, John Hicks, was an advertising salesman for Dallas TV and radio stations who, at age forty-two, purchased a radio station in Port Arthur, Texas, with $115,000 borrowed from friends. The family moved to Port Arthur in the late 1950s, and at thirteen years of age Tom Hicks began working at his father's station, KOLE, behind the scenes. Two years later he was working at the station as a DJ, "Steve King, the Weekend Wonder Boy," earning $20 per week.[1] He briefly attended high school in Port Arthur with the iconic 1960s rock singer Janis Joplin, who was a couple of years his senior.

As Hicks got older, his father bought more small stations, mostly in Texas. But rather than going into business with his father, Hicks, armed with an MBA from the University of Southern California, headed to New York, where he worked in venture capital for J. P. Morgan.

Hicks eventually returned to Dallas and started his own LBO firm with a partner. When his dad announced his retirement, Tom and his younger brother, Steve, pulled a leveraged-buyout deal, reaping three of the older Hicks's stations for $3 million, along with one extra, in Denton, Texas, for $3.3 million. Steve Hicks ran the radio business while Tom kept mostly to LBOs.

Together, in the late 1980s, they cooked up a strategy for radio that stole a page from Tom's prior consolidation of Dr Pepper and Seven Up into Dr Pepper/Seven Up Inc. (sold to Cadbury Schweppes in 1995 for $2.5 billion), leaning heavily on local marketing agreements (LMAs) that allowed them to sell advertising on stations they didn't own. Soon, the Hicks brothers were managing multiple stations in various markets without violating FCC rules that prevented owning more than one AM and one FM in a market.

Like Lowry Mays at Clear Channel, the Hicks brothers saw an opportunity—and smelled deregulation coming. In 1994, Hicks, Muse, their LBO firm, began building Chancellor Media with $48 million in seed money. Unlike Mays, the Hickses didn't always buy low, but they bought smart, knowing that the cost-cutting allowed by the company's growing size would more than make up for the early outlay. They also bought Katz Media, at the time radio's largest advertising representation firm, for $375 million in October 1997.

Tom and Steve Hicks simultaneously grew Capstar Broadcasting, also owned by them, which consisted of small- and middle-market stations. Altogether, the two companies, run separately due to their unique origins but managed together, consisted of three hundred stations in seventy-seven markets—better yet, they had been acquired with nearly 75 percent borrowed money.

In a matter of months, the radio landscape started seeming a lot less crowded. Now just a handful of companies—Clear Channel; Hicks, Muse; Mel Karmazin's Infinity; and Emmis Communications—controlled more than 40 percent of radio's ad revenue. Each had its own specialty. The Hickses' Chancellor became known for its "wall of women," a term Tom Hicks used to describe the New York market it had cornered—women twelve to sixty-four years old. CBS catered to men with shock jocks like Howard Stern and its premier sports programming. Emmis Communications specialized in African-American markets. Clear Channel–Jacor, with its overflow of middle-of-the-country rock and news-talk stations, represented something of a heartland consensus.

Traditionally, at Clear Channel that consensus was arrived at authentically, usually at an executive barbecue out at Lowry Mays's two-thousand-acre ranch just outside San Antonio. "I can remember sitting in a spring-fed creek in a lawn chair with water up to my chest smoking a cigar with four or five other guys in Clear Channel and Mays right in the middle, talking about where we saw the business five or ten years from now," recalls Jim Smith.

But whatever they had talked about in the good old days was certainly nothing like the Clear Channel that existed after the Jacor juggernaut. By the time the AMFM merger was announced on Monday, October 4, 1999, Clear Channel was bleeding internally. Executives like Stan Webb had already plotted their exits, not that anyone outside the company would have known.

Webb, for one, was under strict orders from Mark Mays not to reveal his plan to leave the company in August 2000 until the AMFM deal was fully cleared. It wouldn't have pleased the AMFM brass to learn that the effects of the previous commingling of corporate cultures had set a bomb off in San Antonio. And Wall Street, catching its breath from Clear Channel's meteoric rise since 1996, wouldn't have appreciated news of synergy on the skids.

The terms of the deal were nothing short of mind-blowing. Clear Channel would acquire AMFM Inc. in a complicated stock and debt deal worth $23.5 billion. Nothing else in the history of radio could match the utter totality of the event. Radio was not conceived as a medium that operated on such a scale. It was exciting, scary, and awesome all at the same time.

The pace of new acquisitions had ramped up to a feverish pitch. Clear Channel execs recall Mark Mays's office stacked with papers as he tried to keep as many as fifteen major deals going at the same time.[2] It was not unusual for the young executive to work six or seven days a week.

But as the deals piled up, so did Clear Channel's nascent reputation for nastiness. In the months after the AMFM deal closed, the company instated some new corporate policies that rattled its competitors. One of the more mean-spirited ones involved Premiere Radio Networks, the Clear Channel–owned syndicator of popular news-talk hosts, including Rush Limbaugh and Dr. Laura Schlessinger. In early 2001, Clear Channel informed competing stations in many of its markets that they would immediately lose the rights to broadcast Premiere's content. Instead, the syndicated shows were shifted to Clear Channel stations across town. The move amounted to a huge loss for stations that relied on such name-brand talent to boost their ratings and did little to ingratiate a larger Clear Channel to its fellow broadcasters.[3]

A few months later, Clear Channel announced plans not to re-up its contracts with the radio ratings company Arbitron in 130 markets where Clear Channel owned stations. Arbitron is the main source of listenership data that most radio stations use to price and sell advertising. To use the data, radio groups must purchase costly subscriptions.

Clear Channel's announcement was made on the same day as that of Arbitron's initial public offering, potentially costing the company millions in lost revenues and leading critics to suggest that Clear Channel's mean-spirited competitiveness was to blame.

When the dust finally settled after the rash of acquisitions, Clear Channel was in possession of around 1,233 radio stations, more than thirty times the number that would have been allowed prior to the Telecom Act of 1996. Their closest competitor at the time, Cumulus Media, owned just over 200. Clear Channel stations represented 27 percent of radio listeners nationwide and 27.5 percent of U.S. radio revenues.[4]

Inside the company, which was now essentially a sprawling hodgepodge of former competitors, slashing operations budgets began to take its toll. "Everybody thought there'd be a first round of cost-cutting," says Galaxy's Ed Levine. "When you acquire, there tend to be some duplicated efforts and you move on, but the cost-cutting just kept coming. They were cutting into bone."

Dave Allan knew the feeling. Allan had been working in radio for nearly two decades when the stations he programmed in the Philadelphia market became part of the Clear Channel family due to the AMFM merger. Change of ownership was a way of life for Allan, who began as the program director at Philadelphia's Power 99 in 1987, and over the next fourteen years experienced the bumps of consolidation firsthand. Power 99, an urban-format station, changed hands five times during the period he worked there. The first time, as an independent, it filed for Chapter 11. Then, in 1994, it was bought out of Chapter 11 by EZ Communications, which owned another station in town, WJZZ, which played smooth jazz. In time, Allan became general manager of both stations.

In 1996, Evergreen Media bought the two stations. Eventually they ended up in the hands of Chancellor Media—and Allan ended up vice president of regional urban programming, which made him responsible for, in addition to the Philadelphia stations, urban stations in Miami, San Francisco, Los Angeles, and Orlando. "That was great," he says.[5]

Despite his growing responsibilities, though, Allan was not actually programming all the stations he was responsible for. Each station still had its own general manager and program director. He simply oversaw them.

Then Clear Channel arrived, and general managers began dropping like flies. "I really saw it then," he says. "We weren't getting rid of people, but we weren't replacing them, either." By the time Clear Channel took over, Allan had become vice president of those two stations and senior vice president of programming and marketing for the six stations the company owned in Philadelphia. When Clear Channel restructured, he became vice president of operations for those stations.

All of the stations that Allan was responsible for were profitable under his watch, he says, and none was in danger of folding. In the Philadelphia area, general managers earned upwards of $200,000, and program directors easily cleared $50,000. "These stations were throwing off serious cash flow," he says.

For Allan, the dividing line between the two corporate cultures was blindingly obvious. "When Jimmy de Castro ran Evergreen and AMFM, Jimmy always told us we were in the entertainment business," he says. "But if you go to Clear Channel's website and you look at their creed, it says they're in the advertising business— 'We're in the business of delivering for our clients.' The creed doesn't even talk about employees till the fourth paragraph. So that was a big wake-up call." Clear Channel's baldly ad-centric perspective, a holdover from the early days, was often a shock to employees who came from a more traditional radio background.

Allan says he appreciated Clear Channel's businesslike manner to the extent that there were no surprises about what to expect when working for the company. It was open about its corporate philosophy and carried it out straightforwardly. "The good thing was there was nobody behind the curtain at Clear Channel," says Allan. "It wasn't like this was a big surprise; it just wasn't much fun."

And the Clear Channel way certainly had its hallmarks, many of which were quite different from the ones Allan was used to. As far as he could tell, the Clear Channel brass felt pretty strongly that there was no need to have a general manager for each station. A general manager was expected to juggle multiple stations. There were other cost-saving experiments, too. General managers sometimes were responsible for both programming and sales; other times they just handled sales.

But there came a point when even a good soldier like Allan started getting weary of battle. There were fewer people doing more and not necessarily making that much money. The burnout rate was rising. Cheap Channel was in major ascendancy, and the reality didn't seem that far off from the rumors.

The old notion of leaving stations alone if they were running smoothly appeared to be a nostalgic memory. While Clear Channel never dictated specific changes to Allan's primary market, the company did dispatch a market manager looking for consolidation opportunities. Allan recalls how the first market manager he worked for, Rob Williams, simply changed who was reporting to whom— two senior vice presidents, one for programming and marketing (Allan) and one for sales. Everybody else answered to them. The changes worked well enough that Williams got promoted. In 2001, the next regional manager, Jim Shea, brought in his own marketing guy and sales manager from Allentown—and began the consolidation shuffle.

Soon, there was one market manager, no general managers for the individual stations, a vice president of sales, and a vice president of operations (Allan). Now all of the program directors in the area—which included Philadelphia, Allentown, Bethlehem, Wilmington, and Lancaster—answered to Allan. The added load amounted to twenty-eight stations. Though in reality, they all still answered to Shea. Which was okay with Allan, since he already had his hands full with the six stations for which he was still directly handling programming and marketing.

The irony was that Allan, like other Clear Channel employees at the time, relished the idea of more responsibility. He wanted to do more. "But there came times when too many responsibilities were consolidated under one person to the point where that person was overwhelmed," he says. "At the end of the day they were tired and they were losing motivation for doing all that extra stuff." And it was not a good tired.

Allan found the effects of the consolidation even more dispiriting. Suddenly differently formatted Clear Channel stations in the same market were sharing newspeople, "which we never used to do." Traditionally, each station wanted its own unique sound and approach, a virtual impossibility under the new corporate structure.

The same commercials would show up on all the stations in the market, thanks to one production director shared by all the stations.

The Clear Channel argument, as Allan understood it, was that listeners don't really care. But Allan, who viewed himself primarily as a marketing expert, felt that such repetition watered down the brand of each station.

Then the overnight disc jockeys were replaced by voice-tracked talent from other markets—soon the rule was no live DJs were allowed on the overnight shift.

Voice tracking, the process of pre-recording the DJ's patter between songs, has long been used as a cost-saving measure for radio stations, particularly late at night or on holiday broadcasts. Traditionally, the segments were recorded a day earlier, and then seamlessly added into an automated broadcast, eliminating the need for human presence.

Clear Channel arguably innovated the practice of importing voice-tracked disc jockeys cross-country, whereby a DJ in San Jose, California, would appear on the air in Boise, Idaho, making occasional references to local haunts, news events, and the weather, giving every impression that he was in Boise. In truth, he had recorded his broadcast in San Jose weeks before, aided by a cheat sheet of local reference information.

The company first got a hint at the power of deceiving local radio audiences in 1999, when a group of teenagers showed up at one of its stations one morning in search of the Backstreet Boys, after listening to an on-air interview with them. The fans were simply told the platinum-selling boy band couldn't come out and were plied with promotional merchandise. The interview had actually been conducted at an earlier time in Los Angeles.[6]

The situation in Boise was even more unsettling. A damning article in *The Wall Street Journal* outlined the on-air hoax regularly perpetrated by Clear Channel on KISS 103.3 in Boise (actual call letters: KSAS-FM), one of the forty-seven company-owned stations using the KISS brand. In the name of profitability, Clear Channel took the radical step of eliminating all of the station's on-air talent—a practice it employed at dozens of other small-market stations—and replacing them with DJs piped in from other markets.

What was most jarring was the level of deception employed to give listeners the impression they were hearing a local broadcast. Since there were no DJs, the station hired a student at Boise State University to make public appearances around town, posing as a DJ on behalf of the station. When people called in to the station, they often got a busy signal, purposely programmed to avoid revealing the fact that the personalities on the radio weren't in the studio.

The KSAS program manager, Hoss Grigg, even maintained a guide to Boise for out-of-town DJs, which detailed the main roads, local sports teams, and school names, as well as proper pronunciations of relevant places.

A disc jockey with the unprepossessing name of "Cabana Boy Geoff" Alan, based in San Diego, took on extra shifts to pretape a show for Boise, a place he'd never been. He would get daily briefings on station-sponsored concert events in Boise and pretend in his patter that he'd actually attended them. He also repurposed listener phone calls from his San Diego show by editing out any local references.

On February 15, 2002, according to *The Wall Street Journal*, KISS in Boise broadcast an interview Alan did with the teen pop duo Evan and Jaron, twin brothers from Atlanta who were signed to a record deal by the singer Jimmy Buffett. During the interview, the musicians claimed they had just been skiing at Idaho's Sun Valley and spoke highly of Boise. Alan later encouraged listeners to phone or e-mail the station with questions for the duo. None ever got through. The interview had been done in San Diego weeks earlier.

Alan also did similar ersatz local shows for Medford, Oregon, and Santa Barbara, California. Through this process, Clear Channel saved tens of thousands of dollars in salary and benefits in smaller markets. Voice tracking allowed the company to pay a weekday disc jockey just $4,000 to $6,000 per year extra to fill in the additional shifts.

But Randy Michaels's Clear Channel, in fact, took pride in its voice-tracking strategy. "They did it greater and faster than anyone," says Dave Allan. "It was a movement."

Indeed, Michaels repeatedly argued that demanding that DJs take on extra shifts in markets they had no connection with had nothing to do with saving money. "We can produce higher-quality programming at a lower cost in markets where we could never afford the talent," Michaels told *The Wall Street Journal*.[7] "That's a huge benefit to the audience." Besides, he had the Arbitron numbers to back up his claim that audiences didn't mind. He acknowledged that the practice eliminated jobs for up-and-coming disc jockeys. But those that remained would be better jobs. Sure, some people objected, but Michaels pointed out that the same thing happened when studio orchestras were phased out in the 1930s in favor of records.[8]

But while voice tracking had become common practice at radio companies big and small, Clear Channel seemed to approach it with almost CIA-like levels of secrecy and deception. "I don't have a problem with voice tracking per se," says Galaxy's Ed Levine. "Do we do voice tracking in what we call nonessential day-parts? Yeah, absolutely. The difference is my guys are still in Syracuse doing the voice tracking. They're not in Syracuse voice-tracking to Miami and pretending that they're in Miami. That's where Clear Channel went outside the pale."[9]

Odds are most listeners never suspected any difference, except when a DJ from across the country mispronounced the name of a local town. In Boise, the KISS station easily beat out a competitor that promoted itself as live and local.

Dave Allan understood the benefit of getting the best programming for any market, making it affordable for a name DJ, say, in Los Angeles to log some hours on a station in Shreveport, Louisiana. "What I didn't like about voice tracking was that I thought it was a short-term win," says Allan. "And then in the long term, because we weren't using these small markets to grow new talent, there would be no new talent left. The talent would get older and older. It would be like baseball without the minor leagues."

Another problem was that the practice of deception seemed contagious. In 2000, Clear Channel agreed to pay an $80,000 fine after the Florida state attorney general's office determined that it had deceived listeners of some local Clear Channel stations by running call-in radio contests without making it clear that the contests were running simultaneously in multiple states. Participants, believing they were one of maybe dozens calling in to their local station, were instead forwarded to centralized call centers fielding thousands of calls from across the country, drastically reducing their chances of winning. Though Clear Channel admitted no wrongdoing, it agreed to identify the city and state where contest winners lived when interviewing them on the air. It also vowed to abolish another deceptive practice of dubbing questions from local Clear Channel radio personalities into pretaped interviews with out-of-state winners to make it seem as if they were actually interviewing them live.

Clear Channel was groaning with its extra station poundage, but it remained confident that, at least when it came to improving margins, the rapid growth was a sign of good health.

David Rubin, the dean of the Newhouse School of Public Communications at Syracuse University—a leading destination for budding broadcast journalists—disagrees. Rubin believes the notion that bigger is better in the media business, and particularly radio, is something of a misconception. He attributes the passage of the Telecommunications Act of 1996 to politicians and FCC commissioners who refused to stand up to well-funded industry lobbyists and a "willingness to accept the fiction that because of the Internet and cable television, there is no longer a scarcity of communications outlets and therefore no longer any reason to limit ownership," he says.[10]

Rubin points out that, particularly at the local level, the scarcity of radio bandwidth is made evident by the fact that there are far more people who want to broadcast than there is room in the spectrum. "Therefore," he says, "the people who do have the valuable spectrum space are being given a privilege that millions of others are being denied, and that privilege needs to come with some responsibilities."

Among the other responsibilities that Lowry Mays acquired with his new outsize company was that of political standard-bearer. Politics have always been an important part of the radio business, for the simple fact that radio is regulated by a federal agency. Not surprisingly, as Clear Channel grew larger, politics began to play a larger role, though Lowry Mays had long expressed his interest, having enthusiastically backed candidates at the local, state, and national levels.

In the 1980s, he supported Henry Cisneros, the Democrat who served three terms as San Antonio's mayor before going on to serve as President Clinton's secretary of housing and urban development. Public records show Mays also gave money to the Senate campaigns of other Democrats in that era, including two high-profile U.S. senators, Lloyd Bentsen of Texas and John Glenn of Ohio.[11] For decades, Mays has contributed to the reelection campaigns of another Democrat, senior congressman John Dingell of Michigan. No doubt his generosity has a little something to do with Dingell's longtime role as ranking Democrat on the House Energy and Commerce Committee.

Clear Channel's foes often take issue with the company's strong Republican ties. But, in fact, Lowry Mays's political affiliations for many years seemed to lean whichever way the wind was blowing in Texas. When the Democrats still had control of the governor's office, for example, Lowry did what he could to help out. "Lowry did some fund-raising for Governor Mark White,"[12] a conservative Democrat who won the office in 1982, says John Barger. Not long after, Mays was elected to the board of regents for Texas A&M University, his alma mater.

After Ann Richards, a Democrat, lost the governorship to George W. Bush in 1994, Mays seemed to go with the flow, working his longtime friendship with the elder President Bush to his favor. In 1996, when George W. Bush was governor of Texas, he named Lowry Mays to a state technology council, and Mays donated $51,000 to Bush's 1998 campaign for reelection.

Still, Lowry Mays was not so strongly associated with the Republican Party that when his own name came up as a possible candidate for Texas governor, it was on the Democratic ticket in opposition to Bush.[13] But Clear Channel contributed $106,000 to the Republican National Committee during the 2000 presidential election cycle—Lowry and his wife, Peggy, kicked in an additional $37,000. And President Bush's first antitrust chief, Charles James, had previously run the antitrust department at the Washington law firm that represented Clear Channel during its push for regulatory approval of the purchase of AMFM.[14]

John Barger doesn't deny Clear Channel's solid Republican ties, but brushes off any suggestions that its business decisions are politically motivated. "Who empowered these guys from San Antonio, anyway?" he says. "And the answer to that is they empowered themselves—with the help of a guy from Dallas named Tom Hicks. And who empowered him? It was the putzes in New York who loaned him all the money to acquire all the stuff to begin with. And did the guys on Wall Street care whether they were Republicans or Democrats? Shit no."

Barger says he believes Lowry Mays has always been a businessman first, "a classic American, Southwestern capitalist—McCombs, too."

Still, the labeling of Clear Channel as a Republican-minded company stuck. And in the generally liberal-leaning corridors of the American music business, it only took a few small gestures for that impression to be reinforced.

At one managers' meeting prior to the 2000 presidential election, Rush Limbaugh, an employee of Clear Channel's Premiere Radio Networks division, made an appearance and, together with Lowry Mays, told the assembled employees why the Republicans were good for Clear Channel.[15] Generally, though, within the company, politics were implicit—though they certainly affected news coverage at Clear Channel's stations. "If the nation was at war," says the journalist Eric Boehlert, "you wouldn't propose a series on peace activists. Everyone knew the deal."

Shortly after the terrorist attacks of September 11, 2001, in New York and Washington, word trickled out that Clear Channel headquarters was circulating a list of 150 songs not to be played on its stations across the country. Some of the choices seemed obvious, considering the jumpy state of the nation, such as the Gap Band's "You Dropped a Bomb on Me" and Soundgarden's "Blow Up the Outside World." But other entries on the list smacked of jingoism to the company's critics.

Among the other banned tracks were peaceful pop anthems such as John Lennon's "Imagine," Simon & Garfunkel's "Bridge Over Troubled Waters," Cat Stevens's "Peace Train," and Louis Armstrong's "What a Wonderful World." Even stranger were upbeat songs that seemed to hold only the most tangential of references to the tragedy, such as "Ticket to Ride" by the Beatles, "On Broadway" by the Drifters, "Bennie and the Jets" by Elton John, and Neil Diamond's "America."

While use of the list was not mandatory and was indeed ignored by many Clear Channel stations, the mere fact that it had been circulated in the first place fed the growing animosity toward the company. The banned-song roster, which the company claimed was homegrown from within specific stations—that is, not issued from corporate—seemed to burrow into the collective psyche of the rattled nation. And even if unintentionally, it carried a political statement: this is no time for thoughts of universal love.

As the most passionate gesture about programming that Clear Channel had ever made, it was a troubling message from a company that claimed to program by the numbers.

In the coming years, that message would be reinforced by other actions as well. In the wake of the antiwar rallies protesting the U.S. engagement in Iraq in early 2004, a spate of pro-war rallies began cropping up around the country. While nowhere as prevalent as those objecting to the Bush administration's actions overseas, they nonetheless resonated. After Natalie Maines of the Texas-based country group the Dixie Chicks told an audience in London, "We're ashamed the president of the United States is from Texas," some Clear Channel stations organized Rally for America events, publicized and abetted by Glenn Beck, a conservative talk-show host employed by Clear Channel's Premiere Radio Networks division. Beck's cross-country jaunt, during which he partnered with local Clear Channel stations to promote the rallies, often became a news event in its own right—challenging traditional notions of what role a news provider should play in creating and slanting the day's events.

Rumors also began circulating that Clear Channel had banned the Dixie Chicks' music from being played on their country stations. In the end, it turned out that most of the stations that stopped playing the Dixie Chicks were owned by a rival, Cumulus Media. Clear Channel later cited figures from Mediabase's Airplay Monitor service to back its claims that its stations in fact played Dixie Chicks songs more than any other top radio company, some 10,069 times in the two weeks after Maines made her statement.

11.

CONCERTS

Franz Ferdinand took the stage at the Bill Graham Civic Auditorium in San Francisco at precisely 8:30 on the night of October 6, 2005, and began its show with a signature blast of taut guitar bursts. Dressed casually in peg-legged jeans and T-shirts, the retro-sounding new wave band delivered a rousing version of "This Boy," a track from its brand-new second CD, *You Could Have It So Much Better*. The Scottish rock quintet had the number-one album in Britain at the time, but the band's scrawny lead singer, Alex Kapranos, who strutted around like a punked-out young David Bowie, looked out, with visible dismay, onto a dance floor that was nearly half-empty.

The stage set was spare, just a large projection screen dropped behind the band to display oversize photos of its members and a slide of its new CD cover. A colored light show was the only other entertainment. Long black velvet curtains hung from the auditorium's ceiling, concealing the empty balcony, an important visual device meant to prevent the crowd of around one thousand fans from noticing how few people were actually in attendance.

Bill Graham would have been appalled by the poor showing. Although the venue, a historic, character-filled building dating back to San Francisco's Panama-Pacific International Exposition in 1915, was renamed after Graham—one of the first rock concert producers and promoters, and certainly the most famous one ever, who died in a 1991 helicopter crash—it is totally unlike the magnificent groove

palaces most often associated with the late-1960s icon, such as the
Fillmore Auditorium and Winterland. The seven-thousand-capacity
city-owned auditorium overlooks Civic Center Plaza, one of San
Francisco's historic downtown squares, at the intersection of Van
Ness Avenue and Market Street. The city's opera house, town hall,
and Asian art museum loom nearby. It feels way too establishment
to be named for the late counterculture icon.

Graham, a passionate but often grating figure, was renowned
for his unstinting perfectionism and a penchant for controlling
every aspect of the concert experience, from ticket prices to concession stands to the right combination of opening act and headliner.
Musicians loved to hate him but in the end had to begrudgingly respect him because his nitpicky ways made them look better to their
fans and ultimately made them more money.

From his earliest days as promoter, Graham earned a reputation
as being a near-maniacal organizer who cared deeply about the
quality of the experience at a rock concert, both for the audience
and for the performers. The Who's guitarist and songwriter, Pete
Townshend, once compared him to a concert promoter of the previous era: Murray the K, the legendary New York DJ who would
arrange all-day musical revues at the Academy of Music in New
York. "There was a certain diffidence in the audience to [Murray
the K's] cavalcade approach," said Townshend. "It didn't allow for
any real involvement. I think Bill hit on the fact that people *did*
want to listen. He certainly created what I came to know as the
'electric ballroom syndrome' in America"—creating a scene that
transcended the bounds of a conventional music concert—"which
actually changed the face of rock because it made it *listenable*
music."[1]

"I think he liked to control the environment," says Sherry
Wasserman, who worked for Graham from the time she was in high
school. "And he had more of a passion for the audience and the
artists than the other promoters."[2]

That was many years before Bill Graham Presents, the company
Graham founded in 1966, became a part of Clear Channel in 1997,

along with every other major concert promoter in the country. Shockingly, Bill Graham Presents was not even involved in this evening's show.

Less than a decade before, this fact would have been unimaginable. For more than thirty years, Graham dominated and controlled the Bay Area rock scene to such an extent that many local concertgoers would attend a Bill Graham Presents show even if they were unfamiliar with the group that was playing. Every cool band wanted to work with the master. His imprimatur was like rock and roll's Good Housekeeping seal of approval, a guarantee that the experience would be genuinely fun, safe, and, most important, a good value, while still seeming blindingly hip and, at least superficially, on the edge.

Though the company named after Graham had not presented Britain's hottest act on this night, Graham's ghost hovered above the Franz Ferdinand gig. That was because the show was produced by Another Planet Entertainment, a Berkeley-based concert promoter run by two of Graham's longtime lieutenants, Gregg Perloff and Sherry Wasserman.

The place was half-empty—the Summer of Love's ultimate control freak was probably rolling in his grave. Perloff later explained that the less-than-packed house was the unfortunate result of two factors. First, the band was appearing just two days after their album hit American shores. Second, due to Clear Channel's dominance of the local concert scene, Perloff could only book certain venues in town, none of which his company owned, limiting his ability to control dates, personnel, and other elements of the experience. He certainly couldn't present acts at Bill Graham's legendary Fillmore: these days, the Fillmore is owned by Live Nation, the publicly owned spin-off controlled by its previous owner, Clear Channel.

Perloff operated as co-president of Bill Graham Presents with Nicholas Clainos, Graham's former business adviser, from the time of Graham's death; Wasserman was a vice president and star booker. Self-proclaimed disciples of the Bill Graham rock-and-roll church, the pair weathered two corporate takeovers of the company before leaving to form their own competitor in 2002.

The irony is that, for the first time in thirty years, Bill Graham Presents has a viable competitor in the Bay Area.

When Gregg Perloff first met Bill Graham, he was being interviewed for a job.

"So you've always wanted to work for me?"

"No."

"So would you want to run a club for me?"

"No."

"Did you grow up in the area?"

"No."

Perloff got the job.

The year was 1977. For the next twenty-five years, Perloff worked for Graham and his company, Bill Graham Presents, which arguably invented the modern business of rock promotion and set the standard for a young, shaggy industry. Over time he became co-president and BGP grew into a slick, corporate machine with around $110 million in ticket sales per year.[3] By the time Perloff left in 2002, Bill Graham Presents was part of Clear Channel's newly acquired concerts division, which it bought from SFX Entertainment for $4.4 billion in Clear Channel stock. It was an unlikely pairing by any stretch of the imagination, the most independent of concert promoters linked with a corporate giant.

Decked out in a green-flowered Hawaiian shirt, black jeans, and Saucony running shoes one sunny fall day in Berkeley, California, Perloff—a heavyset, Falstaffian figure with a salt-and-pepper beard and mustache—recalled his long, strange trip. In a spacious office on the recently gentrified Fourth Street, the seasoned talent booker recalled how a homegrown, soulful local institution evolved into the center of a public backlash against Clear Channel's concert division.

"Clear Channel is the Wal-Mart of radio," he says. "They have an arrogance, a squash-the-people mentality. They use that spoke-and-hub model." Gazing at a giant photo blowup of a psychedelic-light-show-bathed audience, Perloff describes the business he grew up in as one in which selling tickets and grossing profits often took a backseat to improving the concert experience for both the audience and the musicians. "Our industry is basically the only industry where if you have a better product," he cracks, "you make less money." One example he mentions is the set of black velvet curtains concealing the balcony at the Franz Ferdinand show: Perloff insisted on them, despite a charge of $5,000 off his bottom line. He wanted the Civic to feel as full and exciting as possible, he says, even if it was at a real cost to him and his company.[4]

Within a period of six years, from 1997 to 2003, Bill Graham Presents was transformed from the ultimate symbol of rock-and-roll hippie do-goodism into an operation best known for raising the prices of concert parking and in-venue beers to stratospheric levels. BGP, along with virtually every other major concert promoter in the country, became part of Clear Channel Entertainment, an industry behemoth that soon would control 85 percent of the concert business in the United States.

One could argue that in an era rife with media consolidation, this was business as normal, but many close to the deal argue that Clear Channel, in an effort to cut costs and boost profits, squandered the formidable San Francisco concert market that Bill Graham Presents had controlled for more than two decades. In its place, the company found itself for the first time with a serious competitor, Perloff's Another Planet, co-founded with Sherry Wasserman, a longtime BGP vice president.

Graham, a Russian-Jewish refugee who immigrated to the United States in 1941, had nothing in his background to suggest he would eventually become a hipster musical icon. But that's what he became, almost overnight, in 1966, after orchestrating a series of rock concerts in San Francisco's Bay Area as a legal-defense fundraiser for an anarchist mime troupe he was involved with. An opinionated and difficult man as well-known for his volatile temper as for his generosity and humanism, Graham soon became renowned for presenting weekly concerts by up-and-coming local rock acts such as the Jefferson Airplane, the Grateful Dead, and Quicksilver Messenger Service at the Fillmore Auditorium, a run-down old ball-room in a rough part of town.

By the early 1970s, he was orchestrating tours by top acts like the Rolling Stones, Bob Dylan and the Band, George Harrison, and Crosby, Stills, Nash & Young. He promoted a rock festival in Watkins Glen, New York, in 1973, starring the Band, the Allman Brothers, and the Grateful Dead, that attracted 650,000 people, the largest paying audience ever assembled. And in 1976 he organized the Thanksgiving concert at Winterland by the Band and guests that is documented in Martin Scorsese's 1978 movie *The Last Waltz*—and served a turkey dinner with all the trimmings to the capacity audience.

In 1985, Graham organized Live Aid, the bi-continental rock festival that raised money for famine relief in Ethiopia. He pursued concert promotion like a religion, worshipping the performers he did business with, or at least courting them as if they were gods. The only concert promoter ever to become a genuine celebrity, Graham dealt with stars like Mick Jagger, Bob Dylan, the Who, and the Grateful Dead as equals and as friends. In 1992, he was inducted into the Rock and Roll Hall of Fame, the only concert promoter to receive such an honor.

A wannabe actor who grew up in the Bronx, New York, Graham ended up in the Bay Area after visiting a sister who lived there. Oddly, his unusual background helped form a personality perfectly suited for finding order in the wild, chaotic swirl launched by 1967's Summer of Love. "He was a real businessman," says Perloff. "He had business savvy; but he was a former actor, so he had a sense of theater and he had a sense of how to do things the right way."

And despite the ecstatic drugs-and-sex-soaked craziness of the scene, Graham presented these bands in as safe and as comfortable a setting as possible. "He always had a better sound system, a better

lighting system," says Perloff. "All of the liquid light shows that occurred—a lot of that stuff was developed out of the Fillmores." (In
March 1968, Graham opened a Fillmore East in New York's East
Village.) Graham instructed audiences to sit down on the dance
floor before the show, to relax before the music started. He was an
early supporter of the Haight-Ashbury Free Clinic, a nonjudgmental
free health clinic founded during the Summer of Love; and helped
start an offshoot, Rock Medicine, which pioneered the availability
of quality medical care at rock concerts. He also co-founded Winterland Productions, the first concert T-shirt manufacturing company, which eventually became a $200 million business. In the old
days, he could often be spotted collecting tickets and handing out
apples at the front of the concert hall. "It was all about treating the
consumer as you would like to be treated yourself," says Perloff.

Though Graham confessed to having little interest in or sensi-
bility for the burgeoning music scene, he educated himself and kept
abreast of the cutting edge. He was adamant about introducing Fillmore audiences to a variety of musical genres, booking top black
rhythm-and-blues musicians like Otis Rush, Junior Wells, Jimmy
Reed, the Staple Singers, and Rahsaan Roland Kirk on the same bill
with leading white rock bands. "Back then, it was a brave move to
mix up soul acts with the most extreme of white music at the time,"
Keith Richards of the Rolling Stones would later say. "Bill was the
first one to do it in a big city on a regular basis."[5]

Into the 1980s, Bill Graham was an innovator in concert presentation. The Shoreline Amphitheatre in Mountain View, California, which Graham and his company built with the city of Mountain
View in 1986, was one of the first venues in the country with an in-
house permanent sound system for better-quality sound.

In the 1950s and early '60s, rock concerts were typically
twenty-five-hundred-seat events. Even Elvis Presley in his prime
never played to an audience of more than nine thousand. For the
first three or four years of his career he played theaters, as did most
other performers. Despite Graham's reputation as a freewheeling
huckster—early in his career, he drove without a license, armed

with a block of concert tickets to bribe officers who gave him trouble—he was something of a business visionary. Over time he expanded into larger facilities and tours, booking three-act shows and charging higher ticket prices.

Graham's devotion to his craft engendered a similar devotion among his staff. Not that they were the best businesspeople. "We were very good at grossing money," says Perloff. "We were very good at selling tickets, but we weren't that good at netting money."

For all of the rage heaped upon Clear Channel in the years since the creation of the entertainment division, at least a fair portion is rightfully due to Bob Sillerman, CEO and founder of SFX Entertainment, the company that consolidated the concert business in nearly one fell swoop before being swallowed up by Clear Channel.

Like Graham, Robert F. X. Sillerman grew up in the Bronx, specifically Riverdale, an elite wooded enclave of New York's most notorious borough. A second-generation radio man and self-proclaimed child of the 1960s, Sillerman was a dyed-in-the-wool salesman said to be driven by the specter of his father, who built the pioneering Keystone Radio Network only to lose it to bankruptcy.[6]

A serial entrepreneur and self-made billionaire who built a discount magazine subscription business while still a student at Brandeis, Sillerman had a knack for seeing value where others didn't. Pairing up with the oldies DJ Bruce "Cousin Brucie" Morrow in the late 1970s, Sillerman acquired two small radio stations in upstate New York for $1.875 million. The pair grew the company with more radio and TV acquisitions, while Sillerman earned a reputation as a ruthless competitor with a brutish sense of humor.

In 1993, he joined forces with Steve Hicks, Tom Hicks's brother, to take a group of stations public under the name SFX Broadcasting. After the Telecommunications Act of 1996, the company gobbled up more stations until it became the seventh-largest chain in the country. That same year Hicks bought SFX Broadcasting, backed by his brother Tom's firm, Hicks, Muse, Tate & Furst, for $2.1 billion. Sillerman personally profited to the tune of $250 million.

One day in the early 1990s, he had an epiphany while planning an annual benefit with the New York–area promoter Ron Delsener for Southampton College on Long Island, where Sillerman served for a time as chancellor. Standing on a football field near his house in the Hamptons, he wondered why rock tours rarely attracted national advertisers. His vision was to pull together the promoters, centralize bookings, and pool the resources of amphitheaters across the country, all in the name of brokering big-league sponsorship deals.

Though SFX Broadcasting owned seventy-two radio stations in midsize and large markets that sponsored concerts nationwide, it had no way of capitalizing the ticket fees and concession sales that made local promoters cash-rich. Then, in 1996, Delsener/Slater Enterprises, the firm co-owned by Delsener and his partner, Mitch Slater, wanted out of a partnership deal with Pace Entertainment of Houston involving the purchase of New Jersey's Garden State Arts Center. Sillerman bought Delsener/Slater for $27 million in cash in January 1997.

Using Delsener and Slater's connections, Sillerman began conversations with other regional promoters around the country. The fiefdoms were as insular as ever, but something was different this time. Sillerman was waving big wads of money. In June, Dave Lucas's Sunshine Promotions in Indianapolis took the bait.

By the end of the year, Bill Graham Presents had been approached, along with Contemporary Productions in St. Louis, Pace in Houston, and Cellar Door in Washington, D.C.

And in typical fashion, Bill Graham Presents took a unique perspective on the offer. For one, it was the only promoter approached that insisted upon keeping full control of its board if the deal went through. In some ways still grieving and angsty over their mentor's death, the partners at Bill Graham Presents had put their lifeblood into the firm and were committed to retaining the flavor and spirit of the operation.

Gregg Perloff and fourteen other BGP executives had purchased the company from Graham's estate for $5 million in 1995—if they were going to sell the thing, they each expected a generous payout. Their expectations were handily met. Sillerman ultimately paid $65 million to the partnership just two years later, making each partner, including Perloff and Wasserman, an instant multimillionaire.

Within months, SFX owned dozens of independent promoters around the country. From Don Law of Don Law Productions in Boston to Gary and Brian Becker of Pace, the entrepreneurs who collectively had created and grown an industry relinquished control to Sillerman's lure of synergy and stock options. The Becker family, for example, received $190 million in cash, stock, and debt for three profitable units, including its concert business and Broadway touring group.[7] While the Beckers expressed concern that the new corporate culture would ultimately harm the intangible magic of their business, they reportedly admired Sillerman's bald ambition. The sale to SFX "was a once-in-a-lifetime chance to score," says one promoter who cashed in.[8]

Sillerman homed in on operations such as Bill Graham Presents that owned their own amphitheaters to hedge against the growing popularity of stadiums and arenas, typically controlled by major sports teams. Promoters that owned amphitheaters had higher profit margins—they made more on tickets and also controlled the venue concessions and parking. Bill Graham loved Shoreline because he could do everything his way: no violence-prone security guards, fair ticket prices, and a separate minimal fee for parking.

Clearly Bob Sillerman had another notion in mind. He apparently was so confident in his deal-making prowess, and the fact that advertising margins could be substantially increased with a national presence, that in many cases he heaped sizable goodwill premiums, money beyond the business's tangible assets, on top of each individual promoter's payout. Goodwill costs totaled nearly $1 billion by the time Sillerman was finished.

An executive close to one of the deals suggested that Sillerman was not initially counting on higher ticket prices for increased revenue. He wasn't even planning to put more tickets on sale. "He just thought he could cut the overhead," the source says.[9]

But skeptics claimed Sillerman had plans to flip SFX from the very start. Sillerman's idea was to capitalize on baby-boomer Wall Street types looking to revisit their teen years. To some extent, his strategy worked. As boomer nostalgia grew, the upper level of ticket prices shot through the ceiling. The best seats at Rolling Stones shows suddenly reached $300. Tickets to Crosby, Stills, Nash & Young's 2000 reunion tour ranged from $30.50 to $201.

Those close to the action saw the endgame pretty clearly. Despite Sillerman's statement to his new employees that his daughter would one day be CEO of the company, many knew better. "Bob Sillerman is a consolidator, but he's not an operator," says Gregg Perloff.

Some critics questioned why SFX wanted to control the live-concert industry in the first place. After all, it was a cyclical, hard-to-manage business heavily dependent on record sales, airplay exposure, and big-name artists' touring schedules. But Sillerman no doubt was aware of the huge revenues associated with the concert industry in the mid-1990s. In 1997, the year SFX began buying promoters, sales of concert tickets reached $1.3 billion in North America, a substantial uptick from $1.05 billion in 1996 and $950 million in 1995.[10]

And though rising ticket prices slowly accounted for a decrease in the number of tickets sold, revenues continued to soar. *Pollstar*, the trade journal of the concert business, estimated that revenues for all major North American concerts increased to $3.1 billion in 2005, up from $2.8 billion in 2004. The top one hundred touring artists sold a combined 36.1 million tickets in 2005, as compared with 37.6 million in 2004.[11]

Some things, alas, remain the same. The number-one-grossing tour of 1997 was the Rolling Stones', which made $89.5 million by selling 1.5 million tickets. In 2005, the Stones also topped the tour-

ing chart, pulling in $162 million for forty-two dates with an aver-
age ticket price of $133.98. But as ticket prices rose, the promoters
got squeezed.

For many years, promoters earned most of their money off a
concert's gross, less the artists' fees, advertising, production, and
other costs. But superstar artists in the 1990s began demanding a
larger and larger percentage of box-office receipts. Promoters had
no choice but to take matters into their own hands and expand into
areas like concession sales, parking fees, and merchandising (the
artists' sales of T-shirts and souvenirs). Similar concerns in the mid-
1980s led promoters around the country to start building their own
amphitheaters, such as Bill Graham's Shoreline Amphitheatre.

Then there was the old-school theory that promoters shouldn't
necessarily want to raise ticket prices as high as they could. This
was for years the way Bill Graham Presents operated—and on business principle, not just some hippy-dippy philosophy. The notion
was that if one firm controlled a market, as did Bill Graham Presents, it wanted the scene to remain healthy. That meant not trying
to maximize profits on any particular show. If that same firm was
booking all the best acts, the more immediate goal would be to generate good ticket sales. As a result, there was some incentive to
charge fair prices for tickets. "In those days, you weren't so worried
about agents selling you the dates," says Gregg Perloff, so promoters could afford to charge lower ticket prices, knowing that more
tours would be coming through town soon.

On top of that, charging high prices just wasn't groovy for
many years, at least in the Bay Area, since most of the promoters
were members of the Woodstock generation.

But while Sillerman was also a member of that generation, his
vibe was from another universe. Sillerman had put Brian Becker,
formerly of Pace, in charge as SFX's chief executive. Thus empowered, Becker acted quickly to install many of his longtime soldiers
in top positions in the new corporate structure. Though Becker was
respected by his fellow promoter-entrepreneurs, the move may have

been as much an act of necessity as anything else: Pace was the only firm in the industry roll-up that had a genuine corporate infrastructure.

By mid-2000, Sillerman and SFX had spent more than $1.6 billion to essentially buy up a whole industry. In the end, SFX owned or operated more than 120 live-entertainment venues in thirty-one of the top fifty U.S. markets, including fifteen amphitheaters in the top ten markets.

When Mark Mays first brought up the notion of purchasing SFX at a Clear Channel board meeting, the idea got a decidedly chilly reception from the directors who were not part of the inner circle. Karl Eller recalls one occasion when he and his fellow board member Bob Crandall had the most to say about why it was a bad move, mainly citing their lack of faith in media synergy.[12] Lowry, during these sessions, was for the most part silent, though his silence implied approval. Mark made the case for synergy. The idea was simple. If Clear Channel controlled venues and tours in markets where it also owned radio stations and billboards, the opportunities to market to national advertisers grew exponentially. Conversely, radio had long been the main vehicle for advertising and promoting concerts.

Randall Mays, in particular, was a strong proponent for the deal. Some former executives with inside knowledge say the idea to buy SFX actually originated with him. "Randall was pushing it," says one who was present at key meetings. "He thought that Viacom was going to buy it, and they had to get it done before Viacom got it."

By most accounts, Lowry sat in the background, probably for the first time, when it came time to go ahead with the purchase. His sons were now fully in command of his legacy.

The early announcements of the SFX purchase were jubilant in tone, partly because they followed on the heels of Clear Channel's second-quarter income report, which was better than expected and indeed the best second-quarter results in the company's history.[13] Revenue had leaped 56 percent over a year, from $617.7 million to $965.9 million, and net income reached $31.2 million, or nine cents a share. Analysts had been expecting only four cents a share.

What bothered Sherry Wasserman the most about the changes Clear Channel began implementing at Bill Graham Presents was that they violated Graham's core precepts. Graham had a say not only in how his venues were decorated but also in who manned the box office and the etiquette of the security staff. If a police presence was deemed necessary, he enforced a no-guns-allowed and no-uniforms policy.

Some of the policies immediately instituted by Clear Channel pushed the outer limits of what was conventionally acceptable in the concert business. At its amphitheaters, it began adding a service charge of around $4 to tickets purchased at the box office—unlike virtually any other theater or arena in the country—effectively blocking the average consumer's only outlet to buy tickets at face value. More troubling, it rarely informed artists of this new policy.

Another Clear Channel "innovation" was VIP parking. Many Clear Channel venues such as Deer Creek and West Palm Beach advertised free parking, when in fact a parking fee was now simply included in the price of the ticket. Then, at the show, Clear Channel would offer VIP parking, whereby patrons could pay an additional $20 to park in the premium lots, those situated most conveniently to the venue entrance.

As ticket prices became padded with additional convenience fees and surcharges, Clear Channel found new ways to siphon profits away from artists. A common tactic employed soon after the takeover involved creating new categories of tiered seating, such as season tickets and corporate boxes that took away from the total number of seats that bands could get paid on, according to one insider.

While the legality of many of the business practices put in place at Clear Channel Entertainment was rarely in question, the ethics of some standard practices annoyed some of the company's own promoters, as well as the artists they were ostensibly promoting and those artists' managers. A typical initiative: corporate instructed promoters, in writing, to shift 10 percent of their advertising budget from print or non–Clear Channel radio and move it to radio stations owned by Clear Channel. More than a few promoters would argue that their agreement with a musical act is to promote the shows they are contracted to produce in the best way possible, an impossibility if they are obligated to advertise on certain radio stations, whether or not they are appropriate advertising vehicles. Such a practice could easily hurt ticket sales.

Clear Channel also applied its Cheap Channel philosophy to the new division, slashing overhead at any perceived opportunity. At Bill Graham Presents, the art department was reduced by half, an odd cost-cutting move at a promoter whose psychedelic band posters arguably invented the notion of rock-and-roll art. Perloff claimed that the Bill Graham Presents advertising department had three times as many salespeople when he ran it as it did in its 2005 incarnation.

Another claim lobbed at Clear Channel corporate was discriminatory employment practices. "Every executive female over forty in my office was fired or forced out," according to Perloff. "Every executive Jew has left in the last three years."

Politics also became a sticking point, particularly in the left-leaning confines of Bill Graham Presents. Perloff recalls attending a meeting in 2000 with the five hundred top executives at Clear Channel where Mark Mays told the audience that the company was better off if they all voted for George W. Bush and not the Democrats. At that moment, Lowry jumped out of his seat to make light of his son's comments. "What Mark meant to say . . . ," the elder Mays assured, as a hush came over the room. Another time, Clear Channel started a political action committee and suggested that all employees earning more than $100,000 should give 10 percent of the money they earned over $100,000 to the PAC. Around 75 percent of the moneys Clear Channel donated to political campaigns went to Republican candidates.

Despite the enthusiasm expressed by the investment community, the reaction to the SFX acquisition by Clear Channel inside the music industry was decidedly tepid and turned almost universally negative within a year. By August 2001, the height of the summer concert season, most of the remaining independent regional promoters across the country were complaining about the company's alleged anticompetitive practices. The biggest issue was the perceived conflict presented by Clear Channel's dual ownership of concerts and radio stations, the very relationships that the company was touting as its crowning achievement.[14]

In the old days, promoters were contracted by touring musical acts and subsequently bought advertising time on local radio stations that played the groups' music to get the word out about upcoming shows. They usually threw in free blocks of tickets to be given away on the air. The arrangement benefited both the promoters, who could shop around the different stations for the best ad rates, and the radio stations, which could select the concert tours that offered the best ticket blocks and the most attractive demos for their audience.

Clear Channel's new dual status changed the dynamic almost immediately. Local promoters began complaining that Clear Channel stations were less than enthusiastic about taking their radio ads, in some cases refusing to run them at all or running them late.

In Denver, the debate took a turn for the worse when the owners of Nobody in Particular Presents, a leading local concert promoter that had booked the Beastie Boys, Pearl Jam, and Sarah McLachlan since opening its doors in 1990, filed an antitrust suit against Clear Channel in a federal court. The eleven-page complaint stated that "Clear Channel repeatedly has used its size and clout to coerce artists to use Clear Channel to promote their concerts or else risk losing air play and other on-air promotional support."

The last straw was the Vans Warped Tour. Jesse Morreale, NIPP's leader and co-founder, had hosted the Warped Tour, a traveling punk-rock cavalcade, for the previous five years in the Denver area, and in 2001 he had the tour again. It had become a key part of his business, particularly since the SFX deal had gone through and Clear Channel began to sap away NIPP's usual tour flow.

One beautiful afternoon that summer, Morreale was happily observing as eleven thousand fans filed in to watch their favorite bands perform on multiple stages when he noticed a van owned by KTCL-FM, a local Clear Channel–owned rock station.[15] Morreale was pissed. He had purchased radio spots for that year's Warped Tour on KTCL, but the station either ran them at the wrong times or didn't run them at all. The tickets he gave to the station never made it to listeners but rather were given to station employees. But the station was on his turf and he was having none of it—he approached the van and ejected the station's representatives from the premises.

Just days later, the other shoe dropped when some of the bands on the tour discovered their songs were no longer being played on KTCL. Only through the efforts of some frantic record company execs did the bands get re-added to playlists.

The message was obvious: Clear Channel played hardball. But Morreale sued anyway. "Somebody had to raise their hand and cry bullshit, and that's us," he said at the time. The lawsuit was the first of its kind for the promotion business.

Clear Channel was unrepentant. Lee Larsen, the head of Clear Channel Radio in Colorado, claimed the missing or misplaced ads were mere oversights.[16] In the case of some promoters being unable to purchase radio commercials, he attributed the dilemma to lack of inventory or the stations' decisions not to feature certain tours that didn't appeal to its audiences, rather than a refusal to accept ads from non–Clear Channel shows.

But the effect Clear Channel's arrival had had on NIPP's bottom line was hard to dispute. A few years prior, NIPP ran 80 percent of the shows at Denver's Mammoth Events Center, a thirty-six-hundred-seat venue. Then Clear Channel took over Mammoth, redubbed it the Fillmore Auditorium, and began booking it exclusively. The company also brokered a deal with the city of Denver that gave it first rights to promoting shows at the twenty-thousand-capacity Pepsi Center. It even built an amphitheater called the City-Lights Pavilion that it booked exclusively.

Then Clear Channel twisted the knife, brokering a similar deal with the city regarding the Red Rocks Amphitheatre, the bucolic outdoor venue made famous by the Irish rock titans U2 in the early 1980s. Red Rocks had never set up such a deal before, though a local promoter, Barry Fey, had long booked most of its shows. More remarkably, this last deal reportedly occurred because the city of Denver was concerned that the CityLights venue would leach bookings and ticket revenues from Red Rocks.

Meanwhile, Clear Channel continued to deny charges that its radio stations bullied bands to play its venues, but anecdotal tales kept cropping up. Mike O'Connor told one reporter, "Our airplay decisions are made completely independent of concert bookings." Yet more than one chart-topping act complained of various shenanigans. One platinum-selling rock band was forced to accept a deal in Denver with Clear Channel, even though NIPP offered it more money to promote its shows. Another was informed that if it didn't hire Clear Channel as its promoter, the artist's shows would not be promoted on Clear Channel–owned stations.[17]

It could work the opposite way, too. Around the same time, Alan Smith, the program director at WOCL-FM, a rock station in Orlando, Florida, owned by Infinity Broadcasting, witnessed a promotional arrangement made by his station surrounding a concert by the band Incubus canceled. "The label said they couldn't afford to piss off a Clear Channel rock station," Smith said. "There's a perception among labels that Clear Channel is willing to yank your band."

NIPP never went to court. In January 2004, Jesse Morreale decided to leave the company. In June, he settled out of court with Clear Channel and later went into the restaurant business. Rumors floated that a financial settlement had been made, though Morreale has refused to talk about the details. The perception was that Clear Channel was winning each battle *and* the whole war. The concert industry was bowing to the Clear Channel way.

Gregg Perloff announced his departure from Clear Channel in July 2003, weary of enforcing business practices he didn't believe in. The last straw was when two longtime BGP employees were fired from over his head. Sherry Wasserman decided to leave along with Perloff. Their stated plan was to start their own promotion firm.

Within days of their departure, they scored their first big concert date, Bruce Springsteen at Pacific Bell Park, perhaps the biggest rock show of the year in the San Francisco area. The show was a last-minute coup but gave the pair enough momentum to jumpstart Another Planet.

Two days later, Clear Channel sued Another Planet, claiming the Springsteen show and other upcoming dates had been scheduled while Perloff and Wasserman were still on Clear Channel's payroll. The suit also alleged that the two former employees had taken in-house trade secrets and tried to hire staffers away from their former employer. "There was a fear that I would start hiring all these people and go national," says Perloff.

Perloff says the Springsteen show fell into his lap days after he left Clear Channel; he adds that he received dozens of unsolicited calls from artists' managers at that time, expressing condolences and asking about future business opportunities. He claims Clear Channel was litigating to solve its business problems. "I didn't do anything wrong," Perloff says. The suit was later settled out of court.

Sherry Wasserman now says she mourns the pre–Clear Channel days of concert promotion as much for the way Clear Channel's involvement has changed artists as it has the promoters themselves. She cites the example of Green Day, a Bay Area band that emerged from the politically liberal Berkeley punk scene of the early 1990s to become one of the top-selling rock acts of the early twenty-first century. Prior to Wasserman's and Perloff's departure from Clear Channel, the band played every tour on their home turf with Bill Graham Presents. But for the tour to promote their 2004 album, *American Idiot*, a President Bush–bashing political tour de force, they chose Clear Channel over Another Planet even though the team they had worked with previously had been wholly transplanted to the upstart company.

While Green Day did not work with Clear Channel exclusively (indeed they played a date for Another Planet in Fresno), the overall effect was unsettling. Wasserman and Perloff ultimately were unable to determine who made the decision to pull the plug on their relationship with the band. Wasserman suspects that Clear Channel had the muscle to suggest that dates in other cities wouldn't come through if Green Day didn't play with Clear Channel in San Francisco. "It's certainly not a money issue," she says. "It's just easier not to rock the boat."

In another instance, Wasserman says she believes the Dead, a band made up of the surviving members of the Grateful Dead, were told they would get a significant bonus if they canceled the three confirmed shows they had booked with Another Planet at Berkeley's Greek Theatre in 2004. Wasserman says a knowledgeable source told her that if the group also agreed instead to play at Clear Channel's Shoreline Amphitheatre, and two other cities where they were up against independents, they were promised five other dates on their terms. The only requirement was that they play in San Francisco with Clear Channel. Around that time, Clear Channel routinely outbid other local promoters just to make sure it got the dates. Clear Channel was likely losing money on that one gig, but for a large corporation, the additional costs were assumable elsewhere. Whatever the case, there was no way a smaller player like Another Planet could compete on that level.

Clear Channel's status as a public company has brought nothing but trouble to the concert business, in Wasserman's opinion.

"They've got to show their shareholders quarterly earnings in a business that is really a gambling business," she says. Promoters have no control over content or when a band tours or how well a band sells. "They're making quarterly assumptions based on voodoo."

In the end, karma appeared to remain on the side of Bill Graham Presents and the other independent promoters who felt wronged by Clear Channel. In November 2004, Clear Channel Entertainment announced it would re-rebrand all of its original concert fiefdoms with their original names. For better or for worse, Bill Graham Presents would remain, at least in name.

By then, Clear Channel Entertainment's bad reputation and rocky profitability had taken their toll. Of greater concern, Clear Channel's stock price was flatlining. In mid-2005, Clear Channel announced plans to spin off Clear Channel Entertainment into an independent public company by the end of the year. In December, an initial public offering took place for a company that became known as Live Nation. While Michael Rapino, the former head of Clear Channel Entertainment, was also chief executive of the new company, Live Nation would have to stand on its own merits.

In October 2007, Live Nation attempted to blaze a new path for the ailing music industry by signing a $120 million, ten-year deal with Madonna. The veteran pop icon, then forty-nine years old, was contracted to produce three albums for Live Nation, and gave the company exclusive rights to promote her tours and to participate in other businesses, including the Madonna brand, website, fan club, merchandising, and TV and film projects.[18]

Says Perloff, "In the concert business, an artist wants someone who is really concerned with every aspect of the show and building better venues and getting places for artists to play and having an overall view."

12.

THE BACKLASH

The mergers and acquisitions community—that is, the influential analysts, lawyers, and assorted deal makers in New York—could hardly contain its enthusiasm for the new and improved Clear Channel. Bigger and better equaled more synergistic in Wall Street's eyes. The bankers and investors gave it their wholehearted seal of approval. As far as the numbers guys were concerned, the conditions that allowed Clear Channel on steroids to suddenly exist amounted to a perfect storm. And despite the fuzzy logic and hasty due diligence surrounding the proceedings, praise for the Mayses' massive multimedia roll-up was nothing short of effusive.

"One of the great powers in this deal is the ability to cross-promote on the local level," gushed Peter Kreisky, then head of the media practice at Mercer Management Consulting. "Many people can get national or international scale, through the use of the Internet, for example, but very few can reach the local level in depth."[1]

Phillip Oleson, an analyst at Warburg Dillon Read, added, "SFX needs to spend money, no matter what, in order to promote upcoming events. It may as well spend that money with Clear Channel's radio stations, and keep a share of the pie, rather than dilute that spending by going to other radio operators."

Even Merrill Lynch's Jessica Reif Cohen, the highest-profile media analyst on the Street, saw some virtue in the new mega-owner.[2] Reif Cohen labeled the SFX and AMFM deals "strongly accretive," adding, "We find these valuations to be quite compelling." At the time, Reif Cohen rated Clear Channel an "intermediate-term, long-term buy" and predicted a $100-per-share stock price within twelve months.

Virtually no one anticipated the host of regulatory issues and dubious business practices that synergy almost immediately seemed to require after one of the fastest roll-ups in media history.

But within the walls of Clear Channel's boardroom, notes of discord had already been sounded. While much had changed in the company's expansion years, the board of directors remained relatively stable. By 2000, the majority of board members were Clear Channel loyalists who rarely questioned initiatives, even major ones, when they were proposed by a member of the Mays family. Three notable exceptions were Karl Eller, who had joined the board as part of his acquisition deal; Tom Hicks, who had joined as part of his; and Bob Crandall, the cantankerous former head of American Airlines and AMFM director who had been grandfathered onto Clear Channel's board.

At one meeting, the head of Clear Channel Outdoor's European division described a plan to lease some of his most valuable sites in England to Van Wagner, a much smaller American rival, for the same price he could sell them for—the problem was, he told the room via speakerphone, he was having a tough time closing the deal. At that point, Eller spoke up, according to someone present at the meeting, and suggested that the deal might not be one worth making. Eller said he knew that Van Wagner would simply turn around and do a sublease deal for double what he was paying. Besides, leasing the company's best sites sent the message that it was considering leaving the business, not one it wanted to telegraph at a time when it was preaching synergy.

Another board member, possibly Crandall or Hicks, piped up and suggested that Eller knew the business pretty well and wondered aloud why the company was doing the deal, if he thought it was such a bad idea.

"Well," answered Mark Mays, "the deal is already done, and

we'll know in two or three years whether it's a good deal or a bad deal." (In May 2006, Clear Channel purchased Van Wagner's U.K. business.)

Eller was hurt that his expert opinion apparently wasn't valued. But he was also stunned from a business standpoint that large deals were being made without an understanding of the fundamentals.

To the few Clear Channel board members who had no prior history with the company, having arrived through one of the big merger deals, every board meeting in the years from 2000 to 2002 was something of an eye-opener. Most came on board enthusiastically, well aware that Clear Channel was on a roll. But for some, that enthusiasm rapidly deteriorated into utter astonishment. One former board member, who spoke on the condition that he remain anonymous, says, "It was clearly a case where there was no appropriate corporate governance."[3]

The number-one point of contention was the infamous employment contract held by the three Mays executives, drafted on October 1, 1999, as a prelude to the AMFM merger. With the agreement's seven-year term, complete with automatic daily extensions, the board—despite Clear Channel's status as a public company—had effectively ensured that it could never appoint anybody except a Mays as chief executive. The inappropriateness of the arrangement never sat well with those who had served on other corporate boards. For all intents and purposes, as far as they could tell, Clear Channel wasn't a public company. It was a privately owned company that was using investors' money to do whatever it wished.

This was not a company that was choosing the best-qualified people to run it. While respect for Lowry Mays continued to run high, there was a growing contingent on the board who felt that Lowry's putting his sons in as the principal officers of a public company was not an appropriate thing to do.

The overall strategy exhibited at board meetings at that time was for Clear Channel to focus on buying stations in markets where it was already a strong presence. Not that the outsiders on the board got any real sense of how business was being conducted. The meetings were more like "nonmeetings" in the sense that no meaningful discussion took place in regard to what the company was actually going to do going forward. Instead, there were long recitations of the financial results for each of the divisions. "I was one of the mushrooms," jokes the anonymous former director. "They keep you in the dark and cover you full of shit."

Indeed, the board at that time made no material difference whatsoever in how the company was being run, since it held a largely ceremonial position. "They've been using the public's money to do what they want to do," says the former board member, who eventually stepped down in disgust, "and they've been doing it badly."

Michael Bracy was a Washington, D.C., lobbyist in the late 1990s representing small cities around the country on telecommunications policy issues when he first became aware of Clear Channel.

Around that time, Bracy founded an advocacy group in support of low-power radio, a low-wattage broadcast format intended to reinvigorate localism in radio that was strongly opposed by the National Association of Broadcasters. Low-power radio was a particular passion of the alternative punk-rock scene, a decidedly anti-establishment movement that prided itself on its independence from what it perceived as a corrupt mainstream music industry.

Through his work recruiting allies to his cause, Bracy met Jenny Toomey, the flame-haired leader of a popular D.C.-area alternative-rock band called Tsunami and co-owner of a small record label, Simple Machines, who also had a history of local political activism. A prolific and critically acclaimed musician who nonetheless had trouble making ends meet, Toomey passionately believed in the notion of the radio as the public's airwaves, not some privately controlled pay-for-play system that systematically excluded artists not caught up in the corporate recording-industry machinery.

In June 2000, Bracy, Toomey, and others founded the Future of

Music Coalition, a nonprofit think tank devoted to the "creation of a musicians' middle class."

Bracy admits Clear Channel wasn't really on his radar until after the AMFM and SFX acquisitions. But as someone who had regular contact with the FCC and other communications operatives in Washington, he quickly noted that no official alarms had gone off after these mammoth mergers. He began to hear the name Clear Channel from fellow grassroots organizers, musicians, and various public-advocacy groups. Was he aware of how big they had become? What was the effect of such a large radio corporation on musicians? What political action could be taken to rein in their influence?

These were the kinds of questions that different groups of people affiliated with various aspects of the music industry had begun to ask about Clear Channel. The newly gargantuan size of the company alone seemed to attract attention.

Meanwhile, a young journalist named Eric Boehlert had found his own way to the story of what was going on at Clear Channel. As a reporter at *Billboard*, a music industry trade journal, and later at *Rolling Stone*, Boehlert had reported regularly on the radio business. For the most part, his work had been pretty arcane stuff, written primarily for those who worked in the music business.

But in mid-2000, he got a new job as a staff writer for Salon.com, one of the first mainstream Internet-only publications. Based in San Francisco, Salon.com presented itself as something akin to *The New Yorker* for the new age. Its perspective was slightly left of center and decidedly provocative. But its main aim was to bring timely, enlightened electronic journalism to the masses.

Initially, Boehlert wrote about media issues relating to the 2000 presidential election, but after the election recount wound down in December of that year, he began to cast about for a new topic to probe in-depth. By January 2001, he and his editor at *Salon*, Bill Wyman, had settled on a story about the pay-for-play system in radio, the institutionalized form of payola that had helped calcify the hit-making machinery but was rarely written about. In the next few months, *Salon* published two articles by Boehlert explaining from a behind-the-scenes business perspective why commercial radio had become so unlistenable.

Boehlert hadn't gotten too far into his reporting when he realized there was another, bigger story to be told about a little old radio company in Texas that had become the world's largest seemingly overnight.

On April 30, 2001, Boehlert's first five-thousand-plus-word Clear Channel article, "Radio's Big Bully," was posted on the site. For perhaps the first time, a journalist documented in great detail the kind of rough-and-tumble tactics the new Clear Channel was becoming known for.

Boehlert vividly described how Randy Michaels and Kraig Kitchin, the head of Clear Channel's Premiere Radio Networks, had taken aside a few AMFM producers at a dinner at the legendary Spago restaurant in Los Angeles celebrating the AMFM–Clear Channel merger in June 2000 and pumped them for dirt on AMFM employees. Days later, after they officially became Clear Channel employees, Kitchin instructed AMFM's president, David Kantor, to fire the same producers. As proof of their bad behavior, he produced a recording of the incriminating conversation made with a cell phone that had been sitting on the table that night.

The article also detailed Clear Channel's involvement in the independent promotion system that enabled payola-like practices, specifically a controversial deal with Tri State Promotions & Marketing. The idea was to hire Tri State exclusively to liaison with the record labels. In essence, the major labels would have to pay steep six-figure fees to Tri State if they wanted their artists played on Clear Channel stations. In return, Clear Channel would reap tens of millions of dollars.

Boehlert also cited Clear Channel's extensive use of voice tracking at the expense of quality programming and its decision to yank Rush Limbaugh's program, which was distributed by Premiere Radio Networks, off all non–Clear Channel stations.

The most resonant image in Boehlert's story, however, related to an on-air stunt involving Todd Clem, the morning DJ at WXTB in Tampa better known as "Bubba the Love Sponge," in which a live boar was castrated and killed in the station's parking lot. Not only did the station broadcast the animal's horrible, bloodcurdling squeals as part of a stunt it dubbed a "roadkill barbecue," but it also posted photos of the butchering on its website. Boehlert dutifully reported it was the third time in a year that an animal had suffered such a fate on the air at a Clear Channel–owned radio station. (Clem later faced legal charges of animal cruelty and was acquitted.)

Then something very peculiar happened: Boehlert says the response to the article was nothing short of astounding. Almost immediately he began getting e-mails from artist managers, record company executives, concert promoters, and even a few reckless Clear Channel employees. And the message from all was pretty much the same: Clear Channel sucks. "Clear Channel sucks" became something of a mantra that started quietly and furtively, mumbled under the breath, but it soon began getting louder, bolder, and angrier. "To anyone in the music business, you'd say, 'Clear Channel,' and they'd just spit—and then start talking," Boehlert says.[4]

The Randy Michaels effect had clearly taken root. It was one thing for Clear Channel to have acquired so many stations, cornered the concert business, and then taken control of a major industry trade magazine and research arm. But instead of conducting itself in a professional, corporate manner, the radio group acted like a Morning Zoo team. "They didn't give a fuck about anyone," says Boehlert. "They just threw people overboard, and they did it laughing."

It was a radical change, certainly in terms of the company's perception within the music industry. By dint of the fact that Clear Channel now had an influence in virtually every aspect of the music business, Michaels's disruptive measures sent ripples throughout an industry that hardly knew anything about the company. Conversely, the Mayses had communicated with astonishing clarity that they had no interest in or concern for the music business. San Antonio's brand of bloodletting combined with Jacor's take-no-prisoners programming style in retrospect was a recipe for a mammoth stink bomb.

Clear Channel's relationship with Tri State, in particular, had thrown the recording industry out of whack. At least two hundred of Clear Channel's stations were top-tier music stations in major markets, and seemingly overnight Tri State's rates to promote records to radio went through the roof. The major labels were furious.

A month later, Boehlert issued his follow-up salvo, titled "Tough Company." This time the focus was the rough corporate climate at Clear Channel and a recent sexual harassment suit. Longtime DJs and producers were allegedly fired without cause. The macho company culture did little to promote women. Employees were actively discouraged from talking to the press. One employee at a station that Clear Channel had recently bought reportedly received an unprompted e-mail from headquarters warning him that if he talked to the press he would be fired.

Other anecdotes described employees being wrongfully terminated, sexist and racial epithets used in the office, and an Indianapolis fund-raiser for the Indiana Children's Wish Fund that Clear Channel pulled out of after learning that the head of Emmis Communications, a competitor, was being honored at the event. Apparently, Clear Channel's general manager for the market even asked for the company's $5,000 donation to be returned.

But perhaps the most insulting allegation, from Clear Channel's perspective, was the claim by a media director at a San Antonio ad agency that Clear Channel's sales teams were bullying her into buying ads she didn't want or need. "You can't negotiate with them because they want to bundle everything," Patricia Bruni of the Atkins/Lord & Lasker agency told Boehlert. "They try to sell you absolutely the wrong format for your demographic and they won't let it die." For the consummate sales executives who built Clear Channel, such tales were evidence of how far their legacy had fallen. They were also a stinging indictment of the media strategy du jour known as synergy.

Over the next two years, *Salon* published more than a dozen articles by Boehlert, each one highlighting in meticulous detail how Clear Channel was damaging the radio and music industries. For those in positions to do something, the series galvanized a movement. Until that time, many musicians, fans, and music executives knew something was going horribly wrong with the music business, but with the rise of Clear Channel there was suddenly a single company that somehow embodied many of the industry's major problems.

A bastard pastiche of homegrown businesses that had all curdled considerably since the idealistic late 1960s, the mainstream popular-music industry had long ago conditioned listeners to expect mediocre, repetitive playlists on radio; filthy, uncomfortable conditions at overpriced live concerts; and more expensive CDs of diminishing musical quality. Clear Channel could hardly be solely blamed for these trends, particularly since it didn't play any direct role in the production of recorded music. But Boehlert's stories, among other press accounts, for the first time put a name to the purely mercenary trend that seemed to have gutted the pop-music biz over the last decade or so.

Unlike with the major record labels, there was no ambiguity about Clear Channel. Clear Channel wasn't actually *producing* any music and lacked any of the perceived glamour associated with the recording world. Furthermore, music fans had no positive historical associations with the name Clear Channel. Indeed, most had never heard of the company before it came to represent something negative.

Subsequent Boehlert stories only served to fan the flames. The early August 2001 installment addressed the antitrust lawsuit filed against Clear Channel by Denver's Nobody in Particular Presents.

When NIPP tried to buy ads on Clear Channel's Denver alternative-rock station, KTCL, the suit alleged, to promote a date in Denver for a popular summer rock tour, the ads did not run during the assigned times. Instead, they aired in late-night or early-morning time slots. In addition, tickets given to the station as giveaways for listeners were instead handed out to Clear Channel employees, such as the head programmer for the company's stations in Denver.

Other, similar stories soon began cropping up. In one instance, the punk band P.O.D. decided to cancel an exclusive concert in Southern California for a non–Clear Channel station for fear of retribution from Clear Channel stations in the area.

"In my mind, everything they were doing was really short-sighted," says the Future of Music Coalition's Michael Bracy. "What they basically did in market after market is they acquired so many properties that they aggressively leveraged to dominate the ad market and really hurt those independent broadcasters. But then the product that came out of it was nothing like you would expect from a real professional broadcast company—it was all second-class products. It wasn't good radio, and it wasn't local radio. And it wasn't well received by audiences."

The Future of Music Coalition was motivated enough by Boehlert's reporting to initiate what became a 147-page study on radio consolidation. Some of the conclusions outlined in the study had never been quantified before. According to the data compiled by the organization, by 2000 ten corporations controlled two-thirds of radio's listeners and dollars. Virtually every local market in the country had a radio environment in which 70 percent of the advertising dollars went to four or fewer companies. Over five years, the study determined, the radio industry had lost a third of its owners.

Bracy says his group's cause was helped, ironically, by Michael Powell, who had been named chairman of the FCC by President George W. Bush in 2001. Powell established himself early as a free-market capitalist bent on dismantling what was left of the media ownership rules. In support of that effort, he commissioned FCC-sponsored studies, including an analysis of the radio landscape that made the case that radio actually supported more programming formats than ever before, proving that consolidation had encouraged diversity. Bracy and his cohorts dug deeper and demonstrated that many of the conventional radio formats overlapped.

Remarkably, Boehlert never got a response from Clear Channel. All of his efforts to interview company executives were rebuffed. No public rebuttals were issued. "They didn't take *Salon* seriously," says Boehlert. "They never, ever, ever—not even after our fourteenth or fifteenth article—believed it had an impact. They thought if they just said the word '*Salon*' out loud that people would just roll their eyes."

Meanwhile, the public movement against Clear Channel continued to gather steam, sometimes in the most prosaic of ways. In 2000, an Austin, Texas–based student and amateur rock musician named Rob Vining started a website called RadioAid.com, as an online clearinghouse for his music, which is computer-based, and that of other musicians who weren't getting played on commercial radio. For a small annual fee, Vining, then in his early twenties, hosted Web pages for emerging artists, where they could stream their recordings and communicate with interested fans.[5] The site eventually featured about five hundred artists from around the world.

As he learned more about the issues surrounding commercial radio from reading news reports on the Internet, it dawned on Vining that one company had contributed more than others to what he perceived as the hostile environment for musicians. "It shocked me how the whole radio industry worked, about the middlemen and the payola going on here and there," says Vining. "I was pretty much blown away at how I didn't know about this beforehand."

Inspired by other popular portals such as WalMartSucks.org, and sensing a business opportunity, Vining decided to register the online domain name ClearChannelSucks.net in January 2002 and began posting links on the site to articles that documented Clear Channel's missteps. He then linked the new informational site to his Radio Aid home page in an effort to attract more traffic. He only chose ClearChannelSucks.net after learning that Clear Channel itself owned ClearChannelSucks.com.

In late 2003, Vining received a letter from Clear Channel's attorneys demanding that he shut down his site. The company's main complaint was that Vining's site containing the Clear Channel name directed users to Radio Aid, which was in effect its competition. Then Clear Channel filed a complaint with an arbitration panel sanctioned by the Internet Corporation for Assigned Names and Numbers.

The panel ruled in Clear Channel's favor; in response, Vining sued Clear Channel for the right to retain the domain name. In the end, Clear Channel backed off, agreeing in a settlement to allow RadioAid.com to retain control of the ClearChannelSucks.net domain, as long as it did not have any advertising on it, that the site stated it was sponsored by Radio Aid, and that it remained separate from Vining's commercial site.

Vining was puzzled by Clear Channel's rapprochement—but not for long. The day after the Radio Aid settlement in February 2005, Clear Channel and Howard Stern dropped their competing lawsuits against each other. "I think they didn't want any negative publicity about it," says Vining.

At the same time, Clear Channel was developing quite a shady reputation, even within the radio industry.

In November 2001, allegations trickled out in the trade journals that Clear Channel had been using "front" companies to hold radio stations that it controlled illegally.[6] David Ringer, a businessman and former broadcaster who advertised in the tiny market of Chillicothe, Ohio, had filed a complaint with the FCC, aiming to prevent Clear Channel from purchasing WKKJ-FM, a country-music station based in Chillicothe, which fell under the Columbus market, where Clear Channel already owned stations. Ringer's petition alleged that Clear Channel had engaged in an "elaborate shell game" with its stations in Chillicothe, in an effort to circumvent existing ownership rules limiting the number of stations a company could own in a specific market.[7] Ringer claimed Clear Channel had been operating the station for years anyway, despite the fact that its name did not appear on the license.

Ringer also argued that Clear Channel's purchase of WKKJ would allow the company to own all four commercial radio stations in Chillicothe, thereby enabling it to raise advertising rates indiscriminately. Ultimately, the purchase went through; Clear Channel argued its actions were legal and that any problems related to WKKJ were "clerical" in nature.

Other radio groups in the industry couldn't figure out why Clear Channel was getting a pass from regulators while they did their best to operate in good faith. "Clear Channel went and said they were not parking stations, that they didn't have stations that they weren't legally allowed to own but they were controlling," says Robert Unmacht. "At the same time that they were saying they didn't do that, I knew of many instances where everybody on staff was working for Clear Channel. I know for a fact they were doing that. I would talk to people in the station and they would all say they worked for Clear Channel, and I couldn't find a general manager or the owner. And they were in Clear Channel facilities and the website said Clear Channel. There was nothing there that anyone couldn't have seen—I'm not talking boardroom secrets."

Clear Channel had something of a track record in this area. As far back as the early 1990s, the company had owned up to 80 percent of the equity interest in Snowden Broadcasting, a small New Orleans radio group owned by Jim Snowden, a general manager of one of Clear Channel's Houston stations. Snowden, as a minority broadcaster, qualified for a minority tax certificate, something that Clear Channel on its own would not have been entitled to. Snowden owned 100 percent of the voting stock but only 20 percent of the company's equity. "Those sorts of things kind of skirted the rules, whether it was legal or illegal," Unmacht says. "Either way, the intent was not what Congress wanted, which was a minority owner."

According to Unmacht, when Clear Channel was ultimately denied the tax break, it sold the stations. "They had a willingness to play games when they said they weren't," he says.

Then there was the case of the dirt-bike races.

On November 7, 2001, Allen Becker, a Clear Channel consultant, wrote an e-mail to his son Brian, Clear Channel Entertainment's president, expressing concern about JamSports, a division of Jam Productions, a relatively small Chicago-area event company. JamSports had recently signed a preliminary deal with the American Motorcyclist Association to become the chief sponsor of Supercross, a dirt-bike competition that traveled to stadiums around the country. In the e-mail, the elder Becker suggested some ways to sabotage the deal, including probing Jam's finances, talking to the motorcycle association, using Clear Channel's concert promotion arm to bargain with the stadiums, and launching a publicity campaign to disparage Jam. "In the past, it has been kill, crush and destroy," Allen Becker added. Brian Becker forwarded the message to three other company executives with the comment "This is good advice. We should be proactive."[8]

Clear Channel subsequently set about orchestrating a strategy to discredit Jam that had the intended effect, even going so far as to contact motorcycle race promoters in Europe and arrange dates for Supercross races overseas that would conflict with those scheduled by Jam in the United States, thus making it in violation of rules set by an international motorcycling association. By early 2002, Supercross had canceled its deal with Jam and signed on with Clear Channel for the next seven years.

These communications were revealed during a federal court case in Chicago after Jam's co-owner Jerry Mickelson sued Clear Channel for its alleged anticompetitive tactics, asking for $32 million in damages. In March 2005, a jury ruled in favor of Jam and awarded the smaller promoter $17 million in compensatory damages and $73 million in punitive damages.

Clear Channel painted a picture of Mickelson as a "disgruntled competitor" and succeeded in convincing a judge to throw out the verdict on damages a few months later and order a new trial, even though several jurors had described Clear Channel's behavior as anticompetitive and scary.

The company's strong-arm tactics also drifted into Spanish-language radio. In 2002, Clear Channel was blamed for scuttling a merger deal between Spanish Broadcasting System, a main competitor of the Clear Channel–controlled Hispanic Broadcasting Corporation, and Univision, the nation's largest Spanish-language television network. Among the bizarre accusations that emerged in an antitrust suit filed by SBS was a claim that Randall Mays had called a Lehman Brothers executive around the time the company was securing the Wall Street firm as a leading underwriter of its IPO in 1999 and told her that SBS's Cuban-born Raúl Alarcón Jr. was a "drug user and/or trafficker."[9] Randall later admitted to parts of the call, but denied that he relayed the unconfirmed rumor with the intent of encouraging Lehman to pull out. Univision later bought HBC for $3.2 billion in 2003, and Clear Channel cashed out its stake to repay debt.[10]

No matter how one sliced it, Clear Channel had developed a reputation as an unscrupulous operator. It was hard to fathom that the company Lowry Mays had built on loyalty and trust had devolved to this, though some close to the company say the shift had a lot to do with the business values of Mark and Randall.

A well-circulated story about Randall Mays gives some sense of how the brothers were perceived in the business world. An enthusiastic golfer, Randall headed out to Pebble Beach, California, in 2002 for the AT&T National Pro-Am, a tournament where amateurs from the corporate world are paired with touring pros. A longtime attendee, he was determined to win this time. That year Randall was paired with the pro Brian Claar, and the team beat Glenn Frey (of the Eagles rock group) and the golfer Craig Stadler by just one stroke, winning with a total score that was 33 under par, the predicted number of strokes it takes to golf a particular course. Mays's handicap was listed as somewhere between 76 and 79, based on a complex formula that averages amateur players' par over a number of previous rounds and then adjusts for variations in course difficulty. But when the tournament judges checked back with Randall's club in San Antonio, they allegedly discovered he hadn't been keeping scores for a whole year prior to the tournament and had essentially fudged his data. The organizers of the tournament reportedly asked him not to come back the next year, though he did return in 2004.[11]

The story, whether apocryphal or not, resonated with those who had dealings with the younger Mays. "That's the kind of guy Randall is," says one insider. "People didn't trust him."

Clear Channel's second-quarter-earnings conference call with Wall Street analysts in 2002 was a bizarre and embattled event. For one, the ever-growing torrent of criticism had prompted the company to hold the conference call somewhat earlier than planned. In his meandering opening statement, Lowry Mays tried to assure the company's stockholders that Clear Channel's core businesses were in fine shape.

"I don't know why the rumors in the market place are malicious," Mays soberly told the analysts, "and I'm in hopes that we can get through those this morning so we can get back to our business, which has always been creating shared value."[12]

But his comments wandered off into stray asides addressing rumors about the company's management style that had clearly found their way back to his office. "I have heard, because of the Adelphia thing [members of the Rigas family had recently been convicted of massive fraud at the cable company], that there has been some concern about this company being a quote 'family company,' " he said. "This is not a family company. This is a company that is run for the benefit of all of our shareholders, not a few of our shareholders . . . We have never, ever embraced anything concerning a super voting class of stock, and we have always been open to a one share, one vote stockholder base."

Mark Mays, who followed his father, made an effort to explain the swift, unanticipated departure of Randy Michaels in August

2002. "I want to emphasize that there has not been a sudden event, or any poor performance within the radio group," he said. "This is a decision that has been contemplated for a long time. This is a simple evolution in the management of the radio division, not moving from an aggregating environment into an operating environment."

Randall tried to bring the focus back to the numbers by assuring callers, in light of the raft of accounting scandals that were ripping through corporate America, that the company's own financial practices were pristine.

"We don't have those issues," he said. "It is very clean. You can walk directly through the financials and follow the cash, and that is going to be true going forward . . . We review every balance sheet account at the end of the accounting period, and any item that does not provide a clear benefit to future periods is expensed."

Despite Clear Channel's best efforts, the odd practices of radio business smashed head-on into Wall Street's antiquated notions of due diligence. The first analyst question came from Mike Russell of Morgan Stanley. "Things seem to be legal, but we are trying to get parameters of the concept of legal payola," Russell began. "For instance, the revenues from the independent promoters, as well as the concept that certain stations that you agreed to operate that are owned by others, that also seems to be legal but of some concern or hence of concern. Could you give us maybe a parameter of how much in terms of total revenues for the radio business comes from independent promoters? Can you give some idea of the number of stations that people might be thinking about in terms of those you are operating, but that you don't own or can't own because of certain FCC issues?"

Randall's response was reassuring, or un-reassuring, depending on one's perspective. "Um—sure," he said. "I think if you look at it, and we don't use the term 'payola,' because it is illegal to take payola. So I will never say legal payola, or anything associated with payola. The revenue stream associated with independent promoters, which is money that is used by the record companies to help market their products, is approximately $10 to $13 million. Record companies utilize different means by which to more efficiently market their product." Randall was trying to explain that these unorthodox payments were not payola since they were not made directly to Clear Channel, but rather to the middlemen, the independent promoters. Such payments had become the norm among the major labels, but in a Wall Street context it was difficult to make them seem legitimate.

Still, Randall Mays gave it his best shot, adding, "My guess is [the record labels] will continue to spend that in a more efficient manner, but it is a *de minimis* amount, as well." In other words, it didn't add up to very much revenue as far as Clear Channel was concerned; and, again, everyone is doing it because it is perfectly legal. "Most every single company in the public domain and in the private domain within the radio industry utilizes LMAs [local marketing agreements] and JSAs [joint sales agreements] because they are very legal and they have been blessed by the FCC. Even so, if you look at those within the radio aspect, it is approximately one percent of revenues."

Anyone who was paying attention might have been pardoned for thinking that something seemed fishy. Why was Clear Channel defending a practice that was responsible for such a small percentage of revenue? The answer most likely was that in a company that paid little attention to its public image, revenue was revenue even if it gave, at the very least, the *appearance* of impropriety.

Clear Channel was drowning in the negative press coverage. One influential radio trade journal, *Inside Radio*, was an unusually sharp thorn in its side. *Inside Radio* and its editor, Jerry Del Colliano, over a period of years had repeatedly attacked the company in a forum regularly read by its peers. Among the charges the publication lobbed at Clear Channel was that its program managers and DJs regularly accepted travel junkets offered by record labels—a clear no-no, according to the FCC.

In November 2000, the company sued Del Colliano, accusing

him of mounting a "vicious and concerted campaign of coercion, public vilification and harassment."[13] Admittedly, Clear Channel's case was weakened somewhat by a parody website owned by the company (and masterminded by Randy Michaels) called Inside InsideRadio.com. The parody site was a dead ringer for *Inside Radio*'s legitimate home page, except for the altered photograph of a man with his head up his behind accompanied by the caption "Jerry checks with an inside source."[14] Articles on the site labeled Del Colliano as a "malicious terrorist" and a "shakedown artist." Another alleged that Del Colliano used unfavorable coverage of radio groups to "extort" advertising or pricey subscription fees from radio executives. The site also claimed that *Inside Radio* was attacking Clear Channel in an effort to convince the company to buy him out.

Del Colliano responded in July 2001 with a $115 million suit claiming that Clear Channel was looking to bury him and his publication's critical coverage.

If a buyout was what Del Colliano wanted, he got what he wished for, though it seems much more likely that he felt unbearable pressure from what had become a very hard-to-combat force in the radio business. Few entities, much less individuals, dared to duel with the Evil Empire at this juncture—and even fewer prevailed. In August 2002, Clear Channel settled with the publisher for an undisclosed amount. As part of the settlement, Clear Channel took over ownership of *Inside Radio*, and Del Colliano agreed to leave the magazine business to become an instructor at the University of Southern California.

Perceptions be damned, Clear Channel certainly knew how to take action when the facts didn't support its worldview. Whether the company could uproot deeply held public perceptions remained far from certain.

13.

CLEAR CHANNEL GOES TO WASHINGTON

Jennifer Johnson was completely lost, even though she was just blocks from her home in Minot, North Dakota. The young mother was frantic, desperately trying to maneuver her pickup truck through a dark, poisonous cloud with her sons Marcus, thirteen, and Matthew, eleven, in the back.

"Mommy, we're gonna die!" someone shrieked from the backseat.

It was 3:25 on the icy morning of January 18, 2002.[1]

Unbeknownst to Johnson, just hours before, at 1:00 a.m., a Canadian Pacific Railway freight train had bounded off the rails, hurling around thirty cars from the tracks just two blocks from the Johnsons' home. Of those cars, a dozen contained anhydrous ammonia fertilizer, of which five had been punctured. The awful sound of the crash echoed for miles.

"The entire house shook," Johnson later told *The Bismarck Tribune*. When she ran downstairs and looked out the window, she saw a giant white cloud approaching. But before she could react, it broke through the window and burned her face, temporarily blinding her. She quickly covered her face with a washcloth and went searching for her children. After getting them down to the basement, she tried calling 911, but the phone line was dead. Then she flipped on the radio, but all she could find was music. There was no station broadcasting details of what exactly had happened or what local residents could do. After an hour of tuning in every station in town, Johnson gave up and shut off the radio.[2] "We didn't know what the chemical would do to us," she said.

Johnson was getting desperate. "The kids were crying," she said. "We were burning up, our eyes were on fire. We were trapped."

That's when she loaded everyone into the pickup and attempted to escape the cloud. But below-freezing temperatures made the cloud dense and seemingly impenetrable. After a few tense moments, she decided to abandon the evacuation plan. Struggling to retrace the tire tracks back to the house, Johnson returned her brood to the basement and waited.

Not far away, her other son, Michael, seventeen, was attempting his own escape. Driving in his Jeep, Michael had heard the explosion, too. He also saw one of the train cars hurl through some trees and into the bedroom of Lee and Carmel Wieland. Followed by a fiery plume, the car ripped through the side of the house, exposing the bedroom and just missing the Wielands' bed. Miraculously, neither was hurt.

The Wielands retreated to their attic, while Michael, driving blindly, attempted to navigate the road out of harm's way. He never made it out of the neighborhood, finding refuge in a nearby home until the air quality improved.

Despite the enormity of the danger, a public warning was not issued over local radio until nearly ninety minutes after the crash occurred. Ultimately, one person was killed, and three hundred more were injured.[3]

When police responding to the catastrophe tried to contact someone at KCJB, the AM radio station designated as the local emergency broadcaster, nobody answered the phone. Instead, the police were forced to contact some of the station's employees at home, seriously delaying the dissemination of crucial information.

The rest of the story is pretty easy to guess. Clear Channel was the owner of KCJB. Indeed, Clear Channel owned all six commercial radio stations in Minot at the time of the accident (there were two others, a public broadcasting station and a religious station). Of the eighty radio stations in thinly populated North Dakota, Clear Channel owned twenty-three.

The local police were later asked by reporters what went wrong with KCJB. They explained that the station was running on auto-pilot at the time of the crash, broadcasting a satellite feed from a remote location. This account was later repeated by Senator Byron Dorgan, a North Dakota Democrat, and became part of the growing public case against Clear Channel.

Over time, the facts have been amended. Apparently, there was one employee on the premises, an eighteen-year veteran of the station. But so many local residents were calling the station that the local authorities couldn't get through. In addition, there had recently been a switchover at KCJB from the Emergency Broadcast System, which operated via a dedicated phone line, to the Emergency Alert System, a more automated digitally based alarm. At the time of the accident, neither system was working.

Both sides disagreed about who was ultimately at fault. The local police didn't have their EAS set up properly, claimed a local Clear Channel manager. A 911 coordinator claimed that Clear Channel's EAS receiver wasn't tuned to the proper frequency. To make things worse, the police had never been notified that the old EBS phone had been turned off.

Lowry Mays later wrote a letter to Senator Dorgan, dated February 12, 2003, in which he stated that the police did not "completely understand the new capabilities of the EAS system," adding that "the government contractor did not correctly install the system" and that "the authorities did not receive complete training on the system."[4]

Regardless of the facts, the blame stuck to Clear Channel. The issue of media consolidation had become a political lightning rod. And Minot, North Dakota's fourth-largest city with a population of thirty-seven thousand, for better or worse, had become the movement's poster child.

It didn't help when Clear Channel stations in other markets experienced emergency-related snafus. During the major Northeast blackout of August 14, 2003, David Rubin, the dean of the Newhouse School of Public Communications at Syracuse University, tuned his battery-operated radio to Syracuse's main news station, WSYR-AM, expecting information about what was happening locally and how the local government was responding. In other words, he expected the station to provide a sense of community within the crisis. Between the hours of 5:00 p.m. and 9:00 p.m. on that day, Rubin later wrote in a letter to a local newspaper, the Clear Channel–owned station instead featured the lone efforts of its news director, Bill Carey, who after a few minutes of local coverage switched to CNN feed reporting on the national situation. Apparently, WSYR had no local reporting staff available to send out to sources for information.[5] Rubin described Carey as "a general without any troops in the field."

Rubin says he was disappointed in WSYR, long considered a pillar of the community, both as a media professional and as a private citizen. "First, it should have had a clearer plan for how to respond during a potential disaster, whether it be a power outage or a natural disaster or a terror attack," he told me. "Second, they have to have enough reporters, so that when they have an all-hands-on-deck, they have a sufficient strength to do something. Third, you have to have people who can do some basic reporting and not simply rely on the whims of public officials who choose to come on the air."[6]

Carey later criticized Rubin's attack, insisting he did have reporters on duty but they were simply putting officials on the air or taping stories. Joel Delmonico, WSYR's general manager, stated publicly that staffing at the station wasn't much less than a decade earlier. Within days, however, the station fired Carey, though it denied the action was in direct response to Rubin's letter; it also claimed to have instituted new emergency procedures. Rubin says he felt somewhat vindicated, though he acknowledged he has no way of knowing if the station has substantively improved its emergency response efforts. "I definitely effected some change," he says.

Rubin was later taken to lunch in New York by Clear Channel's public-relations head, Lisa Dollinger, who told him about some changes the company was making across the board. Clear Channel even later made a $20,000 contribution to the Newhouse School for minority scholarships.

Rubin's experience was apparently not unique. On September 11, 2001, the Future of Music Coalition's Michael Bracy, a Washington, D.C.–area resident, says he tuned in to Washington's WWDC-AM 1260 (now WWRC) for information about the terror attacks. He, too, experienced a CNN simulcast, which mostly described what was going on in New York, where the World Trade Center towers had collapsed. "It's not like they had information on how to escape D.C.,"[7] says Bracy. To this day, Clear Channel owns eight stations in Washington, the legal limit.

"The last time I checked, radio airwaves continued to be owned by the public. We need to remind the FCC that radio is a public medium. It must serve the public good."

Senator Russell Feingold, a Democrat from Wisconsin, made these remarks as a featured speaker at a Future of Music Coalition policy summit at Georgetown University in Washington in January 2003.[8] He recalled how owners of a concert promotion company in his state had complained to him about the anticompetitive business practices of a large radio and promotion company called Clear Channel. He also told the audience that a friend and a local radio station owner had come to him with similar complaints about how these anticompetitive practices were ruining the public service aspect of radio. Feingold delivered these comments from a pedestal of certain moral standing: he was one of only five senators who had voted against the passage of the Telecommunications Act of 1996.

And so with power and influence few Clear Channel critics could match, Feingold laid careful plans to do something.

First, he recruited the support of his old ally from their bipartisan campaign-finance-reform bill, John McCain, the Republican senator from Arizona who had recently been chosen to head the Senate Commerce Committee. Feingold convinced McCain to hold hearings on Capitol Hill regarding media consolidation. Then he assembled a panel of radio industry experts to testify. Two days before the hearing, he reintroduced a bill proposing legislation from June 2002 called the Competition in Radio and Concert Industries Act, intended to help smaller radio station groups and concert promoters by explicitly outlawing anticompetitive practices in the industry.

The Feingold bill never became law. Some observers say the senator never intended it to. But the bill did help frame the argument against media consolidation and forced the Washington power base to slow its push toward even more deregulation. From the time the bill was introduced, the FCC put a freeze on ownership caps. It also helped the Senate Commerce Committee to form a bipartisan consensus that consolidation had probably gone too far, at least as far as the public's interest was concerned. And most significantly for Clear Channel, Feingold's edict shed light on the practice of leveraging unrelated assets—in this case, its concert promotion business—against the possession of a government-issued radio license. Suddenly synergy, at least as mapped out by the folks in San Antonio, didn't seem like such a brilliant idea.

When the Commerce Committee hearing on the concentration of media convened on January 30 at the Russell Senate Office Building in Washington, D.C., it featured Lowry Mays; Eddie Fritts, president of the National Association of Broadcasters; Don Henley of the rock group the Eagles, representing the Recording Artists' Coalition, which he co-founded with the singer Sheryl Crow; Robert Short, president of Short Broadcasting; and Jenny Toomey, executive director of the Future of Music Coalition.

After the members of the Commerce Committee made their opening statements, largely along party lines (Conrad Burns, Republican from Montana, compared payola to grocery stores taking payments from food companies for favorable shelf space, "and I think that needs to be looked at about as much as what we hear of here"), Lowry Mays related his own story briefly. In his hands, it was the humble tale of a businessman who "knew very little about the [radio] business" when he purchased a single radio station in 1972. But there was one core principle he understood back then, he said, as the key to his success: "You must be locally focused and delight and inform the listener every hour of the day." He added, "While radio may have changed in many ways over the past thirty years, the key lesson I learned then still applies today. That means Clear Channel must continue to serve our local communities in the very best way that we can."[9]

Preaching the virtues of consolidation, Mays explained that radio was in fact the least consolidated of any of the media industries, with the ten biggest radio operators accounting for only 44 percent of the industry's advertising revenues. He stated for the record that Clear Channel's twelve hundred radio stations represented a mere 9 percent of all radio stations in the country and that major musical artists in fact wielded most of the power in the industry by the sheer reality that if they didn't want to work with Clear Channel, they could simply go elsewhere. Furthermore, he claimed, a bigger Clear Channel had resulted in more format diversity among the company's stations.

Mays also attempted to dispel the claim that Clear Channel was responsible for the rapid rise of concert ticket prices. He instead blamed escalating prices on the artists, who "are demanding more and more money from touring because their album sales are decreasing."

Mays's statement was surprisingly bland, especially when considering the huge transformation Clear Channel had gone through in recent months, both within the radio community and in the press. It was also oddly out of character. Why would Lowry choose now of all times to preach the simpler pleasures of radio's relationship with its listeners? The tactic, if that's what it was, seemed to betray Clear Channel's very notion of itself and the innovative economic model it devised.

Whatever his intentions, Mays was quickly put on the defensive. Jenny Toomey took issue with his musical diversity plea. "Measuring music diversity by counting the number of radio formats is like measuring the variety of food in your pantry by counting the number of cans without looking at what is inside them," she told the committee.

Of the opposing opening statements, Don Henley's was perhaps the most stinging, if only because it came from a well-known rock star who had, at least theoretically, a lot to lose career-wise. "These days many radio stations are now demanding exclusive promotional concerts from certain artists who are on their way up the ladder of success," he told the panel. "And this is just another form of payola." Henley added that Clear Channel stations were responsible for 82 percent of the popular-music airplay in the United States. Invoking a column by the conservative *New York Times* columnist William Safire (!), Henley explained, "The radio airwaves cannot be equated with grocery store shelves. The airwaves belong to the public, just as the national forests belong to the public, and they are supposed to be used to benefit the public as well as to foster economic growth."

But the exchange that would make the next day's headlines was the dramatic blowup between Senator McCain and Lowry Mays.

McCAIN: "Mr. Mays, does Clear Channel have any plans to obtain more radio stations?"

MAYS: "We don't have any stations pending at this time, sir."

McCAIN: "Do you have any plans to obtain more radio stations?"

MAYS: "I would suggest to you that if we felt there was—"

McCAIN: "Do you have any plans to obtain more radio stations? I'd like to ask the question for the third time."

MAYS: "If we can serve the local community better, and we see an opportunity, yes."

McCAIN: "Do you believe there's any limit to the number of radio stations that a company should be permitted to own?"

MAYS: "I think the 1996 Telecom Act established those limits by limiting the number of stations in each local market."

McCAIN: "I'll repeat my question again, and I haven't got a lot of time, and I'd like you to try to answer the question directly. Do you believe there's any limit to the number of radio stations that a company should be permitted to own?"

MAYS: "I don't think there should be a limit within the Telecom Act of 1996."

Payola, the illegal practice of paying stations to play certain songs without identifying the payments, was also addressed. Senator Kay Bailey Hutchison, a Republican from Texas, asked Lowry Mays point-blank whether artists had to pay to be on the air at a major radio station.

Mays cagily didn't deny that record companies made payments to independent promoters that in turn tried to influence stations. But he implied that the practice was their own fault: "They're not willing to stop that because they're afraid, I guess, some other record company will continue to do it." He also emphasized that Clear Channel had a "zero tolerance to pay for play."

Again Senator McCain made a sharp parry: "What you're saying, Mr. Mays, is that there's no payola. In response to our question, there's no payola?"

"Absolutely none."

Don Henley was livid, noting that none of the radio stations were returning the independent promoters' checks. Though he claimed no direct knowledge of payola, he got billed by his record company for independent promotion. Henley also brought up the so-called charity concerts that Clear Channel often asked artists to play for free. He suggested that in most cases, Clear Channel donated a small sum to the charity and kept the rest of the proceeds while the musicians got paid nothing. "[This] is simply another form of payola," said Henley.

Mays again denied the allegations, saying his company had no policies to that effect, but the evidence told a different story. "I don't care what Clear Channel says, there were clearly many instances where bands were told that if they're touring with Clear Channel and they were coming into a market, they would have to go to [do promotions] on their station," says Eric Boehlert, who wrote about the practice for Salon.com. "And if they didn't go to that station, [the station was] not going to run their ads."

As the press accounts dribbled out in the days following the hearing, it became evident that this was Lowry Mays's Enron moment. That is to say, public sentiment had officially abandoned Clear Channel and gravitated toward "the people." Regardless of the validity of any of the charges hurled at Mays, he had been forced into a position he loathed—having to answer publicly for his business practices. Senator McCain vowed to pursue antitrust legislation against radio, and Mays left the room knowing that Clear Channel would have to make some adjustments.

The first changes dealt with impressions rather than substance, in inimitable Clear Channel style. The company hired Brendan Kelsay, who formerly worked in Representative John Dingell's office, and Robert Fisher, an aide to Senator McCain, as directors of government affairs. Andy Levin, the head of Clear Channel's Washington office (and later the company's chief legal officer), was another former Dingell aide. It also hired the Washington lobbying firm Paul, Hastings, Janofsky & Walker.

From now on, the Evil Empire would have to at least appear to be a little nicer.

In the months both before and after the January 2003 hearing, the FCC commissioners Jonathan Adelstein and Michael Copps, both Democrats, requested that Chairman Michael Powell go on a listening tour around the country and get some feedback at public forums. Powell only held one such hearing, in Richmond, Virginia. So Adelstein and Copps took it upon themselves to hold their own hearings in thirteen different locations nationwide, including Seattle, San Francisco, Chicago, New York, and Atlanta.

The response was remarkable. In many cases, more than five

hundred people showed up. Adelstein says that what he and Copps learned was that there was widespread frustration with radio.[10] Each hearing was held at a local church or community center and consisted of debate among a panel of media experts, followed by an open forum segment that often stretched the gatherings past midnight. Local citizens were allowed only two minutes at the microphone, but the line of prospective speakers often stretched into the hundreds.

The complaints were usually built around a core set of concerns about the rise of big media. The loss of localism. The loss of news coverage. Homogenization of programming. "We got an earful across the country from citizens who had found that radio consolidation was diminishing their experience of radio," says Adelstein. "People pleaded with us, 'Don't let what happened to radio happen to television. Don't allow consolidation in the television field the way that you did in radio or you'll destroy television, too, and make it worse than it already is.' "

Adelstein recalls how an attendee at the event in Albuquerque, New Mexico, approached the mike and described his trip home just before the hearing. As he drove closer, he said, he could see a huge plume of smoke in the area by his house. He wondered if the road was closed. Then he flipped on his car radio, but all he could find was the usual preprogrammed selection of Top 40 and adult-contemporary stations—not a single report about the fire. "It was the top story in the newspaper by the time the next morning rolls around," says Adelstein. "But in real time, he's not getting the information that he needs—and that was just that day."

It was then that Adelstein suspected the incident in Minot was more than a freak occurrence. In his mind, consolidation in radio had strip-mined radio and robbed the medium of its essential communal nature. "The deep sense of accountability to the community has been lost," he says. "A lot of times now, of course, the company that owns the radio station doesn't even come from that community." The FCC continues to license radio frequencies only to local stations, but since those licenses are owned by large national conglomerates, the local connection is severed. "It's different when the owner has to go to the local café in the morning and talk to members of the community," he adds.

Adelstein expresses frustration about the limited means at the FCC's disposal to regulate what he regards as an industry out of control. "The sad story is that the FCC pulled its own fangs," he says. "And now it's a toothless tiger. I don't think broadcasters take us as seriously as they used to. We used to really inspire fear and awe among broadcasters, and now they deal with us because there are major issues in front of them, but they don't feel like their lives are dependent on it."

With the hearings in Washington, Clear Channel had hit rock bottom, at least in terms of the public's perception of the growing company. While no one could give a definitive reason why Clear Channel faced criticism, lawsuits, and bad press where other media companies met with, at the very least, routine coverage, there were a few possible contributing factors.

First, it didn't help that Clear Channel openly flaunted its lack of passion for culture in general. "It might have been a lot more difficult if Viacom were the company doing all of these things," says Jenny Toomey. "The way [Clear Channel] went about their business was so egregious in relation to their mandate."

In this regard, the FCC chairman Michael Powell's arrogant dismissals of those who doubted the merits of consolidation ultimately hurt Clear Channel's cause more than it helped it. "On one hand," says Toomey, "you've got somebody whose job it is to protect the public interest"—Chairman Powell—"who says he has no idea what the public interest is. And then you've got an executive with a clear legal mandate to serve the public"—Lowry Mays—"who says he has no mandate to serve the public, only his advertisers." The incessant stream of complaints that resulted in the hearings on the Hill made clear what even few in the business believed: that the average American still cared about radio.

The second factor was a different kind of culture problem—one of corporate culture. In their haste to assemble a masterpiece of corporate culture, the Mayses seemed to have forgotten to look beyond their spreadsheets and remember that real people run companies. The passion that employees hold for a company's future vision of itself helps that vision become concrete. Toomey points out that when Clear Channel bought SFX, it acted as if it could simply dictate a new way of doing business and that all of its employees would automatically fall into line. "One of the benefits of Clear Channel buying SFX was that these are all people that managers and artists have built up long relationships with," she says. "When they bought these concert houses, they often bought their entire staff. So the guy who gave your artist his first leg up works at Clear Channel now."

Clear Channel once again had the power and resources to reinvigorate a business that had lost its way in a forest of mergers. But the top executives in San Antonio expressed little interest to their new hires in learning the intricacies of what they had purchased. The truth was they were becoming increasingly distracted by the fires burning just outside the company's comfort zone.

14.

PAYOLA

Of the many new practices instituted by Clear Channel Radio under Randy Michaels's command, the one that was perhaps most damaging to its relationship with the recording industry was the innovative wrinkle he brought to the dark art of payola. While Clear Channel had the power to eradicate the system instituted to influence which songs ultimately got played on hundreds of major radio stations, it instead simply tweaked it to favor its bottom line. Under Michaels's direction, the radio division managed to force record labels to make higher payments while at the same time lessening the impact of those payments. It was a strategy that was equal parts brilliant and stupid. In the end, it would catch up with Michaels and contribute to his undoing.

While the practice known as payola has its legal corollaries in other businesses, it remains illegal in radio because the airwaves under American law are owned by the public. The FCC issues licenses to radio stations allowing them to air commercial broadcasts as long as they operate in the public interest. Payola compromises the public interest by encouraging stations to play music based on criteria other than its merits or popularity. Many blame it for the sharp downturn in radio listenership in recent years. If radio stations aren't playing music that people actually want to hear, it stands to reason that people will stop listening, particularly when they have other options. It also hurts the chances of up-and-coming musicians on smaller labels, who usually cannot afford to pay large sums to stations or promoters.

The history of payola, a contraction of "payoff" and "Victrola," is as long as the history of radio itself. And for most of those years, it was hidden enough that it was all but unknown as a concept to the listening public. By the 1930s, however, the practice of paying for airplay was pervasive in both the popular- and the classical-music markets.[1] In those days, it took payments of at least $1,000 to get a composition enough airtime to qualify for *Variety*'s list of most-played songs. While payola was not explicitly illegal, commercial bribery was. Men known as song pluggers, who were employed by sheet-music publishers, held a quasi-legitimate role on Tin Pan Alley, acting as salespeople and sometimes even entertainers, playing the piano in sheet-music store windows and appearing as singers on popular-music radio programs.[2]

In 1960, payola went mainstream after Alan Freed, a popular Top 40 DJ, was indicted and later convicted for accepting a $2,500 payment for airplay. The arrest of Freed and seven other radio professionals was the end result of a long-standing turf war between the American Society of Composers, Authors and Publishers (ASCAP), the original music-licensing organization, and an upstart competitor, Broadcast Music Inc. (BMI). ASCAP, which had its roots in selling sheet music and phonograph records, was an early radio industry foe, and levied high fees for radio play, complaining that playing records on the radio for free would hurt record sales. The broadcasters in turn helped form BMI in 1939 and instituted a payment system to publishers based on the popularity of a song. BMI tended to attract music publishers on the fringes of Tin Pan Alley, in the areas of country and Western, rhythm and blues, and, in the 1950s, rock and roll.

Following the TV quiz-show scandals of the mid-1950s, ASCAP pushed for Washington hearings on payola. The hearings were well-timed with a popular backlash against rock and roll, which was considered a passing fad and feared for its primitive rhythms and sexual innuendo, as well as its African-American influences. ASCAP also had solid economic reasons for wanting to destroy the rock-and-roll industry, whose publishers were mostly represented by BMI.

After Freed was convicted, he received a $300 fine and a six-month suspended sentence and was fired by his various employers; he died of alcohol-related causes a few years later. Dick Clark, another top DJ, was implicated early in the controversy but escaped relatively unscathed and went on to build his *American Bandstand* empire. Following the trial, an anti-payola statute was enacted, making payola a misdemeanor punishable by up to $10,000 in fines and one year in prison, though it was rarely enforced.

Meanwhile, payola persisted. With the rise of FM radio in the 1970s and '80s, the practice went deeper underground, and payments sometimes took the form of marijuana or cocaine. Prosecutors in the 1970s used the Racketeer Influenced and Corrupt Organizations (RICO) statute to combat corporate bribery, forcing the labels to distance themselves from payments. From then on, a group of independent promoters, employed at arm's length by the major record labels, did most of the dirty work through local contacts. In 1981, two of the largest record labels, Warner Bros. and Columbia, upset about rising payments, attempted a boycott of indie promoters. When top artists objected, the campaign fell apart and the promoters only got bolder.

In his bestselling 1990 book, *Hit Men*, Fredric Dannen documented how major labels lost more than $40 million to payola in the 1980s through the influence of a bullying band of promoters called the Network with connections to organized crime. A 1986 feature on NBC's *Nightly News* titled "The New Payola" exposed the scheme and initiated another cleanup. Some majors soon renounced the indies, and Rudolph Giuliani, then the U.S. attorney in New York, began a federal grand jury investigation. Al Gore, then a Tennessee senator, prompted the Senate to examine payola.

From its earliest days through 1989, Clear Channel, according to John Barger, did not engage in payola-like practices as a matter of corporate policy.[3] It required its employees to sign anti-payola affidavits every six months and policed its rock stations in particular, due to its awareness of problems at other companies. "Other stations we knew of had problems—guys who were making less than $175 a week wound up having $3,000-a-week cocaine habits," he says. "It doesn't take long to figure out there's something rotten in Denmark."

But otherwise Clear Channel in the 1980s had little to no presence in major markets and owned few contemporary urban stations, the kinds of stations where the practice was most prevalent. Its big moneymakers were news-talk and country stations. "The ingredients just weren't there," Barger says.

Pay-for-play became less prevalent for a while, and the payments got smaller, but by the late 1990s payola was back and bigger than ever.

While executives who worked at Clear Channel in those days deny that payola was officially sanctioned, the sheer size of the company, particularly after 1999, meant that it was extremely difficult to keep tabs on what was happening at particular local stations. Traditionally, payola occurred at either the DJ or the program director level. Employees in these positions had the greatest ability to impact the playlists and were most amenable to cash payments or perks, due to their lower salaries, especially in smaller markets.

Indeed, the newly humongous Clear Channel received its first FCC fine for payola in October 2000 for a violation at two former AMFM stations that had not even been part of the company when the infraction allegedly occurred. Spurred by a 1998 series of stories in the *Los Angeles Times*, the FCC determined that WKQI-FM in Detroit and KHKS-FM in Dallas had "willfully and repeatedly" broken the law by playing the Bryan Adams song "On a Day Like Today" in exchange for cash payment and a guarantee that he would perform without charge at station-related concert events.[4] The resulting fine of $8,000 was of little consequence for a company of Clear Channel's size, but the incident exposed a new way that payola was being employed.

Randy Michaels, with his encyclopedic knowledge of the radio business, was no doubt well aware of payola's history. As the head of Clear Channel Radio, he publicly stated his distaste for the independent promotion system. "It's not just illegal, but it's also stupid," he said, "because it compromises the integrity of the radio station."

From his new power seat, Michaels believed he could reduce Clear Channel's liability while shifting the entire payment process in his favor. His first idea was to direct all independent promoter payments to Clear Channel headquarters in San Antonio. In a 2002 interview with an industry journal shortly after stepping down as head of Clear Channel Radio, he explained his line of reasoning:

> What we found at an awful lot of stations we bought was that an independent promoter was paying the station based on a formula, so that every time the station added a record they got a credit in the "bank." They could then redeem those credits for concert tickets, promotion items, T-shirts, fireworks shows, or even cash, if they needed some extra money to make the bottom line. To me, there is no difference between paying the manager to play a record and going through the process of getting credits in the bank that can later be converted to cash . . . So what we told the labels was that if they were going to pay the independents all this money, and those independents were going to pay radio stations, we were going to take those payments right to San Antonio. The radio station will never see the money, the manager doesn't get to apply it to his bonus, and the program director doesn't get to spend it in promotion.[5]

Michaels said he believed that such a plan would ultimately reduce payments made by independent promoters to stations. Instead, the reverse happened. Radio stations began adding fewer new songs to their playlists each week since there was little financial incentive to do so and most had long ago abandoned any no-

tions of creative programming. The labels panicked and began raising their payments to promoters in an effort to secure the now-
dwindling number of slots for new singles.

But Michaels, for one, was unrepentant. He liked to point out
that no matter how much the labels paid, it would have a marginal
impact on Clear Channel's profits. Still, he had no intention of putting a stop to the practice. "As long as they pay the money, I'm going to take it," he said. "If they don't want to pay the money, that's
fine."

By claiming to take the moral high ground, Michaels inadver-
tently exposed the hypocrisy at the core of the modern radio business. Consolidation had made operators the engineers of their own
demise, forced to squeeze the quality out of their own content in order to meet quarterly numbers, while listeners slowly migrated elsewhere.

Of course, the labels also had lost interest in promoting variety
in their new releases, instead looking for a few blockbuster hits they
could tout in their annual reports. The labels needed radio, the only
surefire way of creating a hit, more than ever before.

Certainly Clear Channel could not be singled out for what had
become an industry-wide practice, but mass consolidation in radio
had helped give the indie promoters a sheen of corporate re-
spectability. In the post-1996 era, the labels paid millions a year to
established independent promoters like Jeff McClusky & Associates
and Tri State Promotions & Marketing, who in turn made payments
to radio groups, depending on how many songs got played. These
payments often showed up on record label balance sheets as "promotional expenses." Under Michaels, Clear Channel even enter-
tained the possibility of brokering an exclusive promotional deal
with Tri State. The implications of such an arrangement were jolt-
ing to the labels: They would all have to funnel their pay-to-play ra-
tions through one firm to get songs played on Clear Channel,
presumably at whatever prices Tri State wanted to set.

It seems unlikely that Michaels didn't realize that his actions
wouldn't make a dent in payola-like activities. According to the

FCC commissioner Jonathan Adelstein, the payola epidemic had increased to historic proportions by the middle of the next decade.

In May 2002, a coalition of artists' groups and recording-industry trade organizations united by the Future of Music Coalition released a document titled "Joint Statement on Current Issues in Radio," an anti-payola declaration calling for new transparency in the radio business. Endorsed by, among others, the American Federation of Television and Radio Artists, the American Federation of Musicians, the Recording Industry Association of America, and the National Association of Recording Merchandisers—diverse music trade organizations that rarely see eye to eye—the statement, which was later delivered to the FCC and Congress, was one of the first times in modern history that the burdens of payola were laid out so succinctly.

While the letter blasted all of the leading radio companies for the deleterious effects of consolidation, Clear Channel in particular was singled out for its vertical integration of its radio and concert promotion businesses. Clear Channel, the statement blared, "has an interest in limiting the promotional support of bands and artists who are performing for other companies, at other venues or who are sponsored by other stations." It also took a jab at Clear Channel's stated plan to start charging record labels for simply identifying the name of an artist and the song played on its radio stations.

News of the statement got a surprising amount of play, making the front pages of the *Chicago Tribune* and the *Los Angeles Times*. The newsmagazine *20/20* featured a big segment on payola and independent promotion the same day the missive was released.

The flurry of press that followed soon had a real-life effect, though not initially at the FCC. In early 2004, the office of Eliot Spitzer, New York State's attorney general, hot off successful probes of business practices in the mutual-fund and insurance industries, began investigating the major recording labels' relationships with independent promoters and with leading radio companies, after receiving various complaints from within the music business and from lesser-known musicians who said they didn't have access to the airwaves. Initially, Spitzer's office issued subpoenas to some of the biggest recording companies in the world, including Sony BMG, Universal Music Group, EMI, and Warner Music Group, demanding the surrender of all related documents, e-mails, and phone records. At first, radio companies and promoters were not included.

The investigation's supervisor, Terryl Brown Clemons, an assistant deputy attorney general and a ten-year veteran of Spitzer's office, says what she and her team unearthed soon began to surprise her. "Payola was as prevalent as had been described," she says, "but in a different form than what I thought it would have taken."[6]

Instead of cash payments passed off to DJs, the new payola was more corporatized, according to Clemons, relying on program directors at the large radio conglomerates to make contact with the indie promoters. The way of doing business had become much more formalized and legal-seeming enough to appear on the balance sheets of public companies. Promoters now guaranteed the big radio groups annual six-figure payments to represent certain stations.

Over time, payola at pop and rock radio had evolved into an elaborate scheme in which independent promoters made exclusive deals with radio companies to act as liaisons between the labels and the stations. Usually the promoters paid each station an annual fee of $100,000 to $400,000 based on the station's ratings and the size of the market. Sometimes the fee would be paid in monthly installments; other times the deal would promise a six-figure amount of promotional support for the station. In the latter scenario, the station would instruct the promoter to pay the provider of promotional services—a T-shirt manufacturer, for example—directly, thereby enabling the station to avoid having to record the payments on its books.

Deals like these also allowed the stations to bill the promoters on a weekly basis for each song added to that station's playlist. Each addition to an FM station playlist cost anywhere from $800 to

$5,000 with most stations adding between 150 and 200 songs to their playlists per year.[7]

Another new payola wrinkle was the labels' use of phony call-in requests. Marketing companies were hired to pose as listeners calling in to radio stations to request certain songs, creating buzz and encouraging airplay, often unbeknownst to the stations.

In the spring of 2003, in the wake of the congressional hearings, Clear Channel announced that it was terminating its exclusive contracts with indie promoters. With the departure of Randy Michaels, the company apparently lacked the stomach to continue handling the high-profile attacks, no matter how much they had sanitized the pay-for-play process. "You're not going to get Lowry Mays to appear before the Senate trying to defend pay-for-play and make it sound OK," one record company executive told Salon.com's Eric Boehlert. "It might be legal, but just barely and it's basically indefensible."

Jenny Toomey found the announcement puzzling, to say the least. "They got out ahead of the debate when they canceled their independent radio promotion," she says. "But what's interesting about that is that they did that after they testified that there was no payola associated with it. The question then becomes, then what did you cancel?"[8]

Implicit in Clear Channel's announcement was the assumption that the world's largest radio company couldn't police every single program director in its expansive roster. Furthermore, the company never officially said it would terminate all payments to record labels, simply that it would terminate existing exclusive indie promotion contracts.

In July 2005, Sony BMG agreed to a $10 million settlement with Spitzer's office, admitting that "various employees pursued some radio promotion practices on behalf of the company that were wrong and improper." Among the most condemning documents unearthed was an e-mail sent by an employee of the Sony-owned Epic label dated April 7, 2003, to a Clear Channel programmer. "WHAT

DO I HAVE TO DO TO GET AUDIOSLAVE ON WKSS THIS
WEEK?!!? Whatever you can dream up, I can make it happen."⁹ As
part of the settlement, Sony fired the top promotion executive at
Epic.

In October 2005, Clear Channel announced it had fired two
programming executives after conducting an internal review. The
names of the employees were not released. But the Spitzer report
detailed how Diana Laird, the program director of Clear Channel's
KHTS in San Diego, received a flat-screen television in November
2002 from Sony. The TV was recorded as a contest prize in the
record label's accounts.

Another Clear Channel programmer, Donnie Anderson, had accepted a trip to Las Vegas in July 2003 and a laptop computer in
exchange for airplay, according to settlement documents.

It's perhaps not surprising that Clear Channel was the first major radio company to officially sever its arrangements with the independent promoters in late 2003. "Once Washington became
involved, they sort of freaked out, and then when they became involved in pay-for-play, they really freaked out," says Eric Boehlert.
"That's why they were the first to cut ties." Cox Radio renounced its
use of the indies around the same time.

Clear Channel's next-closest rival, Infinity Broadcasting, owned
by Viacom, announced about a year later that it, too, would no
longer use independent promoters, no doubt prompted in part by
the fallout surrounding Janet Jackson's Super Bowl halftime show
and the Howard Stern debacle.

Payments from record companies subsequently declined substantially to around $30 million a year. Spearheaded by the actions
of a newly responsive Clear Channel, the prospect of legal action
from Washington fizzled. "The payola legislation basically died when
they came out and said Clear Channel were ending it," says Boehlert.

Not that the industry as a whole is likely to ever fully eradicate
payola-like practices, at least not as long as getting a song on the
radio is the surest way to musical stardom. The radio industry's
general defense of payola-like practices in recent years is best

summarized as the Rice Krispies defense: When supermarket shoppers see a tower of Rice Krispies at the front of the store, right near the registers, they are not necessarily aware that Kellogg's or somebody else has paid for that placement. Same goes for the stacks of bestsellers that greet book buyers at the entrance to their local Barnes & Noble superstore. Radio is behaving in the same way as many other industries, station groups argue, and none of these other businesses is required to disclose behind-the-scenes financial relationships.

But the airwaves, at least from a legal standpoint, remain different because of their status as public resources regulated by the government. "There's a reason why the FCC and Congress have always required us to insist that the public know who's trying to persuade them," says the FCC's Jonathan Adelstein. "The idea behind these rules is the public can make up its own mind if it knows who is trying to persuade them. It can take into account the fact that if a song is being played, it was sponsored by XYZ Records, that it's there because the record company paid to have it there."

Whether radio will ever be rid of payola is unclear. The fact is, rightly or wrongly, a lot of longtime radio folk find the whole issue tiresome—and even remain skeptical of its effects. "If I record my dog howling, no matter how much money I spend with a radio station, they will not play my record," says Robert Unmacht. "So I refuse to get worked up about it until we eliminate it from every other business. I think it's a crock. If we really want to worry about exposing talent and music and diverse thoughts on the radio, why did we let one company own so many stations?" Unmacht argues that no matter how much money a record label pays to a radio company, there is no guarantee a song will ever become a hit.

The FCC was not convinced. The press that Spitzer's ongoing investigations garnered prompted the FCC to launch its own payola investigations in the middle of 2005. In March 2007, Clear Channel, CBS Radio, Entercom, and Citadel agreed to a consent decree that included a $12.5 million payment to settle payola allegations raised by the agency.

15.

ONLINE, OR ON THE
DECLINE?

I n its March 3, 2003, issue, *Fortune* magazine published a feature story titled "The Bad Boys of Radio," documenting the damage Clear Channel had done in the radio industry. It included this ignominious quotation from Lowry Mays: "If anyone said we were in the radio business, it wouldn't be someone from our company. We're not in the business of providing news and information. We're not in the business of providing well-researched music. We're simply in the business of selling our customers' products."

Just weeks later, *The New York Times* ran two negative stories on Clear Channel: One described the defensive posture the company had been forced to strike after one of its conservative talk-show hosts, Glenn Beck, organized station-sponsored rallies in support of the war in Iraq. The second recapped the 2002 emergency snafu in Minot, North Dakota, and explained how the incident had become something of a political football as the FCC was reconsidering media ownership rules.

Indeed, the *Times* had run nearly a dozen articles in the previous couple of months chronicling various aspects of Clear Channel's alleged bad behavior, including two Op-Ed columns, one by the liberal economist Paul Krugman and the other by the conservative columnist William Safire.

Around that time, Clear Channel decided to hire the New York

City–based corporate spin firm Brainerd Communicators to help manage the fallout. For the first time in its history, the company seemed to be acknowledging it had an image problem. It was a huge step for an operation that had only hired its first communications officer, Lisa Dollinger, two months earlier. Clear Channel's PR problems had grown as big as its bottom line.

Even so, its top executives had some unusual ideas about how to manage the press. When Michele Clarke, a representative from Brainerd, first met with Mark Mays to discuss a new communications strategy, the embattled executive kept hammering on the *Fortune* article's headline.[1] Flustered and frustrated, he insisted that Clarke contact the magazine and demand a retraction. *Fortune* refused, but the headline was eventually toned down in the online version of the story.

Once we're done with this, he asked her impatiently, can they just not write about us anymore?

Clarke politely responded that journalism simply didn't work that way. Silence, she explained, is often worse than attempting to clarify matters. Clear Channel had become a large, publicly owned conglomerate. Its size and influence alone guaranteed constant scrutiny.

Clarke finally cut a deal with Mays to minimize his exposure to a process he obviously loathed. From then on, she would only ask him to do three press days a year, giving access to select reporters eager to interview him. The rest of the year she would call on his deputies to handle any press queries. Mays happily agreed.

The heir to Lowry Mays's throne had plenty of other matters to keep him busy.

By 2004, Clear Channel wasn't what it used to be, by any conventional measure. In just five years, the radio landscape had changed dramatically from when the supersized radio company first landed on mainstream America's radar. For one, the iPod generation had been born, along with music file sharing via personal computers and cell phones (among other devices that would likely tote digitized music in the future). Satellite radio, a subscription-based alternative to traditional radio, began to take off in the form of two fledgling companies, Sirius and XM. And streaming music technology, which allowed anyone and everyone to create his or her own radio stations online, generated a whole new forum for listeners to access programming in a way that didn't necessarily favor advertising-supported media.

Suddenly the company's black hats didn't seem quite so threatening. None of the FCC chairman Michael Powell's media deregulation proposals had come to pass, having been blocked by a Congress increasingly distressed by the past behavior of companies like Clear Channel. (A defeated Powell resigned from his post in January 2005.) In retrospect, though, some of Powell's predictions about the media landscape were astonishingly correct: he was particularly astute in predicting how the Internet would change the equation for media companies. It's unclear, however, that his proposed solutions, which often involved giving free passes to large corporations like Clear Channel, would have stemmed the inevitable tide of digital entertainment.

In February, Clear Channel's Premiere Radio Networks canned the Los Angeles DJ Rick Dees, the most popular radio talent of the 1980s on the flagship KISS-FM station, and replaced him with Ryan Seacrest, the young *American Idol* host whom Clear Channel had tapped just a few months earlier to take over Casey Kasem's legendary host spot on *American Top 40*, which Kasem had created more than three decades earlier.

Kasem read the writing on the wall when his contract was up for renewal, though the new kinder, gentler Clear Channel prevailed in his instance. "They said they wanted to go with Seacrest because of the popularity that he has," recalls Kasem, who says he was treated cordially by the company's executives and who gracefully accepted their decision. As part of Kasem's new deal he was allowed to continue hosting *American Top 10* and *American Top 20*, two shows syndicated to adult-contemporary radio stations popular with older listeners. "It was a win-win situation all the way around."[2]

In the midst of all the bad news, Clear Channel's founder was also hit by a devastating personal blow. In May 2004, Lowry Mays became gravely ill and underwent surgery for a blood clot and bleeding in his brain. Although the operation was successful, recuperation prevented the elder Mays from running day-to-day operations. Mark Mays immediately became acting chief executive.

In September 2004, the company announced it would convert about twenty-five of its stations to Spanish-language formats. In the coming months, Clear Channel stations broadcasting Spanish-language formats, including Regional Mexican, Tropical, and the youth-oriented Hurban format, would represent some of the few bright spots in a portfolio that was essentially flat in terms of ad sales.

To make things worse, the whole radio business was in a slump, and as the far-and-away industry leader, Clear Channel was obliged to do something about it. On December 15, 2004, it started a bold new advertising initiative it dubbed "Less Is More." The basic idea was to cut the number of advertising minutes per hour in an effort to bring back some of the listeners who had been abandoning radio in droves. Research had shown that the number-one reason that listeners switched radio stations or turned off their radios altogether was the annoying strings of commercials, which in some markets accounted for as many as twelve minutes of each hour.

Starting in mid-December 2004, Clear Channel pared back advertising an average of 19 percent on all of its stations. It also began pushing marketers to purchase thirty-second commercials instead of the traditional sixty-second spots in an effort to prevent listeners from switching off and to stabilize the pricing of radio advertising, which had fallen victim to heavy discounting. "Pricing is a product of supply and demand," explained John Hogan, a former Randy Michaels hand who became chief executive of the radio division after his boss left the company. "We're trying to decrease the supply and increase the demand."[3]

Clear Channel, for better or worse, was the only radio group out there with enough reserves and marketing muscle to implement such a dramatic change.

The potential risks were great. The new plan involved raising prices by charging more for two thirty-second spots than the company already did for one sixty-second spot. Such a strategy would almost certainly result in a short-term drop in revenues, jeopardizing Clear Channel's already shaky status on Wall Street.

And while reducing the length of commercials certainly reduced clutter, it had little to offer advertisers and creative directors looking for ways to make their spots stand out on radio.

Many within the radio industry privately expressed cynicism about Clear Channel's claim that the ad-reduction program was something it was doing for the whole industry. Many, in fact, suspected that Mark and Randall had cooked up the plan as a way to impress investors and hopefully give the company's virtually frozen stock price a jolt.

By the middle of 2005, Clear Channel's stock had plummeted to $29 a share, from a peak of around $90 in 2000. And that was after the company bought back around 10 percent of the outstanding shares in 2004.[4] Over the past five years, as of April 2006, the stock had lost around 42 percent of its value, compared with a 26 percent decline for its peers.

"The last thing you want to do when you're selling a commodity that has no real basis for the price that you're asking for it [is] share the integral details of it with the general public," says John Barger. "And I think they may have committed a cardinal sin in how they got from point A to point B and pricing on the Less Is More. But realizing what they're up against, maybe I would have done the same thing. They just need a fresh ball of bullshit to throw on Wall Street."[5]

Coincidentally, programming on Clear Channel stations, as well as stations owned by other radio groups, had reached a creative nadir.

The funny thing is, within about a year, Less Is More actually started to work. That's not to say that revenues were up. In fact, they were down about 5 percent by the middle of 2006. But pricing per minute of ad time on Clear Channel stations had risen around 17 percent, an indication that demand for the company's on-air inventory had increased substantially.

The reality was that the terrestrial radio business, while still fabulously profitable, was in deep water.

One of the problems was a difficulty facing every traditional media source—the impending threat of a digital wireless future. For decades, radio had enjoyed the benefits of a captive audience. Listeners had only one option for live programming in the car, and commuter travel distances weren't getting any shorter. Mel Karmazin famously noted that without traffic, there'd be no radio business.

Satellite radio forever changed the equation. The threat of satellite radio began to seem more ominous as subscriptions to the services provided by XM and Sirius continued growing at triple-digit rates.

Back in 1999, Clear Channel had the foresight to invest heavily in the new medium by sinking $75 million into XM for what amounted to a 19 percent stake in the nascent company. But the interests of Clear Channel and XM eventually hit a snag over what constituted quality programming. At first, Clear Channel provided XM with simulcasts of some of its terrestrial music and talk programming. Then XM decided in early 2004 to make all of its music channels commercial-free, as a marketing tool to counter the commercial glut on traditional radio.

Clear Channel wanted to keep the ads. Commercials were its lifeblood.

The companies went to arbitration, and ultimately Clear Channel prevailed. In March 2006, per the settlement, XM agreed to air four music channels programmed by Clear Channel complete with commercials.

Too bad satellite radio hit a snag. By early 2006, the prospects of Sirius, which was collapsing from within under the weight of

Howard Stern's monstrous compensation package, and XM, which now had lost some of its marketability as a commercial-free alternative to terrestrial radio, looked cloudier than ever as new digital options, such as Internet radio—which had been around for at least as long, if not longer—began to jell.

Also in 2004, Clear Channel cherry-picked the much-respected general manager of America Online's music portal, Evan Harrison, to help create a new online strategy for the company. It was a noticeable reversal in strategy for a company that had viewed the Internet with significant suspicion just a few years earlier.

Clear Channel also went a long way toward dispelling notions that its business decisions were politically motivated when it began broadcasting the left-leaning Air America Radio on KPOJ-AM in Portland, Oregon, in March 2004. The liberal comedian Al Franken and the rest of the Air America commentators represented a new format known as "progressive talk," one of the fastest-growing formats during George W. Bush's troubled second term. By September, Clear Channel was hosting its broadcasts on eight of its stations, including ones in Ann Arbor, Michigan, and Madison, Wisconsin, adding up to a full third of Air America's affiliates. A Clear Channel station in Miami, WINZ-AM, changed to Air America, due in part to the success of Michael Moore's Bush-bashing movie *Fahrenheit 9/11*. Around that time, Clear Channel also gave a weekly syndicated talk show to the onetime Democratic presidential hopeful Jesse Jackson, called *Keep Hope Alive*.

Some critics called these developments a ploy to deflect ongoing attacks. Others called them proof that the folks at Clear Channel were exactly what they said they were: dyed-in-the-wool American capitalists. At the time, Clear Channel executives had contributed nearly $300,000 to GOP causes; the company still syndicated Rush Limbaugh to around 600 stations, including 162 of its own.[6] Collectively, Lowry, Mark, and Randall Mays donated $115,000 to President Bush's 2004 reelection campaign.

The reality was that Air America was niche programming, a lone voice in a vast sea of conservative chat, the bulk of what is profitable in talk radio. Clear Channel's research, however, had shown that progressive talk presented a growth opportunity. Politics, it seems, would not stand in the way of a tidy profit, though Air America filed for bankruptcy in 2006, a victim of its own mismanagement.

By early 2005, Clear Channel had dipped its big feet into the online trend du jour—podcasting. In the name of brand extension, the company planned to offer five-minute, ad-supported segments of its programming for downloading off its station websites. The idea was to find a new venue for short humor bits from its morning talk shows and tap into the rapidly growing online advertising market. Harrison also set out to revamp Clear Channel stations' websites, giving them a cleaner, more user-friendly look and embedding streaming online versions of their radio broadcasts.

Whereas its main rival, Infinity Broadcasting (which was renamed CBS Radio at the end of 2005), had fallen behind in its online strategy, an unfortunate by-product of its former chief Mel Karmazin's hawkish ad-sales perspective, Clear Channel boldly had begun to confront a future that at best appeared uncertain.

By mid-2005, the general hostility toward Clear Channel seemed to have calmed. Not that there weren't situations in which the company made blunders that echoed its previous hamhandedness.

In May, Clear Channel stations in Akron, Ohio, began experiencing what sounded like unauthorized interruptions from pirate-radio operators—that is, unlicensed radio stations broadcasting illegally. Around the same time, a website went up online for something called Radio Free Ohio, complete with a manifesto attacking "corporate-controlled music playlists." The amateurish-seeming website demanded that certain local stations, including some of Clear Channel's, "turn over their licenses to the FCC." The site did not provide any contact information.

It was later revealed by a competing station that Clear Channel itself was behind the fake outlaw barrage. The company was looking to attract listeners to a change on one of its Akron stations from

the sports format to progressive talk, including Air America. "Once
we determined we were going to change the format," the local Clear
Channel market manager told *The New York Times*, "we tried to get
into the mindset of people who would listen to this station."[7] Despite the company's formidable sales acumen, its marketing skills
apparently remained stunted.

But the big announcement Clear Channel made that spring was
surely its most newsworthy of the year. On April 29, the company
revealed plans to spin off Clear Channel Entertainment into a separate public company. It would also sell a 10 percent stake in its outdoor division in a public offering.

It was the first overt admission from San Antonio that Clear
Channel—at least Clear Channel, the media monolith—was crum-
bling. The vagaries of Wall Street had finally forced the company to
admit the ill-advised nature of the SFX acquisition. SFX's founder,
Bob Sillerman, explained to *The New York Times* that the notion of
mixing radio and concert promotion "was something that, intellec-
tually, seemed like it would make sense," adding, "But it's a different time now. Investors viewed things differently in 2000. The most
abused word in the English language was 'synergy.' It was crazy.
Now investors are interested in focus and single purpose."[8]

In late 2005, Mark Mays organized the HD Digital Radio Alliance, a confederation of seven leading radio companies meant to
publicize the industry's rollout of digital radio, its best hope of com-
bating satellite radio, the Internet, and podcasts. Clear Channel,
Infinity Broadcasting, Cumulus Media, Bonneville International,
Emmis Communications, Entercom Communications, and Greater
Media agreed to collectively spend at least $200 million to market
the new medium the following year.[9] High-definition digital radio
permits stations to broadcast their programs digitally and offers listeners improved audio quality, new data services, and more format
options. Stations can also offer more than one channel on the same
frequency.

At the time of the announcement, 585 radio stations had made the leap to digital broadcasts, and 28 stations had introduced HD2 multicasting program options, which featured data to be displayed on new receivers, including song and artist information, as well as traffic and weather alerts. Other benefits of digital radio include surround sound and multicasting (multiple audio sources at the same dial position) and on-demand audio services, such as storage and replay of programs.

Though a few top radio groups such as Citadel refused to participate, there were a few signs that this alliance might be sturdier than most. More important, Clear Channel's John Hogan and Infinity Broadcasting's chief executive, Joel Hollander, who have a well-known dislike for each other, agreed to collaborate on the project.

Certainly there were some hurdles: Digital radio required a new receiver and, at the time of the announcement, the cheapest retailed for about $300. Then there was the fact that digital radios were not yet available as an option in most new cars. Even so, many analysts anticipated that wireless broadband access would be available in new models, a development that would improve HD Radio's chances for survival—and threaten the future of satellite radio.

In April 2006, Clear Channel took the crucial next step by introducing an array of new radio formats to fill its new HD multicast channels, as well as the multicasts and websites of its competitors. Calling the new program Format Lab, the company set out to prove that the radio brand previously associated with turning programming to mayonnaise could produce a far spicier mix. Format Lab consisted of seventy-five new channels featuring genres of music that had long gotten short shrift on commercial radio, such as classical, traditional jazz, and bluegrass. Even its rock formats claimed a new diversity. The selection included Dank—"Hip-Hop and Rock rolled up into one big spliff," boasted an online description— and Vinyl Vineyard, a retread of the original album-oriented rock format.

The company claimed two hundred programmers and production employees developed Format Lab. The idea, according to John

Hogan, was to allow programmers to use their instincts in addition to research.[10] When I checked the Format Lab website in its early weeks of operation, it listed an impressive number of musical options, but a cursory listen showed that more was actually less when it came to the new formats. Relentlessly hits-oriented, many of the narrowly programmed formats seemed overly focused, sort of like the music channels one encounters on plane flights. There was only one classical channel, devoted to the best-known "hits" from Bach, Beethoven, and Mozart. The bluegrass channel was called Americana NewGrass and seemed focused more on today's Nashville hit makers than on traditional mountain music. The serious jazz channel played a mix more suited to a hotel cocktail lounge. All of the channels or stations were in the jukebox format, that is, no DJs or song identifications. More troubling, many of the formats seemed to have substantial playlist overlaps.

Still, it was an admirable first effort from a company whose chairman had habitually professed zero interest in its stations' content.

But despite the company's apparently Herculean efforts to change the overall impression of its activities, its financial reputation—its leading source of corporate pride—had taken a serious beating.

At Clear Channel's annual meeting in September 2005, Fidelity Investments, the mutual-fund colossus and at the time Clear Channel's biggest shareholder with 15.5 percent, voted to give the company's entire board of directors the boot. Fidelity was responding to the board's decision to renew what it viewed as overly generous severance agreements for Lowry, Mark, and Randall Mays worth a total of around $90 million. The board was nonetheless reelected intact, in part perhaps due to an internal conflict of interest—Fidelity also happens to handle Clear Channel's $531 million 401(k) retirement fund.[11]

The following April, the California Public Employees' Retirement System (CalPERS), the country's biggest public pension fund, added Clear Channel to its annual list of companies in its portfolio it believes must improve their financial performance and governance practices. The number-one concern cited by CalPERS's analysts was the same severance issues that had irritated Fidelity. Other issues mentioned were the fact that most of the directors had served on the board for an unusually long time, including two who had been members for twenty-two years, and the board's dearth of technological and international business expertise.

Nepotism has long been a cornerstone of corporate America, as it has in virtually every power structure cooked up since the beginning of civilization. In the media business, the trend of a father handing the reins to his children is a common one and rarely goes without comment. Brian Roberts, the chief executive of the Comcast cable company and the son of Comcast's chairman, Ralph Roberts, is generally praised for his astute management abilities and for putting together the partnership that launched the QVC shopping network.

On the other hand, Edgar Bronfman Jr. suffered the cruel barbs of critics and the ire of investors in the late 1990s after squandering the fortunes of the Seagram Company, a multibillion-dollar liquor company controlled by his family, to get into the media business. He then merged the resulting company, Universal, with the failing French entertainment conglomerate Vivendi, losing billions and clinching his reputation as a laughingstock in the industry.

Yet the possibility that Mark and Randall Mays may be the products of poorly executed nepotistic practices almost never comes up. There exist virtually no press accounts discussing the theory that the brothers' inability to grasp even the basic big-picture precepts of running the leading national radio company, despite their clutch of Ivy League educations, may be the cause of some of that company's largest-scale strategic blunders and the loss of billions in investment capital and revenue.

In the course of my research, I encountered more than a few ra-

dio industry insiders who strongly suggested that Mark and Randall
Mays were not qualified for their jobs. Some of those parties had
their own agendas, but the same message was communicated from
too many unassociated parties to be easily discounted: that the
brothers were in some way to blame for the swift decline in the reputation of the company that their father so assiduously built.

The well-known executive compensation critic Graef Crystal
shed some light on the topic with his dissection of Mark Mays's pay
package in a March 2006 dispatch to Bloomberg News, for which
he writes a column.[12] Crystal noted that although it appeared from
Clear Channel's financial documents that Mays took a huge pay cut
in 2005, since his bonus went from $1.7 million in 2004 to zero the
following year, his total compensation in fact grew at least 72 percent, from $5.8 million to $9.9 million. The difference was made up
in a salary hike, option grants, and a free share award valued at
$5.8 million. Since net sales at Clear Channel were flat for the year
and total return was a paltry 0.16 percent, Crystal argues that
Mays's level of compensation was way out of line.

"Talk about the acorn falling far from the tree," he wrote. "This
particular acorn landed in the next county."

A number of the sources I spoke with also cited the highly ir-
regular employment agreement that binds the Mayses to the company, a seven-year rolling contract that renews itself daily. If any of
the three—Lowry, Mark, or Randall—is pushed out, the contract, in
effect since October 1999 and renewed in 2006, guarantees each of
them a salary and bonus for the rest of the contract—essentially, a
guaranteed seven years' pay.

Moreover, if Lowry Mays leaves the company and neither of his
sons is appointed chief executive, the severance terms for the sons
immediately double to fourteen years' salary and a bonus, plus two
million options and other benefits. For Clear Channel to sever all
ties with the Mays family would cost the company upwards of
$100 million.

"What board of directors would ever approve something that
inane and give them 14 years of pay just because they sprang from

his loins?" observed Graef Crystal. "I wouldn't want to buy the stock if that is how they are going to treat the shareholders. It is shameless, a kind of dynasty thing."

In his 2003 book, *In Praise of Nepotism*, Adam Bellow goes to great lengths to distinguish good nepotism from bad nepotism, arguing that corporate America largely practices the former in contrast to the fiefdoms of yore. He boils down modern nepotism to three rules: the first one is don't embarrass the patriarch, the supreme granter of his largesse.[13] (The second and third are "Don't embarrass yourself" and "Pass it on.")

Had Mark and Randall in effect violated Bellow's first rule, if only by making business decisions that ultimately besmirched the name of their father's legacy? After all, Lowry Mays became known from the earliest days of his radio career as a cautious, conservative investor with a keen focus on the bottom line.

The Clear Channel that made headlines throughout the first few years of the new century was anything but cautious and conservative. Risky bets were taken on huge acquisitions. Due diligence and proper valuations were often tossed out the window. The term "synergy" was used liberally and indiscriminately without an appreciation for its true complexity.

Traditional radio, now more than ever, needed an innovative savior. Mark Mays, at least for the time being, did not appear to be that savior.

This reality was on ample display at a communications policy forum featuring Mays, held in a small banquet room at the Mandarin Oriental hotel in Washington, D.C., on October 3, 2005. A tall, youthful-looking fellow in his early forties with a disconcerting resemblance to Jim Nabors of *Gomer Pyle* fame, he had the conservative, well-pressed look of an investment banker. Neither his mild public manner nor his dispassionate view of his business ("When you link good operations with desire and access to capital, it enables you to grow quickly," he once said of Clear Channel's rapid expansion[14]) suggested the air of someone who has the power to shape radio's future.

Dressed in a gray business suit, white shirt, and baby blue tie, Mays was the focal point of a luncheon on this day sponsored by the Progress & Freedom Foundation, a conservative "market-oriented" (their words) think tank devoted to digital technology that was inspired by Newt Gingrich back in the early 1990s with plenty of backing from the major telecommunications corporations. After a light meal, nine tables of journalists, policy wonks, and Clear Channel flacks watched Mays stand at a podium and stiffly read from a prepared sheet of comments.

First, he touted the virtues of free radio in an era when it faces challenges from new technologies. In the wake of the disaster wrought by Hurricane Katrina, for example, radio came to the rescue on the Gulf Coast. "When television, the Internet and pay radio didn't work," he said, "free radio worked." He also stated that Clear Channel's oft-criticized format selection was more diverse than ever. In D.C., he offered, his company aired both the right-wing commentator Laura Ingraham and the lefty comedian Al Franken. "I think it's safe to say," he joked, "you're going to hate one of our radio stations in Washington." And rest assured, he added, that KISS-FM in Boston has a different playlist from KISS-FM in Los Angeles, referencing one of Clear Channel's best-known on-air brands.

But he quickly changed tack and homed in on his main agenda, describing an industry "crippled by suffocating regulations that hinder free radio." Mays explained how none of these newfangled threats to traditional radio, such as iPods, satellite radio, Internet radio, and mobile phones, were restricted by governmental statutes, as was the radio industry, beholden since the 1930s to the Federal Communications Commission.

His suggestion? Congress should once again relax ownership limits—as it did with the Telecommunications Act of 1996 that first allowed Clear Channel to expand to its current Brobdingnagian proportions—that prevented a single company from owning more than eight stations in a single market. More specifically, he recommended that in markets with at least sixty stations total, the ownership cap should be raised to ten stations and in larger markets with at least seventy-five stations—that is, megamarkets like New York, Los Angeles, and Chicago—to twelve stations.

Mays's reasoning was that a couple of the new kids on the block, XM Satellite Radio and Sirius Satellite Radio, each offered more than 120 subscription-only stations nationwide. Traditional radio, he argued, could hardly compete with such an onslaught—particularly since content on satellite radio was not regulated. Add to this all of the new, unregulated delivery systems, the iPods, music-streaming cell phones, and Internet-based radio stations, and it was almost surprising the folks at Clear Channel didn't just pack it in and go home. As a remedy, Mays also called for legislation to restrict satellite radio firms from offering more local programming.

"Free radio is not asking for a handout," Mays explained. "Free radio is asking for a level playing field."

Never mind that all of these new technologies at this point accounted for just a couple of percentage points of the total advertising pie available to traditional radio. Or that radio remained one of the most profitable areas of the media business in terms of operating margins.

Mays was determined to portray his mega-massive media conglomerate as an underdog, or even a victim.

Meanwhile, Mays continued, Clear Channel and others were investing hundreds of millions of dollars in radio's future, HD Radio.

Despite his influence, Mays is oddly dispassionate about radio, and statements from him regarding his love for the medium are rare. When pressed in a 2005 interview, he admitted he mostly listened to talk radio. "I'm a news/talk junkie," he said, with a somewhat unconvincing note of fanaticism.[15] He also added that he enjoyed country music and soft rock. Not coincidentally, news-talk and soft rock are two of commercial radio's fastest-growing formats, and while country music is losing stations, it remains the most prevalent radio format in America. In other words, Mark

Mays likes what his company determines that America likes. Except, that is, for the hip-hop his kids like. "I can only take that for so long," said Mays. Though there is no official rule in the Mays household demanding the family listen exclusively to Clear Channel stations, the company's leader confessed he never strayed from their offerings.

Still, regardless of what one thinks of Mays's listening tastes, it's safe to say he has a tin ear for the dialogue surrounding the radio business. Hadn't he heard? In 2005 alone, other large media companies like AOL Time Warner dumped AOL (at least from its name) and Viacom split itself into two smaller public companies. Big media was suddenly so yesterday. Clear Channel itself had celebrated this annus mirabilis by spinning off its entertainment division into a separate public entity called Live Nation. Clearly the experience hadn't made much of a philosophical impact.

After reciting his plan for the future, Mays sat down at a banquet table placed atop a small riser at the front of the room right next to three Wall Street types who were there to pick his brain for a few more nuggets.

Chris Stern (no relation to Howard), a financial analyst for Medley Global Advisors and a former *Washington Post* technology reporter with a youthful pageboy haircut and horn-rimmed glasses, bluntly challenged Mays's main assertion, asking, "Why do you think adding more stations will improve business?"

Paul Gallant, a former legal adviser to the ex-FCC chairman Michael Powell and now an adviser on media at Stanford Washington Research Group, came at him from the other end. "Where would you draw the line to put limits on satellite radio? Should it be allowed to sell local advertising?"

Addressing traditional radio again, Blair Levin of Legg Mason, who had previously been the chief of staff to another ex-FCC chairman, Reed Hundt, asked another seemingly ominous question: "Do you think there should be NO ownership limits?"

Mays had pat answers for all these questions, but none of them affected the generally flat mood of the proceedings. Indeed, despite the best efforts of the event's hosts to stock the room with Clear Channel loyalists, there appeared little enthusiasm, and a fair bit of confusion, about the ideas that Mays was putting forth. If the two main perspectives about media consolidation (either it is good or it is harmful) were suitably represented in the room, then neither side fully comprehended Mays's reasoning.

Chris Stern put Clear Channel's dilemma most succinctly when he suggested to Mays that his proposal to "deregulate us and regulate them" held a whiff of hypocrisy.

Even Gallant, who seemed the most sympathetic of the bunch, counseled Mays almost poignantly that "the politics of getting relief [from deregulation] seems tougher than a few years ago."

By late 2005, the chief executive of Clear Channel, once the most intimidating major media force in America, was reduced to pleading for special favors from regulators even as the value and prospects of his company's core assets appeared to dwindle.

16.

TUNING OUT

With its sixty-five-foot ceilings, soaring marble columns, and shadowy lighting effects, the Cipriani catering hall on Forty-second Street in New York looked like the set for some lost scene from *Citizen Kane*. Clusters of mostly older, conservative-looking men, all in classic black-tie attire, greeted each other as good friends and friendly rivals for cocktails and dinner in the cavernous main lobby. Somehow, Cipriani—in the old Bowery Savings Bank Building constructed in 1923, with all its allusions to cold, hard cash—seemed the perfect setting for the twentieth annual Bayliss Radio Roast. This year's honoree: Mark Mays.

Ostensibly a charity fund-raiser to support scholarships for radio-centric college students, the Bayliss is far better known as a chance for industry bigs to get together and let their thinning hair down in a protected environment. When the former Clear Channel exec Randy Michaels was roasted in 1998 (while still a Jacor employee), he mooned the audience of his tuxedoed peers.

On this crisp evening in March 2006, the mood was more formal and muted. With satellite radio and podcasts looming and traditional radio in an advertising slump, the industry was on uncharacteristically shaky ground. "There should be plenty of laughs tonight," announced the emcee, Bill Stakelin, CEO of Regent Communications, which he co-founded in 1996 with Terry Jacobs. "Just run the current stock prices of all our companies across the screen."

Indeed, by mid-2006, Clear Channel's stock price was no laughing matter, its best days seemingly behind it. The company's stock price had fallen from a high above $90 in late 1999 and early 2000 to as low as $27.17 a share by August 2006, an adjusted price the company hadn't experienced since May 1997.[1] Around the same time, rumors began circulating that Clear Channel was vulnerable to a takeover attempt by private equity firms eager to buy out existing shareholders at a discounted price, drastically cut costs, and then presumably gut the company of its most valuable assets and sell them off to the highest bidders. Management had already tried a host of other strategies to give its stock a jolt, but none of them— not the stock buybacks, nor the billboard company spin-off, nor the hiring of the top Internet music executive from AOL, Evan Harrison—was doing the trick.[2]

The radio business as a whole had witnessed its prospects wane dramatically since the late 1990s. Revenue growth was flat in both 2005 and 2006, despite a bump in October 2006, due to the midterm elections.[3] To make matters worse, the amount of time people spent listening to the radio during any given week had decreased 14 percent over the previous decade.

But so far the rumors of a leveraged buyout were just that, rumors. So Clear Channel and, by inference, the rest of the radio industry tried to look on the bright side. A company confidant around that time proudly boasted to me that the mainstream press had even come around and had begun writing about some of Clear Channel's forward-thinking projects instead of its public gaffes and maledicted initiatives.[4]

At the Bayliss roast, Mark Mays, sober-looking and moonfaced, sat at one of two banquet tables festooned with bouquets of white, pink, and purple spring flowers, carefully surrounded by employees and friends. Sitting next to him was Glenn Beck, the Clear Channel–employed conservative radio host. At the other table were Randall Mays, John Hogan, and Peter Smyth, head of the Boston-area radio group Greater Media.

The idea, of course, was to poke fun at Mays, but the makeup of the room made a genuinely embarrassing evening unlikely. It was nonetheless a revealing glimpse inside the still-beating heart of the industry. Among the more than five hundred guests were many of the key figures in the radio biz. In the audience were Jeff Smulyan, president of Emmis Communications; Stu Olds of Katz Media Group; Paul Kagan of Kagan Associates, a top radio research firm; John David and Eddie Fritts of the National Association of Broadcasters; Gary Fries of the Radio Advertising Bureau; Lew Dickey of Cumulus Media; and many others. Arbitron, the radio ratings service that Clear Channel had been actively developing an alternative to, sponsored the evening's libations.

These people were closer than friends: they were enemies and competitors who knew full well that their collective fates became more tightly entwined as the road ahead became more uncertain. Three out of the four roasters were on the Clear Channel payroll. Lowry Mays, in a wheelchair and on the mend from his health scare, and his wife, Peggy, kept watch from the front table.

Still, the pressure to display radio's raucous side persisted. Unlike virtually any other media business, radio seems on a perpetual quest to prove it's the life of the party. Can anyone picture Michael Eisner baring his behind at a Hollywood shindig? Or even Brad Pitt, for that matter? If radio was going down, it would go down in its own inimitably raunchy style.

Stakelin again thanked the guests for coming since, he quipped, "I know many of you are hesitant to attend any event in New York where you have to pay to play," a reference to Eliot Spitzer's ongoing payola investigations. Two days earlier Spitzer's office had released damning documents issued by Entercom Communications that appeared to chronicle a systematized payola schedule in writing. Entercom chose to fight the charges, but later settled for $4.25 million, while admitting no wrongdoing.

Clearly the audience was loose enough to have another laugh at its own expense, but Stakelin nonetheless leavened his patter with bromides suggesting the industry was doing fine. MTV doesn't make hits, radio makes hits. Long live free, over-the-air radio. Let us know when satellite radio has the audience of just one top New York City radio station.

When a video promoting the John Bayliss Broadcast Foundation ran on the giant screen above everybody's head, filled with heartfelt testimonials from scholarship recipients, both Mark and Randall—unlike their fellow dais residents—swiveled their heads to watch. Public earnestness, it seems, came easily to these chaps.

So when Clear Channel's radio head, John Hogan, stood to take his potshots at Mark, one couldn't help feeling a little sorry for Hogan. He was a holdover from the bad old Jacor days, his wire-rimmed glasses and serious demeanor notwithstanding. The man voted least likely by his Clear Channel counterparts to survive the merger had not only survived but thrived, rising higher than those who envisioned his rapid demise.

Of course, he got around all of that by playing into the gag that his job was on the line thanks to his acceptance of Mark's invite to participate in the night's festivities. "Am I going to help a bunch of teenagers I never met?" he asked the audience. "Or keep my job?" Hammering home the gag, he passed out copies of his résumé to the crowd.

After a decade of consolidation only those still standing could make these sorts of jokes.

Far more revealing was a mock 1950s-style educational film Hogan played that purported to explain the origin of those annoying smiley faces Mark famously tacked on to his name when signing memos. Hogan claimed many a Clear Channel employee had come up to him and said, "It's not about the money, I do it for the smiley face." The cartoon portrayed "Smiley the Sperm," the leader of all the sperm, who swims ahead too quickly and splats on a piece of paper in the shape of a smiley face. Endearing and yet raunchy and decidedly male-oriented, it confirmed that somewhere within the sprawling, homogenized, golf-course-traipsing corporate portrait, something, ahem, untamed still lurked.

Hogan's performance cut to the heart of what still irked Clear

Channel. For all of its power, financial brawn, and size, it still lacked a certain gravitas. Mark and Randall didn't carry themselves like keepers of a media empire. To the contrary, they still seemed a little adolescent, least likely to take a stand, settle a score, or make a case for the importance radio had played in the growth of our democracy.

The real truth teller of the evening, however, turned out to be the one professional entertainer on the platform. Looking surprisingly middle-aged and respectable with scholarly wire-rimmed glasses, the talk-radio star Glenn Beck approached the podium with more natural confidence than any of his predecessors had mustered. Leaning on his elbow, he sidled up to the microphone and in the first few seconds described a Mark Mays not unfamiliar to his harshest critics, albeit couched in the driest of satire.

Beck said Mark was the kind of person who thinks "anyone who makes less than nine figures is the little man." He said the real slogan, according to Mark, was "Less Is More . . . Than You Deserve." He began one anecdote by saying, "A lot of people say Mark only cares about money . . . and it's true." Then he described the workplace culture at Clear Channel by saying, "Imagine creative people working at a bank. And it's not just a bank . . . imagine a bank within the walls of Auschwitz." Then, turning to Mark, "I know how important Hitler's words are to you." Beck then once again addressed the audience: "It's more Dachau than Auschwitz— there are no Jews here, are there?"

Those familiar with Beck's usual outrageous routine were likely the few in the audience who choked up a chuckle.

In closing, Beck remarked, looking over at Mark, "This is the wussiest roast I've ever been to. You skated, Jack."

On October 26, 2006, *The New York Times* published a story confirming the rumors that had been floating around for months: Clear Channel was negotiating to be bought by a pool of private equity firms.[5] Clear Channel's stock price had risen 18 percent since August 9, when word of an impending deal first circulated. According to the *Times* piece, a coalition of investment shops, including Providence Equity Partners, the Blackstone Group, and Kohlberg Kravis Roberts & Company, had been talking to Clear Channel for months about a plan to wring shareholder value from a company whose stock now seemed impervious to good news.

The process had been initiated on August 18, 2006, according to a proxy provided by the company, when Mark and Randall Mays approached Goldman Sachs and requested an analysis of Clear Channel's strategic options. The choice of a sale was not ruled out this time, as it generally had been previously.

Certain press accounts disputed the timing and origin of Clear Channel's idea to go private. Andrew Ross Sorkin of *The New York Times* traced the game plan back to a pitch made in May 2006 by Paul J. Salem, a senior managing director of Providence Equity Partners, a Rhode Island–based investment firm.[6] Salem, a former classmate of Randall Mays's at Harvard Business School, according to Sorkin's account, first proposed that Clear Channel think about a leveraged buyout of the company. After some seriously punishing years as a public corporation, the notion of being able to operate far from the intense scrutiny of shareholders and regulators held undeniable appeal. However such a deal were structured, it would likely include an exorbitant payout for the Mays family, likely topping $1 billion, making the risk of not acting greater than that of making a move, at least in the short term.

Most press accounts early that fall, including those in *The New York Times* and *The Wall Street Journal*, suggested that the deal with Providence Equity Partners, the Blackstone Group, and Kohlberg Kravis Roberts & Company was nearly completed. *The Wall Street Journal* went so far as to outline a web of alleged conflicts that Clear Channel's management team had engendered as the deal had progressed.[7] The paramount concern was the astonishing speed with which Clear Channel had gone from the theoretical stage to a bona fide auction.

But a source close to the deal later told me that most of the gos-

sip at the time claiming the Providence Equity group was the favored suitor was mostly propaganda leaked to the press by parties
at the participating firms. In the end, Clear Channel would draw
bids from four different groups. The first group, Providence Equity,
Blackstone, and KKR, which had dropped out by the end, kicked
off the action by making a cash bid of $34.50 per share on Septem-
ber 22, an offer that was rejected four days later by Clear Channel's
"disinterested directors" (that is, everyone except the members of
the Mays family and Red McCombs).[8] On September 27, the same
group raised its bid to $35.50 per share, pending additional due
diligence—but after KKR dropped out on October 18, it readjusted
its offer to $35. The second group, which started with only Thomas
H. Lee Partners, floated an offer of between $35 and $37 per share,
which became a more concrete $36.50 on November 13, after
Thomas Lee joined forces with Bain Capital and Texas Pacific
Group. A third group, consisting of Apollo Management and the
Carlyle Group, but later only Apollo, came in with a maximum offer of $35 per share shortly after. A fourth offer, from a group con-
sisting of Cerberus Capital Management and Oak Hill Capital
Partners that had promised a bid between $37 and $39 per share,
never materialized.

The first two groups, the Providence-Blackstone and the Thomas
Lee–Bain consortia, settled in with final bids of $36.50. Only after
Clear Channel countered with a proposal that discounted the offer
by $300 million (including a reduction of payments due the Mays
family members under their seven-year employment contracts) was
the stalemate broken. On November 17, the Lee-Bain partnership
reemerged with a $37.60-per-share offer that easily topped the
Providence-Blackstone group's modified bid of $36.85 per share.

On November 15, the deal was over, with Thomas H. Lee Partners and Bain Capital, the presumptive underdogs, having emerged
as the winners in a high-stakes contest that resulted in an $18.7 bil-
lion buyout. The final bid also included the assumption of around
$8 billion in debt. In a separate announcement, Clear Channel re-

ported it would be selling off its 42 television stations and 448 of its radio stations, mostly in smaller and medium-sized markets.[9]

But in typical Clear Channel fashion, the company could hardly make a move without generating some controversy. And, as usual, the complaints began quickly and with volume. Most prominent was a news article in *The Wall Street Journal* noting that not only would the Mays family profit handsomely from the buyout but they would also keep their jobs.

In the coming weeks, Clear Channel would become the poster child for the latest scrutiny of private equity buyouts. On January 30, 2007, a source within Fidelity Management & Research, Clear Channel's largest shareholder with around 11 percent of Clear Channel's stock, leaked the news that the mutual-fund giant intended to oppose the company's plan to go private.[10] Fidelity's concerns stemmed from the notion that Clear Channel was being sold at "a significant discount to the true value of the company," much to the detriment of the radio group's shareholders.

On September 25, 2007, Clear Channel shareholders finally approved the merger deal with the group led by Bain Capital and Thomas H. Lee Partners. The price per share to be received by shareholders had by that time risen to $39.20 in cash.[11] In the interim, the company had sold off dozens of its stations in smaller markets, as well as its entire TV division.

Consistent with their longtime antipathy to waging the image battle in public, the Mayses did little or nothing to counteract the impression painted in the press that they were looking to cash out. As far as they had come and as much as they had learned, their distaste for public scrutiny had not abated. Supporters argued that indeed the salaries of Mark Mays and Randall Mays were far from out of line with those of top executives at similar-sized companies.

The irony of this latest public scuffle couldn't have been richer. Despite its recent dive on Wall Street, or perhaps because of it, Clear Channel had begun making some major strides in the realm of new media. That content and commerce could peacefully coexist was hardly a radical concept. But sometime in 2006, Clear Channel started unfurling new creative initiatives on what seemed like a weekly basis. And it presented each with such fanfare as if to suggest it had invented the very notion of original content.

By early 2007, Clear Channel was generating reams of video programming for the websites of its twelve hundred stations.[12] Going against the grain of convention, the company began making available around six thousand music videos and original video content that individual stations could post on their sites and disc jockeys could promote on the air. One program called *Stripped* featured prerecorded performances by artists such as Young Jeezy and Nelly Furtado. Another program, *Video 6 Pack*, invited popular musical artists like Fall Out Boy to act as host and to play their favorite videos. These expanded offerings soon catapulted Clear Channel's Web presence to sixth place in the ranking among music sites, just after big names like MTV, AOL, Yahoo, and MySpace, and indie-powerhouse ARTISTdirect.

Indeed, Clear Channel was making creative strides unimaginable just a few years earlier. But virtually no one, other than some particularly zealous music fans, was taking notice. Regardless of the initial success the company was having in new media, radio was rapidly losing its cachet as a primary medium among young people. Serious music listeners of every stripe had long ago begun abandoning the commercial airwaves for public radio and the idiosyncratic confines of nonprofit college stations. And thanks to everything from iPods to the social-networking hub MySpace.com, younger music fans were becoming addicted to new forms of music distribution at a rate that commercial radio would likely find difficult to match over time. Commercial radio was still the best way to generate CD sales, but hit records no longer meant as much. In 1996, the bestselling album of the year was Alanis Morissette's *Jagged Little Pill*, which sold 16 million copies in the United States. A decade later, the top-selling album of 2006 was the soundtrack for *High School Musical*, a Disney Channel made-for-TV film, with a mere 3.57 million copies.

While it would take years if not decades to determine the true impact of Clear Channel's influence on the radio industry—and the ultimate fate of the radio industry itself, for that matter—it was clear by the time of its sale that the damage had been done. Though its influence had abated, the company once known as the Evil Empire had taken a toll on broadcasting culture. Radio had survived and even prospered under its tenure, but the soul of the medium had been permanently scarred.

In the years since Clear Channel had pioneered its vision of content, popular culture as a whole had shifted its center. The rise of the Internet had primed consumers to expect limitless variety rather than the short list of "hits" that had motivated previous generations to buy product. The expansive cross-promotional marketing campaigns that once provided the conglomerates with their raison d'être were now rendered increasingly ineffective as consumers rebelled against product-driven media juggernauts.

The world of radio on display at the Bayliss roast was already a quaint anachronism. Within three or four years, the medium and the business behind it would likely transform so radically as to render it unrecognizable to the graying veterans who chuckled along with the mildly racist and sexist humor that evening.

Meanwhile, satellite radio was feeling the inexorable pull of progress. In February 2007, Sirius and XM, the two satellite radio services, announced plans to merge, pending FCC approval. As for the HD Radio initiative led by Clear Channel, matters were proceeding slowly and with little fanfare, demonstrating the public's reluctance to trade in their troves of cheap radio sets for better sound quality but similarly uninspired programming.

The very notion of an intimidating Clear Channel seemed, for perhaps the first time, absurd.

EPILOGUE

L ate one sunny February afternoon, I was sitting in John Barger's office in San Antonio. Barger's sparsely furnished suite sits high in a drab modern office tower with large windows overlooking the smog-choked I-10 artery. The folks at Clear Channel, press-shy and suspicious as ever, had decided not to grant me access to the company's top executives during my visit. So I happily stopped by Barger's place for a circumspect chat.

Decades away from his time at Clear Channel, Barger now operates as a broker for other people's station sales; he also still owns a clutch of nine that he runs himself, including KMFR-FM, a classic-rock station in San Antonio. "It stands for 'mother-fucking radio,' " he tells me with a deep, guttural chuckle.[1]

I assume he's kidding, but I'm not fully convinced.

Affable, profane, and prone to entertaining storytelling, Barger seemed relaxed and pleased with his particular fate. Tall and thick in the middle, dressed semi-businesslike in a blue dress shirt and dark suit pants, he could be a senior partner in a law firm. The middle-aged, balding Texan clearly relished his role as an industry elder. Despite his lengthy, successful run at Clear Channel, he says he's earned far more out on his own. Now he makes his own hours and drives a $70,000 Lexus. As it has been for many of Clear Channel's early architects, the radio business has been very, very good to him.

After exchanging some pleasantries, I asked the radio veteran
what he thinks about the future of the radio business and Clear
Channel. Barger looked at me through his expensive wire-rimmed
glasses as if I had just spit my lunch up on his expansive yet tidy
desk. He was acting as if no one had ever asked him such a question
before.

At first he didn't answer it, at least directly. Instead, he explained how he thought consolidation had helped the industry. Consolidation eliminated marginal operators, he said, the very same
independent stations that did not discipline their sales staffs to keep
advertising prices stable and helped plunge the radio business into
dire straits in the late 1980s.

When Clear Channel bought out these smaller operators,
Barger explained, it had incentive to support a more consistent pricing structure, which ultimately made the whole radio industry
healthier. Clear Channel's aggressive sales strategy required the guts
not to offer discounts to advertisers. A larger radio company could
afford to stand up to advertisers and agencies unwilling to pay its
requested fees, and bypass them altogether if it needed to.

After Clear Channel made inroads, its competitors had the market strength to stick with their pricing. Without stabilized advertising prices, many stations would have folded a long time ago.
Instead, under consolidation, many prospered and over time improved their profitability.

Prior to 1992, Clear Channel and Infinity, the two largest publicly traded radio companies at the time, had fewer than thirty stations apiece and broadcast cash flow (BCF) margins at the station
level were approximately 27 percent. In 2005, the BCF margins at
publicly traded radio companies averaged 34 percent. This included
Saga Communications, whose margins were significantly lower.
Without Saga, that average would be closer to 39 percent.

In other words, from the time before consolidation, there has
been more than a 10 percent increase in operating margins at the
station level in radio. There is no question that consolidation im-

proved the economic model of radio. Larger economies of scale such as the one Clear Channel built translated into the most prosperous period in radio's history.

On the other hand, the promise of a lucrative national platform for radio advertising never really materialized. Instead, the homogenized programming that was intended to attract those big advertisers became something of a liability, allowing satellite radio and the iPod and file-sharing culture to thrive. Voice tracking be damned, local programming still mattered.

The ownership of the nation's biggest concert promotion network turned out to be far more trouble than it was worth. And the pricing of billboard advertising in no way was helped by the ownership of radio stations.

"The economic advantage of owning more stations is, if you can run them successfully, good cash flow," says Dan Cohen, a former small-time Florida radio consolidator in Miami and Gainesville who cashed out for fear of competing against the likes of Clear Channel. "As far as creating synergy between markets, the synergies aren't going to be that great. The synergies that really were created in radio happened when you could own multiple radio stations in the same market. And that's what happened with the start of deregulation."[2]

Synergy, in a word—far more profoundly and resolutely than Clear Channel—sucked.

So what are we left with?

Did Clear Channel ruin radio, or is Clear Channel the best commercial radio we can reasonably expect? The answer to that question, of course, depends on exactly how one measures success.

No one outside the radio business will ever argue that the consolidation of the radio business improved the quality of programming. Then again, "quality" is a relative term that few will agree upon. Conversely, few inside the business would argue with the notion that the operating efficiencies pioneered by Clear Channel and others helped rescue hundreds of independent stations from disappearing into the ether. Even fewer would argue that those efficiencies didn't increase profits. For many years they did; and for the most part they still do.

So there it is: What was good for the radio industry and its shareholders wasn't so good for radio listeners. Or concertgoers. Or musicians. Or news junkies. Or sports fans. Or recording labels. Or, let's be honest, the American culture at large. Variety suffered, as did the impetus to improve existing formats.

The location of Clear Channel's San Antonio world headquarters is a perfect metaphor for its current state. The modern glass and limestone edifice overlooks the greens of the Quarry Golf Club in the pristine upscale neighborhood of Alamo Heights. Across the street is the Quarry Market, a tony shopping center containing a cavernous Whole Foods supermarket, a Michael's crafts supply store, and a Borders bookstore complete with cappuccino bar. The environment screams rich yuppie, or rather it whispers it, in rounded, cultured tones.

This side of Texas may be worlds away from Clear Channel's macho, politically incorrect roots, but the new Clear Channel fits right in. Cowed by its horribly bruising encounter with the big time, it is broadcasting's white elephant, a giant ornate network filled with unoriginal content of deteriorating value.

Of course, this means that Clear Channel, the only radio company large enough to affect the entire industry, has a historic opportunity.

"The good thing about Clear Channel's size is that clearly there is a leader in the business at this point," says Jacor's founder, Terry Jacobs. "The industry never really had a leader in the past. Now we have a leader; the question is, are they doing good things as our leader? And for a while I don't think that they were doing good things, but I do think that they've gotten back to doing the right things that will help the industry down the road. It has obviously required a lot of pain in the process to get there."[3]

Chris Anderson, the editor in chief of *Wired* magazine, published a book called *The Long Tail* in mid-2006 that outlines one viable strategy for large media companies looking to capitalize on a fragmented future.

Anderson's theory of the Long Tail is that, thanks to the Internet, our culture and economy are moving away from the "hits" mentality of mainstream marketing. The Web has lowered the costs of production and distribution, reducing the importance of creating homogenized content meant to appeal to the widest possible audience. By not having to worry about the constraints of physical shelf space and other distribution hurdles, companies can now offer countless niche products—the metaphorical "Long Tail"—and make as much money as, if not more than, if they offered only lowest-common-denominator mainstream goods. He uses as examples virtual stores such as Amazon.com, which ekes out 25 percent of its book revenues from the 3.6 million titles it carries that its competitors don't.

Is Clear Channel up to the challenge? As of this printing, its programming strategy is only in the earliest stages of a turnaround, as evidenced by the middling fare offered by its Format Lab project. The Mays boys' tin ear for content is certainly not incurable, but if they haven't understood the value of quality programming up to this point, it is doubtful they ever will—unless it is an economic necessity.

Inklings of a shift are discernible in the company's annual 10K reports.

The radio division's "Company Strategy" section in Clear Channel's 10K from 2000, the year it absorbed AMFM and SFX, begins like this: "Our radio broadcasting strategy entails improving the ongoing operations of our existing stations, as well as the acquisition of stations. Our acquisition strategy has created a national footprint that allows us to deliver targeted messages for specific audiences to advertisers on a local, regional, and national basis. We believe in clustering our radio stations in markets to increase our individual market share thereby allowing us to offer our advertisers more advertising options that can reach many audiences."

The beginning of the same passage from the company's 10K for 2005 reads this way: "Our radio strategy centers on providing programming and services to the local communities in which we operate. By providing listeners with programming that is compelling, we are able to provide advertisers with an effective platform to reach their consumers."

The message: today's Clear Channel, in a radical about-face, is catering to communities and listeners.

Clear Channel is actually ahead of the game technologically when it comes to revolutionizing the way it sells advertising. It has been developing a proprietary online auction system to help streamline its ad-selling process, using TradeWinds trafficking software, among other products, and therefore putting itself head-to-head with companies like Google, which purchased a company called dMarc to develop an online ad-sales infrastructure.

All of this means that as far as radio's future goes, Clear Channel has as good a shot as anybody, if not better.

For all of Clear Channel's history of bullying and consolidation and downright dunderheaded thinking, one begins to wonder if the former Evil Empire is actually the best radio company we can reasonably expect given the current state of the medium.

After all, the notion of a strong leader in the struggling radio industry suddenly doesn't seem like such a bad idea. Radio listeners are no longer the captive consumers on which Clear Channel banked for most of its history. In the not-so-distant future, when wireless broadband service will be available in all new cars, Clear Channel, in fact, may have to *pay* automakers for access to their dashboards.

By that measure, Clear Channel, for all its stations, isn't big enough. It will need the cooperation of its smaller rivals to leverage favorable terms in such situations.

And regarding ownership caps? Maybe the notion of a "level playing field," as Mark Mays calls it, isn't so wacky after all. Regardless of one's political affiliation, it is hard to deny that the Internet has made mincement of traditional notions of media ownership limits and indecency restrictions.

As the media critic Kurt Andersen noted in his weekly *New York* magazine column in June 2006, if any twelve-year-old with even the slightest technological inkling is free to surf billions of Web pages for music, news, and the foulest language and images on the planet, what exactly is the purpose of the federal government trying to regulate broadcast programming?[4]

Media consolidation has undeniably had negative effects, but the economic realities of the current climate suggest that only those companies that compete in terms of both content and distribution will ultimately thrive.

According to a February 2006 technology survey conducted by the research firm Jacobs Media, iPod ownership (including other digital music players) grew 67 percent in comparison to the firm's 2005 study.[5]

Of iPod owners surveyed by Jacobs, about one-fifth said they listened mostly or exclusively to such devices. Four in ten digital music player owners divided their listening between iPods and radio, and another third primarily listened to the radio.

Commercial radio now must compete with a listening option it never imagined—unlimited free choice.

Media deregulation's poster child got that way for a reason. "Clear Channel became symbolic of basically an entire media industry that was just asleep at the switch and not challenging and focused much more on how do we keep listeners, how do we sell ads?" says the Future of Music Coalition's Michael Bracy. "At the same time, you had this company with a massive, massive investment in the public airwaves bragging about their whole orientation is just to serve advertisers, get listeners in the right demographic. Figuring out how they could have the largest possible audience so they can sell the most ad space."

Now Clear Channel would have to find a new path to steady margins.

"If Clear Channel stands for anything, it's that broadcasting is a business," says John Barger. "And business fundamentals, if properly followed, are going to make you successful. And the things that apply in most other businesses do apply. The excuse of 'you don't understand our business' doesn't wash. It's generation of revenue. It's no different than Ford Motor Company."

Barger eases into the subject of Clear Channel's future by referencing radio's past. "In 1956, the Chrysler Corporation put record changers in the glove compartment that handled 45 rpm records," he says. "That gave rise to the eight-track, and everyone said this is going to be the end of radio. Then we went to MP3 and all that other stuff, and it still hasn't punched out radio."

He agreed that Clear Channel had created some of its own problems, particularly when it came to gearing its whole business toward a national strategy. But as long as the company kept to its knitting, he had faith it would prevail.

"We were always accused of being a bottom-line company," he says. "That's not true—we were a top-line company. We deplored waste and unnecessary expense. We didn't focus on cutting costs, we'd come in and we'd push sales—"

Suddenly and finally, it occurred to me how to fit Clear Channel, that gloriously munificent expression of American pop culture, into the media landscape as a whole. Clear Channel had indeed been founded on creativity and innovation. Its founders and executives had exhibited undeniable brilliance. But the fertile minds that conceived of Clear Channel and grew it were creative at business, not culture. All creativity is not created equal, especially when a pillar of American culture is at stake. No matter how many billions Clear Channel had generated for its investors and the Mays family, it had generated precious little content that radio audiences could sink their teeth into. The company had coarsened public discourse at the expense of the public mandate.

While commerce and culture are not incompatible, Clear Channel is the exception that proved the rule. It is quality content, not fiscal prudence, that ultimately stands the test of time—at least as far as cultural legacies go. In the 1950s, when Elvis Presley's manager, "Colonel" Tom Parker, licensed his client's image for everything from guitars to cookware, and marketed Presley via multiple television appearances, he arguably helped burn out a natural talent prematurely. Clear Channel was Colonel Parker without his Presley; in Clear Channel's case, burning out the talent was a given. It was simply a prelude to the ultimate sellout. But by definition one must have something worth selling to sell out. By this measure, Clear Channel's glory days were numbered from its start.

It was already eight o'clock. We'd been talking for over two hours, and John Barger had a dinner date. It was time to lock up and head home.

But before I could say goodbye, Barger directed me into an adjoining office.

"Come in here," he said conspiratorially. "I want to show you something."

As I entered, I was puzzled. There was little in the office other than a desktop computer on top of a standard-issue metal office desk. Then I noticed a spreadsheet filled with song titles running down its flat-screen monitor.

"Welcome to KMFR!" Barger boomed.

I was silent for a minute. Then suddenly I understood.

Barger explained that KMFR was a little experiment of his: the ultimate jukebox radio station. The computer's hard drive was loaded up with an optimized mix of classic-rock tracks by everyone from Creedence Clearwater Revival to, yep, Led Zeppelin, as well as a few prerecorded announcer lead-ins, some of which declared

KMFR the home of "Mighty Fine Rock." He doesn't solicit advertising for the station, eliminating the need to pay a sales force. But he does broadcast commercials from advertisers who hear the station and call in.

"It's 103.7 on your FM dial," Barger told me. "Let me know what you think."

As soon as I got into my rental car, I punched up the station. As I rolled onto the highway ramp, I turned up the volume and waited for the opening bars of "Kashmir."

NOTES

I. THE CONTROVERSY

1. "Fighting for Free Speech Means Fighting for Howard Stern," *New York Times*, May 3, 2004.
2. "Howard Stern, Silenced in Some Cities, Gains in Others," *New York Times*, July 1, 2004.
3. David Harding and Sam Rovit, *Mastering the Merger: Four Critical Decisions That Make or Break the Deal* (Boston: Harvard Business School Press, 2004).
4. Radio Advertising Bureau, RADAR: Arbitron.
5. Michael Wolff, *Autumn of the Moguls* (New York: HarperBusiness, 2003), p. 35.
6. Barry Avrich, *Selling the Sizzle 2: The Magic and Logic of Entertainment Marketing* (Toronto: Maxworks, 2005).
7. Wolff, *Autumn of the Moguls*, p. 94.
8. Graef Crystal, "Clear Channel's Communication Breakdown on Pay," Bloomberg News, March 20, 2006.

2. THE BIRTH OF MODERN RADIO, TEXAS-STYLE

1. Stan Webb, interview with author, April 11, 2005.
2. Gary Stevens, interview with author, May 4, 2005.
3. Paul Starr, *The Creation of the Media: Political Origins of Mass Communication* (New York: Basic Books, 2004), p. 327.
4. Ibid., p. 215.
5. Leonard Maltin, *The Great American Broadcast: A Celebration of Radio's Golden Age* (New York: Dutton, 1997), p. 1.
6. Starr, *Creation of the Media*, p. 216.
7. Ibid., pp. 216–17.
8. Ibid., p. 218.
9. Ibid., p. 219.
10. Maltin, *Great American Broadcast*, p. 2.
11. Starr, *Creation of the Media*, p. 335.

12. Maltin, *Great American Broadcast*, p. 3.

13. Starr, *Creation of the Media*, p. 344.

14. Maltin, *Great American Broadcast*, p. 15.

15. Ben Fong-Torres, *The Hits Just Keep On Coming: The History of Top 40 Radio* (San Francisco: Backbeat Books, 2001), p. 17.

16. Ibid., pp. 19–21.

17. The Handbook of Texas Online, www.tsha.utexas.edu/handbook/online/articles/RR/ebr1_print.html.

18. Ronald Garay, *Gordon McLendon: The Maverick of Radio* (New York: Greenwood Press, 1992), p. 7.

19. Ibid., p. 19.

20. "End of Liberty," *Time*, June 9, 1952.

21. Garay, *Gordon McLendon*, p. 18.

22. Stan Webb, interview with author, April 11, 2005.

23. John Barger, interview with author, May 27, 2005.

24. Garay, *Gordon McLendon*, p. 28.

25. "End of Liberty."

26. Garay, *Gordon McLendon*, p. 68.

27. Ibid., p. 73.

28. Stan Webb, interview with author, May 11, 2005.

3. CLEAR CHANNEL'S BEGINNINGS

1. *International Directory of Business Biographies: M–R* (Detroit: Thomson Gale, 2005) (see www.referenceforbusiness.com/biography/M-R/Mays-L-Lowry-1935.html); "Lowry Mays: The Quiet Empire Builder," *San Antonio Express-News*, October 12, 2003.

2. "Lowry Mays."

3. "Exec Tunes in on S.A.," *San Antonio Light*, August 10, 1975.

4. "Full Speed Ahead for Clear Channel," *Broadcasting*, October 1, 1984.

5. "Mays Scores with Goals," *San Antonio Light*, March 10, 1985.

6. "Clear Channel: An Empire Built on Deregulation," *Los Angeles Times*, February 25, 2002.

7. U.S. Bureau of the Census, Table 20. Population of the 100 Largest Urban Places: 1970.

8. "Officials Snip the Ribbon on Toyota Plant's New Driveway," *San Antonio Express-News*, January 31, 2006.

9. Tom Frost, interview with author, January 31, 2006.

10. Jim Smith, interview with author, May 20, 2005.

11. "Lots of Static over Radio," *San Antonio Express-News*, February 2, 2003.

12. "A Major Voice in Broadcasting," *San Antonio Express-News*, August 4, 1996.

13. *San Antonio Business Journal*, October 31, 1988.

14. "Welcome Reception," *Dallas Morning News*, July 28, 1996.

15. "The Accidental Broadcaster," *Forbes*, June 8, 1992.

16. Stan Webb, interview with author, April 4, 2005.

17. "Lowry Mays."

18. John Barger, interview with author, May 27, 2005.

19. "Radio's Resurgence Has It Singing a Happy Tune," *Dallas Morning News*, November 8, 1998.

20. "Avco: Back from the Brink," *Forbes*, November 1, 1976.

21. John Barger, interview with author, May 27, 2005.

22. "A Major Voice in Broadcasting."

23. John Barger, interview with author, February 1, 2006.

24. *San Antonio Light*, August 10, 1975.

4. WAR STORIES

1. Stan Webb, interview with author, May 11, 2005.

2. Rex Tackett, interview with author, May 4, 2005.

3. Robert Unmacht, interview with author, October 12, 2005.

4. Ralph Guild, interview with author, June 23, 2005.

5. Ralph Guild, interview with author, June 23, 2005.

6. "Mays Scores with Goals," *San Antonio Light*, March 10, 1985.

7. "Full Speed Ahead for Clear Channel," *Broadcasting*, October 1, 1984.

8. "Changing Hands 1984," *Broadcasting*, January 8, 1985.

9. "The Fall of the House of Bingham," *New York Times*, January 19, 1986.

10. "Bingham Family Radio Stations Sold to San Antonio Company," Associated Press, June 11, 1986.

11. Jim Smith, interview with author, May 20, 2005.

12. Robert R. Scherer obituary, *Variety*, June 11, 1999.

5. ANARCHY ON THE AIRWAVES

1. "Clear Channel's Performance for 1987 Praised," *San Antonio Light*, April 22, 1988.

2. Dan Sullivan, interview with author, January 17, 2006.

3. "Clear Channel Reports Loss of $685,000 for First Quarter," *San Antonio Express-News*, April 28, 1989.

4. *Electronic Media*, July 10, 1989.

5. "Abry Chooses Dan Sullivan," *Daily Variety*, September 27, 1995.

6. Reed Hundt, interview with author, July 27, 2006.

7. "Bitter Feud Fouls Lines at the F.C.C.," *New York Times*, November 20, 1995.

8. Ibid.

9. Paul Starr, *The Creation of the Media: Political Origins of Mass Communication* (New York: Basic Books, 2004), p. 355.

10. Ibid., p. 360.

11. Ibid., p. 381.

12. Nicholas Lemann, "The Chairman," *New Yorker*, October 7, 2002.

13. Michael Bracy, interview with author, August 16, 2005.

14. Robert Unmacht, interview with author, October 12, 2005.
15. Jonathan Adelstein, interview with author, September 30, 2005.
16. Blair Levin, interview with author, October 17, 2005.

6. A BRILLIANT IDEA

1. "Clinton & GOP: Telecom Law Will Create Jobs," CNN.com, February 8, 1996.
2. "Radio's New Wave," *Chicago Tribune*, March 10, 1996.
3. Andrew Schwartzman, interview with author, September 23, 2005.
4. Lee Abrams, interview with author, July 27, 2005.
5. Rex Tackett, interview with author, May 12, 2005.
6. Stan Webb, interview with author, May 18, 2005.
7. "Signal Strength," *Vanderbilt Magazine*, Spring 2005.
8. Jim Smith, interview with author, May 20, 2005.
9. Bob Turner, interview with author, July 20, 2005.
10. "GE's Pension Fund Ventures to Be Different," *BusinessWeek*, November 14, 1994.
11. George Sosson, interview with author, May 23, 2005.
12. "Clear Channel to Buy Owner of 19 Stations," *San Antonio Express-News*, May 10, 1996.

7. SUCCESS (THE NEW RADIO UNIVERSE)

1. Ed Levine, interview with author, July 13, 2005.
2. Lee Abrams, interview with author, July 27, 2005.
3. "Oldies Formats Can't Get Ad-vantage," *New York Daily News*, March 21, 2006.
4. "N.Y. Station Suddenly Dumps Oldies Format," Associated Press Online, June 4, 2005.
5. www.millerkaplan/Summary05/Summary05.htm.

8. BILLBOARDS AND BEYOND

1. Karl Eller, interview with author, November 15, 2005.
2. Catherine Gudis, *Buyways* (New York: Routledge, 2004), p. 104.
3. Karl Eller, *Integrity Is All You've Got* (New York: McGraw-Hill, 2005), p. 3.
4. "Clear Channel's Pending Buy-Out of Eller Is Part of Industry Trend," *San Antonio Business Journal*, March 14, 1997.
5. "Clear Channel Buying Up $1.15 Billion in Billboards," *San Antonio Express-News*, February 26, 1997.
6. "Billboard Firm's Sale Sign of Big Changes," *Crain's Chicago Business*, May 26, 1997.
7. "Radio Giant Clear Channel Buying Ackerley Group, Leader in Outdoor Ads, for $500 Million," Associated Press, October 8, 2001.
8. "The FCC's Powell: Defying Labels, Like Famous Father," Associated Press, November 12, 1997.

9. "Powell Power: F.C.C. Commissioner Takes First Restrained Steps," *Telephony*, November 24, 1997.

10. Reed Hundt, interview with author, July 27, 2006.

9. THE MERGERS THAT TRANSFORMED CLEAR CHANNEL

1. Terry Jacobs, interview with author, October 28, 2005.
2. "Sex Harassment in Focus and R&R Meet," *Billboard*, June 27, 1992.
3. *20/20* transcript, February 28, 1992.
4. "Michaels' Antics Crank Up Fun and Trouble," *Greater Cincinnati Business Record*, March 9, 1992.
5. Eric Boehlert, "Tough Company," Salon.com, May 30, 2001.
6. Robert Unmacht, interview with author, October 12, 2005.
7. Lee Abrams, interview with author, July 27, 2005.
8. Eric Boehlert, "Radio's Big Bully," Salon.com, April 30, 2001.
9. "Making Noise in Radio," *Dallas Morning News*, October 27, 1996.
10. Robert Unmacht, interview with author, October 12, 2005.
11. "Jacor a Rising Star Among Radio Networks," *New York Times*, June 23, 1997.
12. "17-Station Deal Moves Jacor into Big Cities," *Cincinnati Post*, October 28, 1997.
13. George Sosson, interview with author, May 23, 2005.
14. "Clear Channel Snares Jacor for $4.4 Billion," *Electronic Media*, October 12, 1998.
15. "Clear Channel Plugs In Jacor for $4.4 Billion," *Variety*, October 12–18, 1998.
16. "Chancellor Acquiring Capstar," *Billboard*, September 5, 1998.
17. "Clear Channel to Take Over Jacor," Associated Press, October 8, 1998.
18. Ralph Guild, interview with author, June 23, 2005.
19. Dave Allan, interview with author, September 14, 2005.
20. Jim Smith, interview with author, May 20, 2005.

10. THE WORLD'S BIGGEST RADIO COMPANY

1. "Radio-Active Men," *Forbes*, June 1, 1998; "When Dealmaker Hicks Shoots, He Usually Scores," *Dallas Morning News*, July 11, 1999.
2. Rex Tackett, interview with author, May 12, 2005.
3. Eric Boehlert, "Radio's Big Bully," Salon.com, April 30, 2001.
4. "Radio Deregulation: Has It Served Listeners and Musicians?" report published by the Future of Music Coalition, November 18, 2002.
5. Dave Allan, interview with author, September 14, 2005.
6. "From a Distance: A Giant Radio Chain Is Perfecting the Art of Seeming Local," *Wall Street Journal*, February 25, 2002.
7. Ibid.
8. "Randy Michaels: The Noise You Can't Ignore," *Radio Ink*, September 9, 2002.
9. Ed Levine, interview with author, July 13, 2005.
10. David Rubin, interview with author, June 14, 2005.

11. www.newsmeat.com.

12. John Barger, interview with author, February 1, 2006.

13. "Democrats Weigh Pros, Cons of Mauro's Possible Run for Governor," *Dallas Morning News*, June 22, 1997.

14. "Clear Channel: An Empire Built on Deregulation," *Los Angeles Times*, February 25, 2002.

15. Eric Boehlert, interview with author, March 29, 2006.

II. CONCERTS

1. Bill Graham and Robert Greenfield, *Bill Graham Presents: My Life Inside Rock and Out* (Cambridge, Mass.: Da Capo, 2004), p. 189.

2. Sherry Wasserman, interview with author, October 5, 2005.

3. "N.Y. Firm Pays $65 Million for Bill Graham's Company," *San Francisco Chronicle*, December 17, 1997.

4. Gregg Perloff, interview with author, August 8, 2005.

5. Bill Graham and Robert Greenfield, *Bill Graham Presents*, p. 180.

6. Kevin Gray, "Ticketmaster," *New York*, November 15, 1999.

7. Ibid.

8. Author interview with confidential source, July 26, 2005.

9. Ibid.

10. "Concentrated Rock," *Boston Phoenix*, March 19–26, 1998.

11. "Stones Score 2005's Top Tour," Pollstar.com, December 30, 2005.

12. Karl Eller, interview with author, November 15, 2005.

13. "Clear Channel Results Hailed," *Hollywood Reporter*, July 28, 2000.

14. "Clear Channel's Dominance Obscures Promotional Conduit," *Los Angeles Times*, August 3, 2001.

15. "Backstage Brawl," *Fortune Small Business*, February 2002.

16. Ibid.

17. Eric Boehlert, "Suit: Clear Channel Is an Illegal Monopoly," Salon.com, August 8, 2001.

18. "Madonna, Live Nation Link Up on Deal," Associated Press, October 16, 2007.

12. THE BACKLASH

1. "Clear Channel Exploits the Synergies Between Radio and Live Events," *Mergers & Acquisitions*, May 1, 2000.

2. "Sell-Side Tunes In to Clear Channel," *CBS Marketwatch*, October 6, 2000.

3. Author interview with confidential source, December 3, 2005.

4. Eric Boehlert, interview with author, March 29, 2006.

5. Rob Vining, interview with author, April 19, 2005.

6. "A Cloud over Clear Channel," *Broadcasting & Cable*, November 26, 2001.

7. Eric Boehlert, "Washington Tunes In," Salon.com, March 27, 2002.

8. "Suit Against Clear Channel over Racing Goes to Jury," *New York Times*, March 21, 2005.

9. Eric Boehlert, "Habla Usted Clear Channel?" Salon.com, April 25, 2003.
10. "Hispanic Radio Is Boosting Clear Channel," *San Antonio Express-News*, September 11, 2005.
11. Author interview with confidential source, November 16, 2005.
12. "Q2 2002 Clear Channel Communications Earnings Conference Call," Fair Disclosure Wire, July 24, 2002.
13. "Clear Channel and Mag End Long Court Battle," *New York Daily News*, August 6, 2002.
14. "Static from Clear Channel," *Columbia Journalism Review*, January/February 2002.

13. CLEAR CHANNEL GOES TO WASHINGTON

1. "Family Describes Surviving a Nightmare," *Bismarck Tribune*, January 19, 2002.
2. "Anyone Listening?" *Nation*, May 6, 2005.
3. "On Minot, N.D., Radio, a Single Corporate Voice," *New York Times*, March 31, 2003.
4. "What Really Happened in Minot, N.D.?" Slate.com, January 10, 2007.
5. "When the Power Went Off, WSYR Failed Listeners," *Syracuse Post-Standard*, August 24, 2003.
6. David Rubin, interview with author, June 14, 2005.
7. Michael Bracy, interview with author, August 16, 2005.
8. feingold.senate.gov/%7Efeingold/speeches/03/01/2003107832.html.
9. Hearing of the Senate Commerce, Science, and Transportation Committee transcript, January 30, 2003.
10. Jonathan Adelstein, interview with author, November 30, 2005.

14. PAYOLA

1. Russell Sanjek, *Pennies from Heaven* (New York: Da Capo, 1996), p. 199.
2. Ibid.; Ben Fong-Torres, *The Hits Just Keep on Coming: The History of Top 40 Radio* (San Francisco: Backbeat Books, 2001), p. 93.
3. John Barger, interview with author, August 8, 2005.
4. "Company Town: Clear Channel Fined Just $8,000 by F.C.C. for Payola Violation," *Los Angeles Times*, October 20, 2000.
5. "Randy Michaels: The Noise You Can't Ignore," *Radio Ink*, September 9, 2002.
6. Terryl Brown Clemons, interview with author, April 13, 2006.
7. Eric Boehlert, "Payola Is Dead! Now What Will We Listen To?" Salon.com, January 6, 2005.
8. Jenny Toomey, interview with author, August 15, 2005.
9. www.oag.state.ny.us/press/2005/jul/payola2.pdf.

15. ONLINE, OR ON THE DECLINE?

1. Michele Clarke, conversation with author, January 20, 2006.
2. Casey Kasem, interview with author, September 15, 2005.
3. "Static on the Radio," *Daily Variety*, July 26, 2004.
4. "Antenna Adjustment," *BusinessWeek*, June 20, 2005.
5. John Barger, interview with author, May 2, 2005.
6. "Left Is Gaining in San Diego, a Rightist Bastion," *New York Times*, August 28, 2004.
7. "That Rebellious Voice Is No Pirate After All," *New York Times*, May 30, 2005.
8. "Clear Channel to Spin Off Its Entertainment Division," *New York Times*, April 30, 2005.
9. "HD Radio Alliance Formed," *Mediaweek*, December 6, 2005.
10. "Clear Channel Unveils 'Format Lab,' " Dow Jones MarketWatch, April 24, 2006.
11. "Fidelity Votes to Oust Clear Channel's Board," *Boston Herald*, September 9, 2005.
12. Graef Crystal, "Clear Channel's Communication Breakdown on Pay," Bloomberg News, March 20, 2006.
13. Adam Bellow, *In Praise of Nepotism* (New York: Doubleday, 2003), p. 471.
14. "Signal Strength," *Vanderbilt Magazine*, Spring 2005, p. 42.
15. Ibid.

16. TUNING OUT

1. "Broadcast Radio Is Scrambling to Regain Its Groove," *New York Times*, September 15, 2006.
2. Richard Morgan, "Tell All," *Daily Deal*, February 7, 2007.
3. "Radio Revenue Flat for Second Straight Year," *Mediaweek*, February 2, 2007.
4. Author interview with confidential source, November 31, 2006.
5. "Radio Chain Is Said to Be in Sale Talks," *New York Times*, October 26, 2006.
6. "Bid for Radio Giant Started with Talk Between Classmates," *New York Times*, November 14, 2007.
7. "Clear Channel Buyout Talks Fuel Concern of Management Conflicts," *Wall Street Journal*, November 14, 2007.
8. Morgan, "Tell All."
9. "In a Big Bet on Radio, Private-Equity Group Buys Clear Channel," *Wall Street Journal*, November 17, 2006.
10. "Fidelity Voting No on Clear Channel Deal," Associated Press, January 30, 2007.
11. "Shareholders Approve Clear Channel Buyout Offer," *San Antonio Business Journal*, September 25, 2007.
12. "Is Radio Still Radio If There's Video?" *New York Times*, February 14, 2007.

EPILOGUE

1. John Barger, interview with author, February 1, 2006.
2. Dan Cohen, interview with author, April 28, 2005.
3. Terry Jacobs, interview with author, November 8, 2005.
4. "What the [Bleep]?!" *New York*, June 5, 2006.
5. jacobsmedia.com/042406-techipod.htm.

ACKNOWLEDGMENTS

I owe thanks to many people for the completion of this book, but the original source of inspiration was my agent, Paul Bresnick, who presented the earliest idea of it to me with much enthusiasm and flair. Paul convinced me almost immediately that Americans still had a passion for radio, and that interest in Clear Channel far transcended the confines of the broadcast industry. And I owe special thanks to Kathy Belden, who convinced me it was time to do another book and that Paul was the one to make it happen. Also fueling that early flame was my editor, Denise Oswald, who, in an initial hour-long phone conversation, helped me unlock my own personal passion for the subject. Her continued interest and insight helped make this book as good as it could be.

As much as I knew about the recording industry, my understanding of the commercial radio business qualified it as foreign territory, requiring the need for numerous translators. Warren Bodow served that role first and most dramatically, by pointing the way to invaluable industry resources with assured calm and aplomb. Gary Stevens, another radio industry vet, helped explain the ins and outs of modern radio without condescension. He also provided some key early history and contacts, as well as deeply knowledgeable insights.

I reserve a special thank-you for the dozens and dozens of inside sources who agreed (some anonymously) to be interviewed for this book, most notably the former veteran Clear Channel executives who talked freely and generously, giving up countless hours of their time, including Stan Webb, John Barger, Jim Smith, Rex Tackett, and George Sosson. Their reminiscences and observations most notably helped bring my story to life and provided its historical and emotional center.

Thanks to Robert Greenfield, author extraordinaire, for hooking me up on the West Coast and showing me the way to reportorial gold. Bob's own work—meticulously researched, engagingly sprawling volumes of alternative history—also provided creative inspiration.

Michele Clarke of Brainerd Communicators, Clear Channel's New York public relations outpost, offered advice, background, and other information, sometimes against her better judgment, and was helpful in many ways she perhaps did not even realize at the time.

My wife, Erica, gave me everything else I could ever want for this project. Her constant support and reassurances, as well as her razor-sharp insights, made the seemingly impossible somehow possible and allayed my darkest doubts. She also was quick to question anything that didn't make sense, or that wasn't that interesting to begin with. Finally, her love and caring made it all matter.

My parents, Ken and Norma Foege, also did their part by reliably providing contacts, news clippings, and reminders to "take a break." And last but certainly not least, my children, Charlotte and Henry, contributed to this project by supplying their dad with much-needed downtime fun and escape from the hard work and long hours that writing this book oftentimes entailed. Charlotte, this is the book I kept telling you about.

INDEX